TAMING MANHATTAN

TAMING
MANHATTAN

Environmental Battles in the Antebellum City

Catherine McNeur

Harvard University Press
Cambridge, Massachusetts
London, England

2014

First printing

Library of Congress Cataloging-in-Publication Data
McNeur, Catherine.
Taming Manhattan: environmental battles in the
antebellum city / Catherine McNeur.
pages cm
Includes bibliographical references and index.
ISBN 978-0-674-72509-6 (alk. paper)
1. Urbanization—New York (State)—New York—History—19th century.
2. Manhattan (New York, N.Y.)—Environmental conditions. 3. City planning—
Environmental aspects—New York (State)—New York—History—19th century.
4. New York (N.Y.)—History—1775–1865. I. Title.
HN80.N5M36 2014
307.7609747'1—dc23   2014003557

To Dan, Nora, and Julia

Contents

Introduction

When John Randel, Jr., and his fellow surveyors set out in 1808 to map Manhattan Island, they surely anticipated having to wade through salt marshes and red maple swamps, climb rocky outcroppings, and make their way through thick forests of hickory, pine, and tulip trees. The island was ecologically and topographically diverse, and this would have been par for the course. They might not, however, have expected to be pelted with cabbages and artichokes while they worked. The commissioners charged with developing a plan for New York City had hired Randel to draw the map that they would use to stamp the gridiron street plan onto the land. Randel cut through overgrown woodlands, broke off branches, and planted markers at the intersections of future streets. The story goes that small landowners who spotted the surveyors and engineers marking up their property were so outraged that they set their dogs on the trespassers or united with their neighbors to drive them

away. When a "venerable old woman" who had sold vegetables downtown for over twenty years saw the engineers plot an avenue through her
farm and kitchen, she apparently attacked them with her cabbages and
artichokes until they retreated.[1]

Regardless of whether the story is true or a colorful urban legend
passed down through histories of the city, the farmer's attack demonstrates the contested nature of urban growth and progress. Antebellum
Manhattan struggled with a wide range of environmental battles that
involved everything from street surveys to animals, parks, manure,
food, and shantytowns. Neighbors from all social classes found in the
urban environment a means for controlling the dramatic physical, social,
and economic changes facing the city. It made the uncontrollable seem
controllable.

Fast-paced urbanization between the War of 1812 and the Civil War
wrought dramatic social and environmental changes for New York. The
United States, as a whole, was becoming increasingly urban, and New
York was a magnet for Americans and immigrants alike. From a city of
96,373 in 1810, when the densest part of the city sat below Chambers
Street, New York grew by nearly 750 percent to house 813,669 in 1860.
By that point, the city, which still consisted only of Manhattan Island,
stretched four miles north to 59th Street. Despite the signs of material
prosperity associated with this growth, the city's small municipal government and hodgepodge infrastructure failed to meet the needs of its
densely packed residents. Garbage filled the streets and sewage contaminated the drinking water. Epidemics, fires, and endless inconveniences
made the city practically unlivable.[2]

Antebellum Manhattan would hardly be recognizable to modern
New Yorkers. Pigs and dogs freely wandered the streets, cows foraged in
the Battery, and the dirt was so thick that pedestrians often forgot that
the streets were paved. New Yorkers rebuilt the dense downtown buildings to hold more people, while simultaneously pushing the boundaries
farther north up the island. Those living through this era were keenly
aware of how quickly their city was changing. When John Randel, Jr.,

reminisced in 1864 about his time spent surveying Manhattan, he re-
called traveling to his office in Greenwich Village, "*then* in the country." It was also common for bourgeois men of this era to look back at
their childhoods in the city and wistfully remember how they used to
collect blackberries along the Bowery or fish with their friends in a spot
now covered by buildings. Urbanization was a tangible part of their lives.
The boundary between city and country, between blocks filled with
buildings and open space with sparse development and room for farms,
was constantly shifting during this period.[3]

Poor New Yorkers and wealthy New Yorkers had very different
ideas about what belonged in the city and in many ways efforts to
tame the city were attacks on an informal economy that supported a
large segment of the city's poor. The city's notoriously filthy streets
served as an urban commons for the poor, who used the piles of trash
to feed their animals, recover salable materials, and make ends meet.
They were trying to survive in an evolving but unstable market economy that offered few safety nets. These women and men adapted to
growing heaps of waste and found innovative ways to use the resources
at hand to scrape by. As politicians and reformers pushed to improve the
urban environment with better sanitation and greener spaces, the ability
of the poor to use this de facto urban commons as they liked began slipping away. Still, the continued importance of the urban commons
through the nineteenth century reveals the dynamic power play between
neighbors over how the urban environment could be used.[4]

What we understand today as rural land uses were a consistent, if
contested, part of city life. While we might smirk at the idea of pigs wandering the streets of Manhattan, their disappearance and eventual home
far from the city center did not seem inevitable to antebellum residents.
This is a study as much about the battles to maintain or erase urban agriculture and other uses of the city's environment as it is about the development of our modern conception of what properly belongs in the city
versus the country. Not only is the city impossible to understand without
the country, but the country was also very much a part of the city.

To explore the processes involved in fighting for control of the city, this book looks at a range of environmental battles, from attempts to control the hogs and dogs running loose on the streets to struggles over the development of Central Park. The efforts by some New Yorkers to tame the city at the expense of others revealed contemporary tensions between spaces of leisure and spaces of labor. Parks supplanted shantytowns, and police removed livestock for the sake of the city's cleanliness and reputation. While some social battles erupted publicly and violently, as was the case with controversies over loose animals on the streets, others occurred almost silently in taxation and funding structures that planted parks in only the wealthiest neighborhoods. The stories also occurred across different scales, involving everything from New Yorkers personally consuming corrupt food to the city's efforts to sell manure regionally. The project of taming the city involved a combination of public and private efforts from diverse groups of residents, real estate developers, public health officials, journalists, reformers, and politicians. Some efforts were public while others were private. After decades of struggle, the city government gained the tools necessary for control in the wake of terrifying epidemics. Yet the attempts to improve and perfect the city in terms of both its environmental and its social conditions often created new, unexpected challenges. The various cases, characters, and outcomes of these stories not only reveal the changing role of nature in cities but also the social, cultural, legislative, and economic underpinnings of environmental inequality, from access to parks to the control of public and private property.[5]

Of course, New York City was not alone. Many of the stories about the city's struggle with its expanding population and environmental conditions could be told about other cities to varying degrees. Boston and Atlanta contended with urban cows, St. Louis dealt with its own smelly offal problem, San Francisco and New Orleans struggled with filth, and epidemics plagued nearly every nineteenth-century city as well as small towns. Many American cities struggled with fast-paced urban growth in the nineteenth century. Yet New York was the country's largest metropolis, and it experienced many of these issues earlier and more intensely than most other American cities. New York's problems were well known and newspapers across the country and occasionally the world reprinted articles about its environmental issues, both to poke fun at New Yorkers and to compare notes about how to tackle the issues of urbanization. New York was at the forefront of many public health and environmental reforms, thanks to the extent of problems facing the growing city.[6]

Urban landscapes continue to be contested, though debates over topics like urban animals have profoundly changed. While urban agriculture was far from fashionable in the nineteenth century, today it is not uncommon to find chicken coops in upper-middle-class backyards and even on Fifth Avenue rooftops of the wealthiest city residents. For the past several years, the *New York Times* has had a column offering advice about foraging weeds and flowers from sidewalks and parks. Even the New York City municipal government is on board, offering unprecedented support for community gardens and other ways to tap local food sources. This is a national phenomenon that is slowly transforming urban dwellers' relationships with city land. The media, however, give much less attention to stories about how poorer city residents continue to garden, fish, and forage in ways to make ends meet. Whether rich or poor, urban Americans are fighting against the boundaries drawn in the nineteenth century when they plead with their municipal governments to permit them to keep chickens, pigs, goats, or bees. Today, proponents argue that urban agriculture and local food sources promote "sustainable cities." In the nineteenth century, many Americans would have believed the opposite.[7]

Antebellum New York underwent a period of profound transformation. In many ways the seeds that propelled Progressive Era reformers were sown during this period as a range of city residents tried to take hold of what was changing, make sense of what was at stake, and wrestle with their neighbors for power over the urban environment. Ultimately, this is a story about the inextricable ties between social control and environmental control, and the desperate impulse to seize such power during times of overwhelming change.[8]

1

Mad Dogs and Loose Hogs

On a sunny spring day in 1817, a New Yorker stepped out of his house to enjoy a stroll through the city. Along his route he experienced "sufferings and mortifications" that would have embarrassed any metropolis but had become increasingly common in Manhattan. First, he found a cluster of nine hogs cavorting about the street, along with "several smaller congregations." The smells were too much to bear. As if this were not painful enough, he "was twice docked by chamber-maids cleaning windows . . . and once inundated by a grocer emptying his moptub on the pavement." Looking for a country escape from all this chaos, he wandered to the upper part of Broadway, where he encountered a wooden shanty blocking the street, "rendering passage equally disagreeable and dangerous." Disregarding the laws governing public spaces, the owner of the "miserable old hulk" had erected his home less than a week before, "obstruct[ing] and deform[ing] the principal avenue of this great city."

After his disappointing walk, the New Yorker returned to his home that night exhausted. However, as soon as he lay down to sleep, his rest was disturbed by "the discordant notes of a concert of bull-dogs." Sleep-deprived, he composed a letter describing his frustration with the city's nuisances and sent it to the conservative *New-York Evening Post,* hoping to rally the support of other New Yorkers and shame the municipal government into taking control and enforcing its ordinances governing public space. Whether or not he dramatized or condensed his experiences to make his argument stronger, the author was annoyed with what had become typical nuisances in one of the foremost cities of the country.[1]

One man's nuisance, of course, was another's livelihood or even cherished pet. Livestock, such as the foul-smelling hogs the letter writer encountered, helped to feed New York's poorest residents. The dogs that howled at night were a mix of strays, beloved companions, watchdogs, and hunting dogs. The owners took advantage of the filthy condition of the streets to find free food for their animals. With the municipal government struggling to keep up with the growing city, the streets were left in disarray, which allowed for the creation of this de facto urban commons where animals grazed freely. Yet New Yorkers like the author of the letter, who had other visions for what the city might become, fought to have the "corporation" (as New Yorkers called their government) close the commons once and for all, in order to make the streets cleaner, more convenient, and ultimately respectable. With such strong feelings on both sides about how the streets ought to be used, political debates remained extremely contentious.

Just over a week before the *Evening Post* published this letter, the outgoing members of the Common Council took advantage of their impending exit to pass a number of controversial laws and ordinances, including a ban on loose dogs and hogs. Similar laws had been on the books previously but had met with resistance from owners and were rarely, if ever, enforced by the police. The Common Council regularly tinkered with the laws hoping to find the key to the city's problems. However, the lack of enforcement continued, to the chagrin of our letter writer.

FIGURE 1. Baron von Klinckowström, *Broadway and City Hall, New York, 1820.* Hogs and dogs mingle with carriages, carts, and pedestrians on Broadway right in front of City Hall. (Collection of the New-York Historical Society.)

In the opinion of many who sympathized with him, Manhattan seemed to be an ungovernable space riddled with unpleasant nuisances and ineffective politicians.[2]

New York's uncontrollable growth was partly to blame for the chaos on the streets. Immigration to New York from the countryside and from Europe picked up rapidly in 1815, after the end of the War of 1812. New York was in the process of intensive urbanization, and the municipal government had a hard time keeping up. Not only were there more people around to own animals, but those people were also creating more garbage that, left uncollected on the streets, fed a burgeoning, free-roaming animal population. The battles that erupted over animals in the streets exacerbated tensions among New Yorkers over class, race, and national origin. As wealthier, native-born New Yorkers began wringing their hands about the fate of the city, they typically tied the chaos of the animals to impoverished newcomers. To them, the city seemed to be declining rapidly.

While it might not have appeared so to its critics, New York's municipal government had adapted somewhat to the city's growth. The completion of a monumental new City Hall in 1812 marked a period of significant growth for the municipal government. The building testified to the government's expanding role in controlling the city's public spaces and consequently its population. While the government had long focused on New York's commercial needs, it was increasingly turning its attention toward the services necessary to maintain the public's welfare. By the end of the War of 1812, the city had begun to parcel out responsibility to more departments and administrators, in an attempt to expand urban services. Yet the government struggled to stay on top of these tasks. City officials touted their efforts to manage public markets, docks, and commerce; maintain order; keep the streets clean, in good repair, and lit at night; and safeguard public health. Unfortunately, they had a difficult time doing any of these tasks well.[3]

Success was difficult for several reasons. The councilmen, for instance, were overworked and had few incentives to improve government efficiency. During this era, representatives were primarily patricians rather than career politicians, and wealthy enough to afford unpaid government positions. Many continued their legal and mercantile work after being elected, convening once a week for Common Council meetings. It was not particularly surprising, then, that these part-time representatives could not meet the needs of a rapidly growing city, let alone restructure the government to be more efficient and effective. New York City had the largest population-to-councilman ratio among contemporary American cities. In 1830 the ratio was a remarkable 14,471 New Yorkers per councilman, more than three times higher than that of its nearest competitor, Philadelphia. These councilmen had to represent the interests and needs of a vast and dramatically changing population—responsibilities too enormous for their part-time positions.[4]

The municipal government expanded to handle the growing needs and complications of the city, but an increased number of departments did not always mean better services. As a measure of the corporation's growth, between 1800 and 1840 city expenses increased twenty-four-fold. The government's growth sometimes resulted in overlapping juris-dictions, as was the case in the handling of public health and nuisance issues such as loose animals. In fact, the disorderly expansion often caused more confusion, less efficiency, and continued issues with the enforcement of laws. While the city's commerce and culture thrived, its public spaces suffered from ineffective ordinances and impotent leader-ship. Those New Yorkers who relied on the urban commons to supple-ment their incomes benefited directly from this chaos.[5]

The inability of New York's government to control its public spaces had major implications for the fate of free-roaming animals. Citizens held enormous power over the success of any laws that politicians passed about these animals. Given that New Yorkers were so divided over how public space ought to be used, this resulted in intense battles that both exposed and amplified class and racial tensions. In many ways, the ani-mals came to symbolize their owners in these debates. Characterizations of the animals served as a means for New Yorkers to either criticize or praise their owners. The ways New Yorkers classified and understood these animals played an important role in their treatment and the de-bates that resulted. While both free-roaming dogs and hogs were clas-sified as domestic animals, they were actually half-wild. These animals foraged on their own and bred with other animals on the streets; they were in many ways beyond the control of their owners, let alone that of politicians and city employees. Yet while dogs and hogs were in many ways similar, the various ways New Yorkers treated them reflected not only their respective statuses as pets and livestock, but also their associa-tion with specific groups of New Yorkers.

The municipal government struggled to catch up with its growing constituency and gain control of the city's free-roaming animals, but its attempts were unpopular and often failed. Balancing a desire to polish a growing city with a reluctance to burden an impoverished lower class, city leaders half-heartedly enforced laws or completely ignored them—that is, when they had the power to enforce them at all. Those like the letter writer resorted to penning frustrated articles or tongue-in-cheek humor pieces for newspapers that mocked the inefficient city government while also begging for reform. They worried about how New York could ever compare to London or Paris, let alone Boston or Philadelphia, when dogs and hogs ruled the streets. Though Boston and Philadelphia were not exempt from loose animals, they controlled them far more effectively, and New York's journalists often wrote enviously of their cleaner streets. At the same time, those New Yorkers who owned the animals and relied on their ability to use the streets as a public commons fretted over the implications of losing these rights. The stakes were high for both groups. Newspaper campaigns, heated Common Council debates, and a number of riots would help to define the future of New York's urban environment and public spaces.[6]

Mad Dogs

New York's canine residents had long faced trouble on the city streets. Regular panics washed over the city, instilling fear that mad dogs were on the loose and eager to infect innocent passersby—both pets and humans—with rabies. These four-legged, foaming terrorists inspired fearful newspaper stories that helped to rally support for restricting dogs' ability to roam the streets freely. Yet not all New Yorkers supported this universal ban, let alone the government-sponsored slaughter of all dogs found at large. City residents, rich and poor, owned these animals and considered them pets, guard dogs, or hunting companions.[7]

Though strays, known as "tramps," made up a good number of the free-roaming dogs, New Yorker's pets often mingled with them indiscriminately on the sidewalks. In an era before flea and tick control, dogs typically had to stay outdoors, especially during the summer, in order to keep their owners pest free. While some owners kept their dogs chained in yards, others let them out to roam the city and mix with dogs of all classes and ranks. Middle- and upper-class dogs were typically fed table scraps, but they, too, joined the lower-class dogs in foraging among the city's heaps of garbage. The animals and their owners took advantage of the bounty left on the streets due to the city's ineffective garbage removal contracts. This urban commons was filled with ripe piles of organic matter, such as offal and kitchen waste, so dogs and other free-roaming animals could essentially find their entire day's diet within a few blocks of their residence.[8]

To those who feared death by dog bite—a fear fueled by word-of-mouth stories and newspaper accounts—the origin and pedigree of these dogs did not matter. In the opinion of such people, *all* dogs, especially those left to wander freely through public spaces, posed a threat to the lives and well-being of New Yorkers. Reports of rabies outbreaks came primarily from newspapers, which inspired terror by emphasizing the unknown factors in the contagion. It was impossible to know the exact number of dogs on the streets, let alone the number of those infected, as the dogs were nomadic and therefore uncontrollable and uncountable. Rabies was also difficult to diagnose in the offending dogs, mainly because they ran off after biting their victim. Bystanders felt justified in tagging particularly aggressive or erratic dogs as "mad." Without having reliable information about the attackers, every dog bite victim could worry about the possibility of rabies. Savvy salesmen marketed a series of potions that claimed to cure hydrophobia if taken prior to its onset. The long delay before victims developed signs of the fatal disease left many imagining symptoms and panicking. "Epidemic terror" infected more people than rabies itself and inspired some to support drastic measures, such as banning or even killing all urban canines.[9]

However rare dog attacks and the incidence of rabies were in reality, the newspaper reports that built up their presence made them a larger symbol of the breakdown of civility. The streets, like the dogs, were uncontrollable and lives were placed at risk. Critics associated rabies with disorder and considered loose dogs to be a kind of pollution that could spread and contaminate, challenging the purity of New York's public spaces and its citizenry. In the absence of clear medical solutions, government policy was necessary to purify the streets and maintain order.[10]

For decades, the Common Council passed law after law restricting dogs' access to the streets following various outbreaks. Such laws, instituted in 1785, 1802, 1803, and 1808, ultimately proved to be ineffective, though they temporarily mollified alarmed residents. In 1811, however, fear over rabies was growing as newspapers continually reported the deaths of people both locally and nationally from dog bites. New Yorkers, fearful to walk down the street lest they encounter an uncontrollable dog, wrote to newspapers and petitioned the city government. A petition from 1,347 New Yorkers helped to solidify the Common Council's position, and on the very day it was read, the aldermen passed the most effective law to date.[11]

The 1811 "Law Concerning Dogs" was effective because it created the job of Dog Register and Collector, an official who was given significant monetary incentive to collect a new, $3 tax from each dog owner and kill all dogs found roaming at large. The councilmen appointed Abner Curtis, a police marshal, to the position. He pocketed 20 percent of the tax and 50 cents for every dog he or his employees killed and buried. The law permitted anyone to kill free-roaming dogs outside the Lamp District (the very dense downtown area), as well as any dog that bit or attempted to bite a person or animal on the street. Predicting resistance from dog owners, the law established a steep fine of $30 for those who tried to "hinder or molest" the Register or his staff when they carried out their business.[12]

In establishing the 1811 dog law, the aldermen had decided to create the new post of Dog Register rather than incorporate the responsibility for monitoring loose canines under the City Inspector's jurisdiction. A state law of 1807 had created the position of City Inspector. The job entailed investigating and removing nuisances, as well as protecting and monitoring the public health. Though the dog law was written specifically in response to concerns about rabies, the Common Council saw fit to keep it separate. Perhaps they did this because they classified dogs apart from other nuisances, since dogs were pets; or perhaps they did it because they wanted to design a position where the pay itself was dependent on the number of dogs taxed and killed, thereby establishing an incentive to enforce the law, something they would have had difficulty controlling with the salaried City Inspector's department. Whatever their logic, the Common Council ultimately divided jurisdiction over public health and the control of public nuisances among several departments.[13]

One thing that is clear from the 1811 law is that the Common Council aimed to regulate the ownership of dogs. The dog law was financially oppressive for poorer New Yorkers, who not only had to pay the $3 tax but also had to buy food for their dog, when previously they had been able to let their animals forage in the streets. A writer to *The Columbian*, judging himself a representative of wealthier New Yorkers, remarked: "We object not to the tax, as there are few persons who justly appreciate the good qualities of the dog but would pay it with pleasure." The implication was that those who could afford to pay the tax had a refined appreciation for their canine companions, unlike their neighbors who kept curs or mutts and let them out on the street to forage. While most of the newspaper reports about mad dogs did not go into detailed descriptions of the dogs that attacked, there was a general implication that the most dangerous canines were the mongrel wanderers who congregated in packs on the streets. In short, strays and the dogs of poor New Yorkers seemed to pose the greatest threat.[14]

Unlike other urban animals such as horses and swine, dogs played only a minor economic role. Owners of hotels, warehouses, and other buildings kept terriers to combat rat populations. Occasionally, artisans, such as a paint maker or the operator of a "machine for raising water," employed dogs to power their equipment, but these were rare cases. One dog-law supporter estimated that "perhaps nine-tenths of them are kept from whim, oddity or some trifling or selfish motive, equally useless to the public as the animals are troublesome to the neighbors." Their value to most owners, of course, went beyond economic worth. While dogs served as status symbols for some, guard dogs for others, and income makers for the occasional artisan, most New Yorkers kept their dogs as companions and pets. Though it would have been logical to shun these "useless" animals that might carry fatal diseases, the owners loved and valued these animals.[15]

Dog owners typically expressed great affection for their pets. Though dogs had long been kept as pets, their status in American families was rising as part of the developing interest in domesticity and gentility. Owners considered them to be friends, loyal servants, and playmates for their children—in short, part of the family. Even though urban dogs lived most of their lives outside, there is no lack of evidence that nineteenth-century dogs were prized, beloved companions—whether you look at obituaries, journal entries waxing on about pet activities, relics like toys, or even family portraits that included the family dog. It was exactly this kind of devotion to their faithful canine friends that caused dog lovers to rise up against the city's attempts to clear them from public spaces.[16]

The city streets were not safe for dogs the summer after the 1811 law passed. Between June 1, when the law was enacted, and September 9, Abner Curtis and his staff of collectors killed 2,610 dogs and registered 1,085. Though many New Yorkers heeded the new law and rushed to Curtis's office to pay the dog tax, their dogs were not necessarily protected. The *New-York Evening Post* complained that the law was imprecise. Would dogs whose owners had paid the tax be allowed to wander the streets, or were they likely to be killed as well? How could collectors tell the difference? A self-described "friend to humanity" wrote to the *Columbian* complaining that mischievous boys were taking great pleasure in killing "poor harmless and unoffending animals" in the outer neighborhoods of the city. The law offered little protection to these creatures or their law-abiding owners. The councilmen revised the law accordingly, calling for dogs to wear metal collars with the names and addresses of their owners clearly marked, in order to protect registered dogs from the dog catcher's bludgeon.[17]

Dogs pulled at the heartstrings of many New Yorkers. While it might be assumed that free-roaming dogs would be more closely associated with the city's poor, given the benefits of letting them loose in search of food, the wealthy also had a stake in the dog population. According to one literary magazine, dogs were as frequently the topic of gentlemanly discussion as horses, women, money, and heritage. As hunters' companions, dogs held a status in the city that other urban animals lacked, with the exception of horses, whose characters, features, and economic value were similarly celebrated. Sportsmen paraded to the outskirts of the city with rifles propped on their shoulders and dogs following closely behind. They attempted to replicate the aristocratic culture popular in England while hunting for foxes, grouse, and other prey in the city's hinterland.[18]

Wealthy critics of the dog law expressed their disapproval in newspapers and magazines. The *New-York Evening Post,* for instance, which was typically aligned with causes favored by wealthier New Yorkers, openly questioned the value of the 1811 dog law. A writer to the *Public Advertiser* asked readers "whether the whole race of that useful and excellent animal, the DOG, is to be sacrificed to the fears and frightful visions of the credulous and timid?" To these New Yorkers, urban dogs were not pests; they were pets. The municipal government was targeting all dogs indiscriminately, and wealthy owners and sympathizers rallied to save their animals. In fighting the dog law, they ultimately had to defend *all* urban dogs, not just purebreds. This was less a battle of class than a battle between dog lovers and rabies fearers.[19]

Less wealthy New Yorkers also resisted the law. Instead of writing to the newspapers, they blocked the dog catchers who drove carts through their neighborhoods. When dog catchers began to police the streets in June 1811, resistance mounted. On June 6, a crowd of nearly one hundred men, many of whom were artisans such as blacksmiths, coachmakers, and tobacconists, gathered around the cart of dog catcher Garret C. Van Horne, jostled him, and released the dogs. The next day, as two catchers brought their cart to the Potters Field to exterminate and bury their captives, a crowd met them with insults and threats. One rioter called a dog catcher a "Damned Murdering Bugger," threatening to

FIGURE 2. William Chappell, *The Dog Killer,* ca. 1870. A dog catcher carries a dog carcass to his cart while he polices the Fourth Ward, a neighborhood known for working-class residences, in the 1810s. (Image copyright © The Metropolitan Museum of Art. Image source: Art Resource, NY.)

throw him into the ditch with the dead dogs. The crowd then broke the dogcart and released the animals. Abner Curtis was troubled enough by these riots to hire protection for the catchers so that they could complete their business unhampered. The $30 fine for obstructing the catchers seemed to be of little use in preventing such resistance.[20]

Anti-dog New Yorkers saw the riots as a crime against "humanity and civilization." By the end of June, a writer for the *New-York Spectator* was reporting that a number of dogs still dominated the streets, to the detriment of the city's residents. Not mincing words, the writer declared that "no dog ought to be allowed to exist. The life of one single person is worth more than the lives of all the dogs in the United States; and while there is one dog living, there is danger that one or more persons

may suffer the most cruel of all deaths in the course of a year." Again, this
fell squarely against the arguments of those who defended urban dogs as
faithful companions and guardians of property. The fearmongering author preferred full extermination to any threat of hydrophobia.[21]

Abner Curtis continued his campaign to control the city's dogs, but
his efficiency seemed to dwindle as the years passed. Critics charged
that the number of canines was on the rise. Although riots appeared to
stop after 1811, individuals continued to protect their dogs from being
taken. When dog catchers William Bouker and Israel Lawrence tried
to seize a loose dog on Elizabeth Street in 1815, the owner, Bernard Bailey, "came out of a yard adjoining and furiously seized said Dog &
swore he would sooner loose [sic] his life than they should have him."
Bailey and the catchers had a heated discussion that ended with their
returning the animal and taking Bailey's name so that he could be fined
for not registering his dog. In another case, the Common Council,
when reviewing a petition from someone fined by Curtis's office, found
that the fine might very well have been "unjust and oppressive" if "the
greatest part of the community do with impunity resist the operation
of the dog law." New Yorkers who were growing increasingly enraged at
the number of dogs still on the streets pressured the government to protect the city from rabid animals. Facing criticism, Curtis submitted a
letter of resignation to the Common Council that was finally accepted
two years later. With limited support from the council and limited compliance from dog owners, there was little that he could do to control the
streets.[22]

When the council appointed Benjamin Watson to the post of Register and Collector in 1818, the renewed vigor in enforcing the dog law was
met with increased resistance from dog owners and sympathizers. The
mayor published a special notice in the local newspapers warning the
city's residents that anyone who hindered or molested the dog catchers
would be fined $100. He added that due to the recent cases of hydro-
phobia, "citizens are earnestly requested to co-operate with the public
officer in measures which are so necessary to avert the calamities which

the law of the Corporation is intended to guard against." A few days later, Watson reported to the Common Council that "from the opposition he has met with he is not able to enforce the laws respecting dogs without some aid." Despite these warnings and precautions, riots occurred that summer and fall, leading to diminished enforcement and a continuing presence of dogs on the streets.[23]

In the years that followed, stories of rabies outbreaks continued to inspire public pressure for enforcement. Stuck between panicked citizens and dog-law resisters, Watson realized that a compromise had to be made with the dog-loving public if the law was ever to be properly enforced. Since much of the public's resistance had to do with the immediate killing of the dogs, Watson proposed establishing a pound where captured dogs could be kept for a short time before extermination, giving owners ample opportunity to claim their animals. The council never followed through, though. In fact, by 1820 it had cut most of Watson's funding, making enforcement even more difficult.[24]

By the 1830s the battle over loose dogs had grown increasingly fierce. As in the past, well-publicized dog attacks and rabies outbreaks led the government to reinforce the dog law and make it more effective. In 1831 the Common Council upped the dog bounty from 50 cents to $1. The response was so huge that the Dog Register and Collector had to set up a special meeting location to receive dog carcasses and pay the citizen killers. One alderman spoke out in opposition to what he saw as "the most wanton, cruel, and arbitrary [law] that he ever knew." His objections did not have an immediate impact, however, and bounty hunters killed nearly 3,000 dogs in just two months.[25]

These mass, citywide killings inspired critics to charge the city with animal cruelty. Eager for the generous bounties, citizen enforcers, who were typically lower-class men and boys, grabbed any loose dog they could find and clubbed it over the head, often in clear sight of passersby. Some of the horrified onlookers feared that this spectacle might influence the children who witnessed it. The *New-York Spectator* published an article expressing its concern that the cruelty of the dog law had a "demoralizing effect . . . upon the character of boys in particu-lar." After a particularly severe "dog war" in 1836 that involved the kill-ing of over 8,000 dogs, the Board of Aldermen reevaluated the brutal-ity of their law. In explaining why they were ending the policy of paying New Yorkers a bounty for the dogs they killed, a committee of aldermen wrote: "The exhibition of cruelty before the young, and their gradual and progressive participation in it, has always been considered by every moralist, to blunt every finer perception; to harden the heart and prepare the individual for the perpetration of crime. Habitual cru-elty to animals, conducts with slow and certain steps, to the entire ex-tinction of all those moral sentiments, which make and keep a man a good neighbor and a good citizen." The popular writer and activist Lydia Maria Child similarly wondered, while visiting New York from Mas-sachusetts, about the effect that such government-sponsored violence would have on the city's children: "Whether such brutal scenes do not prepare the minds of the young to take part in bloody riots and revolu-tions is a serious question." The fear that animal cruelty would have a lasting effect on the younger generation was becoming a serious issue for the growing chorus of critics.[26]

The idea that a depraved child would become a depraved man was hardly new to the nineteenth century, but the concept was gaining a firmer foundation in popular culture, especially with its presence in widely read child-rearing books, such as Lydia Howard Sigourney's *Letters to Mothers*. Sigourney warned mothers that it was important to in-still kindness toward all creatures from an early age. There was a fear that if a child was permitted to hurt animals, he or she might turn out like the traitor Benedict Arnold, "who in his boyhood loved to destroy insects, to mutilate toads, to steal the eggs of the mourning bird, and torture quiet, domestic animals, who eventually laid waste the shrink-ing, domestic charities, and would have drained the life-blood of his endangered country." Preventing animal cruelty was not only important for the welfare of animals and the child perpetrators, but also for that of the young republic. Witnessing the savage deaths of dogs had the double threat of not only inspiring children to participate in similar actions but also of permanently recalibrating their moral compass.[27]

Battles over animals had a way of highlighting the tensions over class and race that were seething in the city. Bourgeois Victorian culture increasingly embraced an ethic of kindness to animals, and the outspoken critics of dog killings believed that some of the central tenets of gentility were at risk in the bounty hunters' violent displays. The citizen enforcers of the dog law tended to be poor. They were typically boys and men looking to earn a side income by collecting the bounties. Even the city's official dog catchers were typically from the lower class. The critics who cried out against the cruelty occasionally made derogatory references to the class of the dog killers, as if this alone were an explanation for why they transgressed the rules of gentility and respectability. In an 1830 issue of the *New-York Mirror: A Repository of Polite Literature and the Arts,* a writer bemoaned the loss of beautiful dogs at the hands of "boys, negroes, and all the 'list of landless resolute,' who are pleased with an opportunity to gratify the natural ferocity of their disposition with impunity." The writer lingered on descriptions that made the dog killers themselves seem savage and animal-like. Similarly, in 1837 journalist Asa Greene wrote that the dog killers were "loafers," both "black and white," who collected just enough bounties to pay for their daily expenses. With the dog law promoting the capture and killing of any seemingly dangerous dog, wealthy dog lovers perceived a threat from their poorer neighbors who might kill a dog for the reward they would receive from the city, or for perverse fun, as the *New-York Mirror* writer presumed. The aldermen who were responsible for establishing the bounty system even called the dog killers "idle and unfeeling," and denounced their open practice of violence in the presence of "wives and children."[28] Such writers seemed to believe that these boys and men were a threat not only to dogs but also to civilization.

These dog-killing campaigns were not the only venues for cruelty toward dogs in New York during this period. A masculine culture that prized dogfighting and the mischievous torture of animals alongside boxing, drinking, and gambling dominated tavern life in the early republic. This culture, however, was increasingly marginalized as gentility, religious revivals, and economic improvement led many men, especially elite men, to value respectability and restraint. The growing class-based disdain for this tavern culture and its associated animal cruelty certainly flavored the criticisms aimed at the lower-class dog killers.[29]

While part of this outrage certainly had to do with the danger and indecency of exposing impressionable or delicate people to the butchery, it also was tied to the idea that dogs could very well be faithful, beloved members of bourgeois families. These dogs, in essence, were representatives of their families and were being killed at the hands of poorer New Yorkers who had a monetary incentive to act violently and seemingly ruthlessly. Even if the dogs caught were "curs of low degree," onlookers would likely show sympathy toward them, as they resembled their favored pet at home. The attacks on pets, such as dogs, evoked far more outrage from bourgeois New Yorkers than attacks on pigs, which they typically saw as pests. Watching these brutal killings time and time again throughout the city must have made the bourgeois spectators feel not only as if the virtuous principles of gentility and compassion were being transgressed, but also that to some degree the upper class itself was being attacked by the "idle and unfeeling" lower-class bounty hunters.[30]

While upper-class dog lovers might pin blame on lower-class "loafers" who clubbed the creatures for bounties, making it seem as if the campaigns against dogs were clearly divided along class lines, in reality dogs' defenders came from all economic classes. The bounty hunters were poor, but so too were many dog owners. These poorer owners who rioted or threatened dog catchers defended their canines as staunchly as the eloquent writers who used newspapers, magazines, and other literature to broadcast their arguments. With such widespread resistance, the Common Council could not effectively clear the streets of potentially dangerous let alone rabid dogs. To New York's dog lovers, rich and poor alike, the urban commons ought to have remained open for "the people's favorites" to roam and graze. Owners of the less charismatic animals who shared the streets with dogs had difficulty gathering similar political support.[31]

Loose Hogs

The differences between the ways New Yorkers considered hogs and dogs were stark. Pigs had far fewer defenders than dogs in nineteenth-century New York, especially among the middle and upper classes. Authors did not publish poetry in literary magazines waxing romantic about the beauty of the neighborhood sow or the loyalty of the piglets down the street; no one stood up in outrage at the death of a hog. Humor pieces abounded, but nothing nearly as earnest as what was penned in honor of canine New Yorkers. Hogs were livestock, not pets, and ownership did not cross social class, as was the case with dogs. The city had its share of wandering livestock, including cows, goats, and fowl, but hogs were by far the most numerous and attracted the most attention. They were everywhere.[32]

New Yorkers had been arguing about hogs for centuries. In 1640, the Dutch West India Company complained that its properties had suffered "great injury of cultivation and serious damage" at the hands (or hooves) of hogs and goats. A decade later, a desperate Peter Stuyvesant, the Director-General of New Amsterdam, threatened to shoot any hog found rooting near the fort. The English who succeeded the Dutch also found it difficult to deal with roaming swine; they struggled to enforce impoundment laws and organize government-regulated hunting of loose hogs on the streets.[33]

Hogs became an even bigger problem after the American Revolution. Following the war, the city's population boomed, garbage piled higher, and the hog population thrived. One 1820 estimate suggested that there were 20,000 hogs in the settled parts of Manhattan, or approximately one hog for every five humans in the city.[34]

By the 1810s, the controversy over hogs had become a hot topic for New Yorkers, revealing friction between wealthier and poorer neighbors.

While hogs had been owned by residents of all classes in colonial New York, in the early nineteenth century they were typically the property of poorer city residents. Wealthier New Yorkers had been able to abandon gardening and livestock raising in exchange for purchasing their food with cash at their local markets. Poorer New Yorkers with lower wages had a harder time making that transition. In consequence, as these issues with swine intensified, they began to reflect growing class tensions in the city.[35]

The role of hogs as livestock did not help their situation. They were not coddled or praised, the way pets such as dogs were. Certainly, some of their owners bonded with them, but their potential to be eaten or sold probably helped to limit the depth of that bond. Potential bourgeois allies did not have a propensity to sympathize with the plight of the urban hog, as they may have with the vagrant dog about to be caught or attacked, since they did not have similar creatures at home to compare. With real estate development pushing farms ever farther from the city's center, critics increasingly viewed hogs as foreign invaders in a human-centered environment. At best, they were seen as a food source; at worst, as stubborn, filthy impediments on streets and sidewalks. The hogs hardly garnered the same level of respect that dogs did.

The fact that hogs were domesticated animals, and therefore tied directly to human owners, made their omnipresence on the streets not only an environmental nuisance but also a social problem for New Yorkers who wanted them gone. Hog owners, being poor, certainly exacerbated these tensions. In anonymous letters to newspapers, critics of loose hogs routinely drew parallels between pigs and their owners, using Edmund Burke's phrase "the swinish multitude" to describe both populations. In his *Reflections on the Revolution in France* (1790), Burke, a conservative Whig politician in Britain, referred to the French masses as the "swinish multitude" when he warned readers of the perils of allowing the lower classes to gain political power. The controversial phrase gained notoriety in antebellum America and elsewhere. For the New York authors who appropriated the phrase for their swinish situation, urban hogs were as much of an "other" as the Irish immigrants and African Americans who owned them. The fact that people associated pigs with the city's lower classes led to many vicious, tongue-in-cheek poems and letters by critics who saw the animals and their owners as interchangeable. Through these comparisons, whether drawn in humor or in anger, critics of loose hogs emphasized the ridiculousness of allowing outsiders—base pigs and their similarly base owners—to run their city.[36]

Yet when Europeans visited the city, their criticism of the roaming hogs condemned *all* New Yorkers, not just the poor who owned them. In 1819 an English tourist found the city to be "miserably dirty," with "innumerable hungry pigs of all sizes and complexions, great and small beasts prowling in grunting ferocity, and in themselves so great a nuisance, that would arouse the indignation of any but Americans." Worried about such reactions, a group of concerned New Yorkers pleaded with the Common Council to refine the city. Discussing a vacant lot filled with rubbish, swine, cattle, and beggars, a neighbor appealed to the city to clean it up: "[The Common Council's] interference becomes doubly urgent, in this instance, from the consideration, that the nuisance above mentioned exists in the section of town which is most frequented by our citizens, and by strangers who visit New York." The city's image was at stake.[37]

Critics of loose pigs frequently referred to the city as being "disgraced" by the presence of the animals. Ironically, many American cities, such as Philadelphia, Washington, D.C., and Baltimore, as well as many smaller cities, had roaming hog populations. One traveler, who derogatorily referred to hogs as America's "favorite pet," declared that he had "not yet found any city, county or town where [he had] not seen these lovable animals wandering about peacefully in huge herds." Many European cities and towns likewise struggled with their hog populations. New York's situation was not exceptional, though it seems that New York had a larger population of hogs than most other cities. Pittsburgh, for instance, faced similar troubles with both hogs and dogs, though on a smaller scale. Regardless of the hog's universality in cities, New Yorkers were concerned about the influence of swine on the identity of *their* city. To visitors and local critics alike, the hogs symbolized all that was backward in New York. They represented the city government's inability to effect change and promote the progress of the city. When critics complained about hogs, they were also in many ways complaining about the undesirable classes that impinged on *their* public space and municipal government.[38]

The hog owners, however, saw these issues more in terms of survival than in terms of modernity or progress. Whereas in the eighteenth century laborers lived and ate in the homes of master craftsmen, with the growth of wage labor most of these men had to find separate housing and pay rent. Food was rarely cheap, and over time prices became less predictable with the gradual demise of government price protections, such as the bread assize. Jobs for day laborers were hardly stable, often seasonal, and completely dependent on weather and economic conditions. Municipal welfare programs, which expanded in a haphazard fashion in response to emergencies and immediate pressures, assisted some of the poor with food and fuel but could not keep up with New York's ballooning population in the early nineteenth century. During periods of economic crisis, such as after the War of 1812, alternative sources of income and food were especially crucial.[39]

New York's laboring poor used hogs as a cheap and efficient way to make ends meet. Avid consumers of food waste, the hogs utilized the garbage on New York's streets in an even more practical way than the dogs: they turned it into protein that New Yorkers would eat. They foraged among the heaps of garbage in the de facto urban commons, finding their day's diet within a few blocks of their home. While butchers certainly took advantage of this situation to fatten their soon-to-be-butchered hogs, this urban commons was crucial for the survival of New York's poorest families. When the hog owners argued for the right to keep their livestock, they maintained that hogs made it possible for the poor to "pay their rents and supply their families with animal food, during the winter." By selling a pig or two, poor New Yorkers were able "to procure some other articles necessary for their comfort and convenience." They pleaded that without their livestock, they would be forced to rely on the charity of the city and become a "public burden."[40]

These poorer New Yorkers argued in petitions to the city that swine played an important role in cleaning the streets of garbage. Since the city did not have the resources to hire enough street sweepers to collect trash, hog owners contended that sanitation and public health problems actually would worsen without swine to keep them under control. Pigs were "our best scavengers, as they instantly devour all fish guts, garbage, and offal of every kind, which is suffered to remain during the summer months, would be very offensive and might very probably be injurious to the health of the inhabitants." Garbage collecting in the poorer neighborhoods was irregular at best, and allowing hogs to forage was one method for removing trash and preserving the health of these residents.[41]

New Yorkers who wanted hogs off the streets countered that the municipal government ought to fund and regulate street cleaning more effectively, creating jobs for people, not swine. They believed that taking care of the streets would solve multiple problems. In 1809, a self-styled "friend to order and improvement" wrote to the *Republican Watch-Tower* pleading with the city to get rid of the trash so that the "hogs would disappear." If the city would just clean the streets, the hogs would have less to subsist on and the owners would essentially be forced to take them off the street and either give up the hog business or find alternative food sources for their animals. Critics linked the existence of hogs to a chaotic city where neither the government nor the citizens had control of the situation. With the dramatic transformations occurring during this period, many residents hoped the city would evolve into a more organized, manageable environment. If "progress" for these New Yorkers meant the municipal government's maintaining control over its nuisances, pigs stubbornly grunted in resistance.[42]

Hogs also disrupted city life with their constant rooting, which made the roads "unfit for driving over in wagons and carts." They dug up cobblestones with their snouts, creating traffic disruptions, accidents, and muddy holes for pedestrians to dodge. In 1812 the Common Council noted that pigs were tearing apart a sidewalk near the Battery, one of the more prestigious residential neighborhoods at the time and a popular tourist destination: "Every description of filth is there deposited & the swine by rooting up the ground & wallowing there in the mire, make the passage to the Battery from Broadway not only very unsightly but very offensive." As the city became more populous, the number of problems and severity of the accidents only increased. Horses would either get scared by or stumble over pigs loitering in the streets, causing carriages to tip over, often injuring passengers and bystanders.[43]

Critics of loose hogs also complained about the danger they posed to public health. Swine were closely tied to the filth and unpleasant smells that characterized the streets and public places of the city. Hogs and garbage, after all, went hand in hand. The nineteenth-century medical community generally believed that the offensive smell of the animals, their exhalations, and their environs fostered epidemics. After each outbreak of yellow fever and cholera, complaints about hogs increased in number both in newspaper articles and in letters to the government. New Yorkers even blamed mundane aches and illnesses on the hogs. It was not uncommon for those suffering from headaches and nausea to attribute their ailments to their neighbors' fondness for swine. While hogs certainly had the ability to transmit epizootic diseases, the connection between hogs and these health issues was much more tenuous than the connection between dogs and rabies.[44]

Critics argued that the threat of these urban hogs was even greater because they were consumed as food. Ham and pork, as well as other porcine products, were staples in the diets of Americans, rich and poor, in the early nineteenth century. Butchers and consumers could easily preserve pork through salting and smoking, which was an enormous advantage, since refrigeration was both difficult and expensive. Not only were hog owners able to eat their street hogs, they could also sell them to

FIGURE 3. Hyde de Neuville, *Bridewell, and Charity-School, Broadway, Opposite Chamber Street—February 1808*. Loose animals mix with pedestrians behind City Hall, near the Office of the Board of Health. (I. N. Phelps Stokes Collection, Miriam and Ira D. Wallach Division of Art, Prints and Photographs, The New York Public Library, Astor, Lenox, and Tilden Foundations.)

the butchers of the city. Critics, however, complained of the potential dangers of eating these "walking sewers" that regularly consumed the waste left on the streets, though the reality of this threat was less clear. One writer for the *Evening Post* claimed that "when they become diseased, from high feeding on dead cats and the vermin in the gutters, or any other cause, they soon find their way to our butcher's stalls. Knowing this may be the case, if in fact it is not, many people of my acquaintance whose stomachs are rather squeamish, would as soon taste a broiled rat as the finest looking griskin [pork loin] or roaster that can be brought to the table." Wealthy New Yorkers who had the choice preferred to eat the pricier, country-raised hogs from Long Island and New Jersey.[45]

Critics of loose hogs found that one of the most effective ways to enrage voters—more effective perhaps than complaining of objectionable meat—was to expose the danger hogs posed to women and girls, a tactic which started to appear in the newspapers in 1815. While boys mischievously rode hogs down the streets and men caned hogs to get them to move, women and girls were more often attacked by the creatures. One observer happened to be passing by as a "bristly invader, in his precipitate retreat across the pavement, upset a lady in full dress for a party, and landed her broad-side in the filth of the gutter! The result was, no bones were broken; but her dress so soiled as to require an entire change." The roles of women and girls remained almost constant in the anecdotes used by those pleading for the removal of the swine. Burly hogs threw women off their feet into mud puddles, and angry sows threatened the lives of little girls. Through tales that were likely exaggerated for dramatic effect, authors invited the men of the city and specifically the aldermen to be valiant heroes and make the city safe for genteel womenfolk. Just as elite New Yorkers were concerned that women and children should not witness the brutality of bounty hunters clubbing dogs, critics here argued that women and children should not have to encounter loose hogs in a respectable, civilized city. Loose animals endangered the spaces presumed safe for genteel families.[46]

Yet hog owners would perhaps argue that the women in these stories represented only a specific population of the city. Many working-class women owned and cared for the hogs that were the villains of these tales. The hogs contributed to their household economy, and female members of the family were likely the ones who tended the swine when necessary. These women were also actively involved in protesting the laws and rioting. While critics might argue that *all* women were threatened by the quadrupeds, they were not accounting for those who depended on them.[47]

While the complaints critics lodged against dogs dealt almost completely with the rabies threat and very occasionally with nighttime howling, the complaints against hogs were manifold. New Yorkers angling to ban loose hogs developed their various arguments in newspaper articles, letters, and government petitions in an attempt to compel the government to act. Compared with dogs, hogs posed very little immediate threat to public health, so critics chose to focus on the threats they posed to decency, food quality, traffic, pedestrians, and the city's image. Supporters of hogs and dogs likewise differed. Dog lovers tried to elicit sympathy and compassion from readers in their pleas, while hog owners made economic arguments. Hogs and dogs may have mingled indiscriminately among the city's heaps of trash, but the debates they provoked differed markedly.

The arguments between those who were for and those who were against free-roaming hogs had fully matured by the mid-1810s, when hogs had become so numerous that their presence could no longer be ignored and real estate pressures began to transform neighborhoods. Following the War of 1812, the city fell into an economic slump. Facing unemployment or underemployment, many of the poorest New Yorkers scraped by using alternative means of subsistence and income. At the same time, the city's population was growing rapidly, and stylish neighborhoods were pushing into the outskirts of town where these working-class New Yorkers lived. This clashing of neighborhoods and classes, along with the rising number of hogs, brought the conflict to a boiling point.[48]

In November 1816 Abijah Hammond, one of the city's wealthiest landowners and merchants, rallied a group of approximately 200 like-minded New Yorkers and submitted a petition to the Common Council calling for the removal of all free-roaming swine from the streets. The councilmen themselves were not unlike Hammond in terms of class, the majority being lawyers, merchants, and a few successful master craftsmen. The Common Council had been debating the wording of a new law pertaining to free-roaming swine in the months before Hammond's petition, but progress came to a standstill that October, when it was tabled. Hammond's petition may have been an attempt to break the deadlock and get the ordinance passed. Following the presentation of the petition, the aldermen continued to hesitate. They considered drafting a law but twice postponed voting on it: the first time because it would "oblige the poor owners" to kill off their herds before the usual butchering season in the fall; the second because it would jeopardize their own political careers if discussed before the April elections. That May, however, the council returned to the issue and resolved to be done with pigs once and for all. Hog owners got word of the council's intentions and united quickly under the leadership of Adam Marshall, an African American chimney sweep. In merely two days, they drew up a petition containing eighty-seven signatures and marks of both men and women that implored the city to "pity the poor" and allow the hogs to remain, as they were a necessary resource for the destitute. The *Evening Post* reported that the petitioners read the remonstrance in such a dramatic fashion that the aldermen felt the need to adjourn for a week.[49]

Hearing about this display, critics belittled the hog owners' efforts in the newspapers. One author mocked the petition as being "signed, or at least *marked* by the principal master chimney sweeps, who generally keep droves of hogs for our amusement." By mentioning the chimney sweeps, this writer was signaling to readers that Marshall and the other petitioners were African American, since chimney sweeping was commonly known to be an African American occupation. In fact, only about half of the petitioners were African Americans. Hog owners were mainly united by their economic status as unemployed or unskilled laborers, rather than by their race. They were typically recent Irish or English immigrants, as well as African Americans. The author's reference to "chimney sweeps," however, helped to emphasize the outsider status of hog owners and the ridiculousness of their animals. Prior to the 1821 revision of the New York State constitution, African Americans held the same voting rights as all other New Yorkers. It was not unusual to find men such as Adam Marshall actively involved in petitioning the Common Council to protect their interests and those of other working-class New Yorkers. Yet in the eyes of critics, Marshall and the other hog owners had little right to influence the aldermen, and, in doing so, dictate how public space should be used.[50]

When the council reconvened on May 27 and avoided the contentious topic of the hog law, New Yorkers campaigning for the removal of hogs used humor to criticize what they saw as the impotence of the government. One writer remarked that in battling the government, the hogs and, by implication, their owners had "kept their ground, grunting a sturdy defiance." Hog owners seemed to have the Common Council's ear. Satire remained an important way for the elite critics to address what they saw as an embarrassment to the city. It served as an entertaining and artful technique for criticizing the city government and its poorest citizens while also wooing like-minded New Yorkers to join their cause. Critics interchanged stereotypes about hogs with racial and ethnic stereotypes about hog owners.

The aldermen waited for the dust to settle before they debated the proposed law a month later. The document stipulated that hogs running at large would be impounded and their owners would pay $10 plus costs to recover their property. This was an exceptionally steep fine at a time when the average artisan earned approximately $1 per day. In contrast to the dog law, the hog law did not legalize the killing of swine, as they were not an immediate threat to the lives of New Yorkers in the same way rabid dogs were. They also had an economic and nutritional value that enabled them to be resold at auction or used by the city's almshouse to feed paupers. Regardless, the law was defeated by four votes, only to be considered again that October at the behest of numerous constituents pushing for hog-free streets. This time the Common Council passed the ordinance on the same day it was proposed, leaving the hog owners with no time to assemble and draw up another petition. The aldermen scheduled the law to take effect January 1, 1818. In the meantime, the supporters of the hog law celebrated their long-awaited success.[51]

The hog owners, however, fretted about the implications of this new law. Adam Marshall again rallied his hog-owning compatriots to sign a

petition calling for the city to repeal the law, but they were less than successful. Once more, the anti-pig press ridiculed the efforts of "a black
man and chimney sweep" to challenge "common decency." The tension
over class and race embedded in these battles over hogs was hardly hidden. Regardless, Marshall was undeterred and tried yet again on behalf
of the hog owners, presenting a third petition to the Common Council
just a month after the law had taken effect. This document was much
more substantial than the petitions they had presented before, containing 140 signatures of only white men, and rolling out to be nearly five
feet long. Marshall, though African American himself, likely felt he
could be more effective and avoid the predictable ridicule of the press
by excluding African Americans and women from the list. The petitioners also responded to the criticisms in the newspapers by including only
signatures and no marks (such as an X), which had earlier indicated the
illiteracy of some of their supporters. Addressing the especially unfair
nature of the law that allowed private individuals to take pigs off the
streets in exchange for a reward, the petitioners claimed that "unjust
and rapacious men have prowled through several parts of the upper
wards, and under colour of this Law seized on the property of the poor,
and even appropriated it to their own uses." The city had essentially "let
loose a swarm of informers upon the defenseless poor." After this petition and another were read before the council, the persuaded aldermen
repealed the law.[52]

Opponents responded in kind, mourning the repeal and calling on
voters to oust the aldermen at the next election. One poet, angered by the
repeal, mused that the rulers of the city were four-legged:

> But now the hogs,
> Those grunting dogs,
> Have made their sway complete;
> A voice they have
> In Council grave,
> And rule in ev'ry street.

Those, like the poet, who were against the presence of loose hogs were frustrated that the city government was not supportive of their vision for New York City's public spaces. While the aldermen themselves hailed primarily from the city's mercantile elite during this period, they did not represent only elite interests, as evidenced by their responsiveness to the pleas of the hog owners. Their critics returned to publishing satirical and humorous pieces in the newspapers, ridiculing the government's friendliness toward swine while pleading with the city to reissue a strict hog law.[53]

Aggravated by the uniquely nonpartisan nature of the debates, one critic suggested "designating the ticket for aldermen and assistants that contains the names of such as are in favor of the hogs as *The Hog Ticket*" at the upcoming municipal election. Those voting for the repeal of the hog law certainly included more Republican aldermen than Federalists, but the division was geographic rather than political. Aldermen and assistant aldermen from the outer wards typically supported the interests of hog owners. Representing wards with lower land values, these aldermen counted many hog owners among their constituents. In the postwar economy, with limited municipal resources for welfare and many constituents struggling, the removal of their ward's hogs would probably have caused more immediate problems than it would have solved.[54]

While the aldermen attempted to balance the needs of the city's destitute with the demands of the increasingly vocal anti-pig faction, Mayor Cadwallader D. Colden considered himself above the fray. Unlike the aldermen, Colden had been named to his post by the state's Council of Appointment rather than elected, and therefore was not subject to the same political pressure by constituents. Colden, who descended from an elite New York family, was decidedly against loose hogs. In 1818, soon after he took office, Colden decided to use his position as judge of the Court of General Sessions to break the Common Council's stalemate by calling a grand jury to hear evidence on urban pig-keeping. The jury returned an indictment charging two artisans with creating a nuisance by keeping hogs on the street. One defendant offered no defense, was quickly convicted, and paid a nominal fee; but the other, Christian Harriet, maintained his innocence and hired lawyers, thereby sending the case to trial.[55]

Mayor Colden hoped *The People vs. Christian Harriet* would be the legal end for the city's roaming pigs. Harriet's lawyers, however, claimed that he had the right to keep pigs in the streets, as this was a practice of "immemorial duration" and "our ancestors had never been troubled with any excessive notions of delicacy on the subject." The attorneys pleaded with the jury to recognize the importance of the pigs, whose exile would cause the poor to be driven deeper into poverty. They argued that the case should be dismissed, since the council had repealed the law earlier that year. Mr. Van Wyck, the prosecutor, and Mayor Colden, the judge, argued that despite the absence of a municipal law, the city was still obliged to follow English common law precedents against nuisances. Hogs, regardless of their benefit to the poor, qualified as a nuisance, which Colden defined as "an offence against the public order and economical regimen of the state, and an annoyance to the public." To Colden, public order meant controlling how people used the streets. Apparently, Colden's "public" did not include the hog owners who depended so heavily on these animals. By declaring loose hogs to be a "nuisance," Colden was unleashing the authority of the city to limit the hog owners' property rights. Nuisance law was one of the primary ways nineteenth-century cities exerted control over private property in order to protect public welfare. Responding to the defense's claim that barring pigs from the streets would harm the poor, the mayor declared, "Why, gentlemen! Must we feed the poor at the expense of human flesh?" He played on the fears that loose hogs were not only a nuisance but also a threat to the welfare of the city's women and children. With the mayor's urging, the jury found Harriet guilty.[56]

The People vs. Christian Harriet set a precedent that was followed for at least the next two years. Instead of struggling to pass laws against all pig owners, the prosecutors focused on indicting random, individual offenders for their negligence. The New Yorkers fighting for safer, cleaner streets praised the efforts of the courts in newspaper articles and hoped that the cases would have a significant impact. The mayor had used his position as judge to circumvent the Common Council's deadlock. As one newspaper put it, "We must look to our courts for the remedy; it is considered too unpopular for the corporation to meddle with it." Mayor Colden found this to be the easiest way to avoid dealing with petitioners and voters who did not support his vision for streets cleared of pigs.[57]

It is noteworthy that a similar tactic was not used to target owners who let their dogs run freely. On the one hand, such a piecemeal, labor-intensive method would have done little to appease critics during the widespread rabies panics, when a quick and effective method of removing the dogs was crucial. On the other hand, hog owners came almost uniformly from the lower classes, and perhaps the mayor would have faced less resistance throwing these men and women in jail or fining them than he would have if he had attempted to do so with the dog owners, who came from all classes, including the wealthiest.

After a few years, it had become apparent that the hog owners had not been frightened into compliance by the threat of indictment. In 1821 Mayor Stephen Allen took office, ready to tackle the hog problem. Realizing that Colden's tactic had been unsuccessful, Allen brought the issue back before the Common Council. The council then passed a law requiring that all pigs collected on the street be brought to the almshouse, where they would be served for dinner. Though the law was already on the books, little was being done to enforce it.[58]

As was the case with the dog law, the hog law did not place the enforcement of the law under the jurisdiction of the City Inspector, who was typically in charge of public nuisances and protecting the public health, but instead assigned the job to the almshouse commissioners. Tasked with caring for the city's growing ranks of impoverished residents, the commissioners could hardly be expected to effectively clear the city's streets of its thousands of hogs. The logic behind this decision never made it into the records, but the Common Council seems to have reasoned that if the almshouse commissioners were benefiting from all that ham, pork, and bacon, they should be in charge of collecting it.

Since the almshouse commissioners were unable to enforce the new law fully, New Yorkers saw little improvement in the state of their streets after its passage, a situation that was not out of the ordinary for most laws during this period. A few angry constituents wrote to the newspapers a month later pleading with the city to take action, claiming that "unless [the aldermen] wish to make fools of themselves and expose themselves to the contempt and ridicule of the public, they will cause all their laws to be strictly enforced." Determined to make the ordinance effective, the Common Council resolved that it "be carried into full operation against the offenders."⁵⁹

A mere four weeks later, the council once again ran into problems. The almshouse commissioners announced that they had tried to collect the hogs, but the hog catchers had been violently resisted by the hogs' owners. Mayor Allen called the collectors together a few weeks later and warned that if they did not execute the law, they would forfeit their licenses. When the hog catchers resumed their tasks later that week, they were immediately resisted by hundreds of hog owners. Locals assaulted the hog catchers with mud, rotten food, hot water, and broomsticks. A riot had begun. The rioters were a diverse group of women and men, largely made up of working-class Irish and African Americans.⁶⁰

Perhaps the hog owners resorted to violence this time because a large number of them—namely, the African Americans—had lost the ability to use more customary means of political protest, such as petitioning, with the restriction of their suffrage under the 1821 New York State constitution. Prior to the 1821 convention, race-blind property requirements had restricted suffrage. There was a push among many white, upstate residents, who saw the limits to suffrage as undemocratic, to amend the constitution. With full emancipation of New York's African American population planned for 1827, rural representatives at the constitutional convention feared what full black suffrage might mean. Ultimately, the convention decided to raise property requirements for black men to $250, while white men could vote as long as they had served in the military, worked on the roads, or met tax requirements. Even these meager limits on white suffrage would be eliminated five years later. The race-based suffrage restrictions, however, left African Americans legally unequal and gave them fewer ways to reach their politicians. While petitioning to save their hogs might have been ineffective, rioting could still grab a politician's attention and block a hog catcher.[61]

In response to the riot, the Common Council decided to limit the hog law so that it excluded the outer wards, where resistance was particularly strong. Clearly frustrated, supporters of the hog law belittled the riot as a feeble attempt to "oppose the execution of this salutary ordinance." Feeble or not, the hog owners were successful. By April 1822, the papers were noting that the Common Council indulged the hog owners, "who openly disregarded the ordinance, and set it at defiance." The editors of the *Evening Post* complained that pigs were still found trampling through piles of garbage on the streets a year later, in 1823, "notwithstanding the prohibitions against them." The law was as good as dead.[62]

When the city tried to reinvigorate its efforts to collect hogs in 1825, the resistance of the hog owners remained strong. The government extended the hog law into the Eighth Ward, a neighborhood that had predominantly housed working-class New Yorkers but was experiencing gentrification. Some of the ward's wealthier residents had petitioned the Common Council that March to get rid of the swinish nuisance. They planned to polish up their streets, and the first step involved getting rid of the pigs that sat on their stoops and blocked their sidewalks. The aldermen eagerly obliged. The aldermen anticipated some resistance from the neighborhood's hog owners, so they sent four officers, including Abner Curtis, the former Dog Register, to accompany the hog catchers. By the time the six men reached the upper end of Hudson Street, near Vandam, their cart teemed with squealing swinish captives. Angry men and women had gathered around them—a crowd the newspapers referred to as "a large mob of disorderly people." With their demands for the return of the livestock unmet, the protesters became violent. Henry Bourden—an Irish laborer who lived in the Eighth Ward with his wife, four children, and likely several pigs—grabbed a four-pound weight, perhaps a brick, and hurled it at the officers. He hit Abner Curtis in the face, knocking him down. After the crowd had overpowered the hog catchers and officers, they broke open the back of the wooden cart and "let loose all of the hogs, who quickly scampered off in different directions." The hog catchers were so effectively blocked in the Eighth Ward by Henry Bourden and his neighbors that the law was again considered obsolete.[63]

The hog owners continued to protect their property and their right to use public space each time the city government enforced the hog law. Thomas F. De Voe, a butcher, wrote that he had witnessed many scrimmages in 1825 following the Eighth Ward riot "where the negro hog-catchers, and also the officers who attended them, were either cheated out of their prey, or obliged entirely to desist, . . . [and] almost every woman, to a man, was joined together for common protection in resisting their favorites from becoming public property." Additional riots occurred in 1826, 1830, and 1832 following the same pattern, with several hundred people emerging each time to block the passage of the hogcart by whatever means necessary. While their opponents continued to complain about the city's inability to implement the laws, the pig owners had successfully prevented the city from enforcing them, at least for the time being. The hog law was not just being imposed repressively from the top. Hog owners played an active role in amending the laws by fighting them with petitions and riots. The Common Council made exceptions when residents in the outer wards lobbied to have the hog law lifted. The city government, which was better at creating hog laws than enforcing them, lacked the organization, power, and will to make a concentrated effort to take charge of the city's public spaces. The near-constant frustration of those trying to get rid of loose hogs was evidence that elite New Yorkers did not exclusively control the urban environment.[64]

By 1841, though Manhattan had grown remarkably, become the home of countless immigrants, and seen its commerce flourish following the opening of the Erie Canal, the city's streets remained in a state of decay. The editors of the *New-York Tribune* complained that they were growing tired of calling on the Common Council to reform the streets: "We are daily required again and again to remonstrate against the horrible condition of our Streets, and the great numbers of Dogs, Hogs, and other forbidden animals by which they are so thickly infested. We heartily agree with those who address us on the subject; but what is the use of writing about it? Officers of the City! do your duty this year, or you will provoke the People to do *theirs* next Spring!" The *Tribune's* complaints replicate almost exactly the grievances of the letter writer in 1817, who found his trials in the city so exhausting. Little seemed to have changed in nearly a quarter-century. New York's aldermen still struggled to control public spaces, and New Yorkers continued to fight over how these spaces should be used. When the scores were tallied, poorer New Yorkers had perhaps the most control over the urban environment in this instance. When their petitioning efforts failed, they took to the streets to free their hogs physically. They fought and won their ability to use the urban commons by getting the laws repealed or by frustrating enforcement.[65]

New York's municipal government was unable to establish effective control over the city's loose animals during the first half of the nineteenth century, and this failure resulted from a number of factors. If constituents were not on board with a new law, there was little hope for effective enforcement. While dogs certainly benefited from having a range of supporters across the economic spectrum, hogs were not doomed simply because they lacked wealthy backers. With inadequate resources and organization and a city expanding beyond its reach, the Common Council had a difficult time taking control of the urban environment. In both cases, any sort of resistance to the laws helped to dismantle whatever attempts the city made at clearing the streets. The municipal government could not effectively enforce the laws without compliance from New Yorkers. It would take widespread public outrage to bring about a sweeping end to the problem of free-roaming urban animals.

As they wrote and revised the dog and hog laws, members of the Common Council decided for various reasons to delegate responsibility for the laws' enforcement to separate offices—whether a Register and Collector's office, as in the case of the dogs, or that of the alms-house commissioners, in the case of the hogs—according to what seemed most appropriate at the time. Unfortunately, this haphazard expansion of government services helped to complicate and confuse the bureaucratic process and in most cases made efficiency and enforcement even more difficult. Instead of assigning these tasks to the City Inspector's office and expanding its funding and power so that they could effectively control the free-roaming animals as part of their other responsibilities in minding the streets, the aldermen blurred the jurisdictions. In this way, they essentially reduced the level of responsibility in each of the departments and hampered efficient management of the city's issues.

Institutional inertia proved to be an effective force in keeping the urban commons open for hogs, dogs, and other foragers, to the chagrin of those who campaigned tirelessly for its closure. New York's filthy streets had cultivated an informal economy and a fertile environment for roving creatures, and for the time being the inability of New York's municipal government to effect long-lasting change made it possible for New Yorkers and their animals to continue using the streets as they had before. Without the services necessary to remove the garbage that made the streets so welcoming to foragers, and without the organization to enforce their ordinances, city officials provided an environment that allowed New Yorkers to set their dogs and hogs out to roam the streets.[66]

There were brief moments, to be fair, when the government managed to enforce its ordinances, especially in the case of the dog law, but citizen outrage made long-lasting success impossible. New Yorkers and Americans more generally were coming to see beloved animals such as dogs in a new light, and cries of animal cruelty were growing louder as they reacted against the government-sponsored dog-killing sprees of the 1830s. Though the founding of the American Society for the Prevention of Cruelty to Animals would not occur until 1866, more and more people were coming to believe that violence toward animals was harmful not only to the animals themselves but also to the society that accepted it. While hogs, as less-beloved livestock, did not elicit the same compassion, dogs pulled at the heartstrings of owners and sympathizers, who winced at the open displays of brutality seen daily on the streets.[67]

These battles over loose animals provide a glimpse into how New York's classes interacted. When New Yorkers described these animals, their descriptions moved beyond the specific dogs and hogs to include their owners. When an author in a literary magazine wrote effusively about a "large dog, black as the raven, and of fine form: his head was such as sometimes looks down on you from the silent study of the painter; his body was covered with a profusion of glossy black curls," he clearly meant to celebrate members of his own elite class—the type of people who would own and respect such a refined creature. And when another author described a hog as "the filthiest part of the brutes," his disdain for the city's poor shone through. Hogs, often considered to be among the lowliest of farm animals because of their ravenous, greedy behavior, were ripe for insults. When newspaper writers grumbled about the power of the swinish multitude, they were making a statement not only about the state of the city's streets but also about its residents. While wealthier New Yorkers were perhaps hesitant to insult their poorer neighbors directly, insulting their animals provided an outlet for airing class tensions. The streets were a place where New Yorkers had to face off not only against animals, but also against one another.[68]

When the pedestrian of 1817 took his walk through the city that spring day, he was as much bemoaning the nuisances of the city—the hogs, dogs, shanties, and general filth—as he was complaining about the changing character of New York. With out-of-control growth and an almost constant flow of new immigrants, the city was almost unrecognizable when compared to what it had been even a decade before. The city government needed to adjust to its new demands, and New Yorkers had to determine what—and *who*—belonged within city limits. These considerations would continue to play a large role in the development, distribution, and use of the city's parks during the real estate boom of the 1830s.

2

Unequally Green

Amid cannons roaring, guns saluting, church bells ringing, and fireworks bursting, New York City ushered in a new era. On November 4, 1825, the city celebrated the opening of the Erie Canal, the engineering marvel that would reroute much of the nation's commerce through its port. New York City was the final stop on a ten-day-long jubilee that involved handsomely decorated boats, extensive festivities, and countless political speeches in every major town from Buffalo to New York. The highlight of the celebration in Manhattan was the marriage of the waters, when Governor Dewitt Clinton poured a cask of water from Lake Erie into New York Harbor. Carefully choreographed by city leaders, an extensive parade of city and state politicians, soldiers, merchants, professionals, and artisans followed the aquatic procession. Late-night fireworks in front of City Hall capped off a busy day of speeches, songs, and citywide revelry. The city had reason to celebrate. In his speech that day, Governor Clinton declared to New Yorkers: "There will be no limits to your lucrative extensions of trade and commerce." Newspapers proclaimed that the celebration marked the "commencement of a glorious era for New-York." Everything *was* changing for the city. The country as a whole was enjoying a real estate boom thanks to the easing of credit and an upswing in the business cycle, and the Erie Canal only helped to increase the benefits for New York. Indeed, in the years that followed, the artificial river did have a significant effect on the state's environment, but it also altered the face of the city. The city's enhanced prosperity led to significant social and environmental changes, evident in its new parks and tree-lined streets.[1]

Before the Erie Canal opened, New York City had only a handful of parks. In 1823 the *Evening Post* referred to the scarcity as "one of the greatest blemishes on the face of New York." Guidebooks routinely apologized to tourists for the deficiency. With land values on the rise, almost every square inch was developed downtown. The *Evening Post* railed against this "parsimonious disposition of [New York's] population which leaves no spot of ground in the settled part of the city unoccupied with buildings." With two of the city's major parks on former burial grounds, it seemed as though the only way to preserve open space was to fill it with corpses. Real estate interests had a strong influence on the workings and mind-set of municipal leadership, an influence that would only grow as property values skyrocketed following the opening of the canal and the city's subsequent rise as a commercial center for the country.[2]

New Yorkers' understanding of the role that parks and street trees played in the urban landscape changed dramatically during the late 1820s and 1830s, as politicians and speculators dreamed up ways to develop and refine the city. Advocates believed green spaces could solve several of the city's problems by making it healthier, creating elite spaces, and raising real estate values. After the cholera outbreak in 1832, the idea that parks provided a way to counter polluted, disease-ridden air certainly enhanced their popularity. Dense development blocked the sea air from circulating through New York's streets as it once had. Though boosters had long touted New York's wonderful situation between a river and an estuary, with a harbor ushering in fresh air, in the 1830s New Yorkers were coming to realize that their location was not enough. Advocates increasingly argued that parks were essential to the survival of the city. In addition, elite New Yorkers, who saw their control of the city slipping away as immigrants moved in and strangers grew wealthy, believed parks could help them regain their position. Perhaps the biggest incentive that drove the parks craze of the 1830s, though, was the benefit they brought to real estate values. Parks had the power to draw elite residents and raise the city's tax base. As a result, speculators and landowners proposed countless public and private parks for their neighborhoods. The ways that the aldermen handled these requests show exactly where their priorities lay.[3]

The new parks did not benefit all New Yorkers equally. As a result of the funding structure adopted by the city government, they existed almost exclusively in wealthy neighborhoods and in new housing developments designed to attract wealthy purchasers. Yet, despite the unequal distribution, park creation did not lead to riots in the ways that hog and dog catching did during this period. The growing inequalities in the greening of the urban landscape were buried in tax policies and ignored due to the seemingly indisputable belief that any new park was a boon to the city. Invisible yet pervasive policies such as these had as much influence over the distribution of environmental resources as did the public battles over loose animals and access to the urban commons. Whereas the 1850s champions of New York's more famous Central Park would argue for the benefits parks provided for the city's poor, the park promoters of the 1830s were not concerned about that. They were explicitly interested in creating exclusive, elite spaces that would lift real estate values and the city's tax base.[4]

Erasing the Grand Parade

Central Park was not the first big park proposed for the city. In 1807, when the mayor and Common Council asked the state legislature for permission to lay out a plan for the entire island, the map they approved four years later not only created New York's famous grid, but also designated land for its largest park yet: the Grand Parade, a 260-acre space that extended from 23rd Street to 34th Street, between Third Avenue and Seventh Avenue. Even though the commissioners had reserved it for military assembly and exercises, New Yorkers who were accustomed to mixing recreational and military uses in public parks saw this as a potential ornament for the city.[5]

A park like this would not have been possible without the municipal power to organize and purchase such a large swath of land. With the 1807 act, the state legislature authorized the city to use the power of eminent domain to purchase any land set aside on the official map for a street or park. The city's power over such enormous swaths of private property was unprecedented. The state appointed three commissioners with the task of laying out the city's future: Gouverneur Morris, the statesman and founding father; Simeon DeWitt, New York State's surveyor-general and a cousin of politician DeWitt Clinton; and John Rutherford, former New Jersey senator and respected New York businessman. Morris and DeWitt also served on the Erie Canal Commission, another project that would shape the future of the city. The appointment of these men was likely strategic: such elite and influential New Yorkers might wield the power to quiet discontented landowners. The commissioners had convenience, simplicity, and business on their minds as they plotted the future of the city onto the map drawn by John Randel, Jr., their hired surveyor.[6]

When the commissioners submitted the map to the Common Council in 1811, they intended it to aid the growth of the city and ease real estate transactions. They did not extend the older, narrow, twisted, and angular streets from downtown, but instead imposed a rational, right-

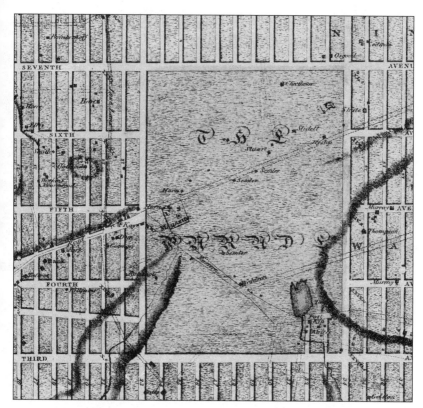

FIGURE 4. Detail of the Commissioners' Map of 1811, published by William Bridges, showing the Parade, along with the buildings and roads on the property as of 1811. (Collection of the New-York Historical Society.)

angled grid on the island. By having the streets planned out in advance, speculators and landowners could feel confident enough to develop their property without fear that the city would lay a street through it. The grid, which completely ignored the topographic and geographic irregularities of the island and required significant leveling to realize the plan, made it easier for developers to build "straight-sided and right-angled houses," according to the commissioners. Since its implementation, critics

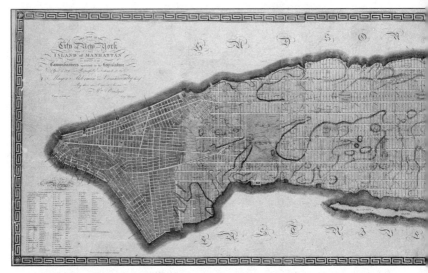

FIGURE 5. The Commissioners' Map of 1811, which plotted out New York's rectilinear future, left few breaks for parks. (Collection of the New-York Historical Society.)

including residents and scholars alike have characterized it as boring, monotonous, profit-centered, and "entirely deficient in sentiment and charm." John Randel, Jr., looking back at his life's work, defended the plan as it facilitated "buying, selling, and improving real estate, on streets, avenues, and public squares." With the 1811 plan, the commissioners sought to exert control over New York City's spontaneous, unregulated urban growth. Despite the plan's benefits for real estate interests, some New York landowners and developers still found reason to complain: there were just too many parks. Critics charged that the public squares set aside on the map cut into private property and limited development.[7]

The commissioners felt that they had kept public space to a minimum. Expecting the opposite criticism—that they had reserved too little open space—they explained that New York did not need much:

"Certainly, if the City of New-York were destined to stand on the side of a small stream, such as the Seine or the Thames, a great number of ample spaces might be needful; but those large arms of the sea which embrace Manhattan Island, render its situation in regard to health and pleasure, as well as to convenience of commerce, peculiarly felicitous; when, therefore, from the same causes, the price of land is so uncommonly great, it seemed proper to admit the principles of economy to greater influence than might, under circumstances of a different kind, have consisted with the dictates of prudence and the sense of duty." De-Witt, Morris, Rutherford, and Randel all noted that, in their minds at least, public spaces were intended more for the circulation of air than for beauty or recreation. Not only did New York not *need* park land, it would be a luxury given the price of real estate. The commissioners were interested in a simple, utilitarian design for the city, and that design did not include any of the fashionable "circles, ovals, and stars" that embellished plans for cities such as Washington, D.C., nor did it include many parks. The commissioners laid out six new squares, which they located far from the center of town in an attempt to anticipate the city's needs in the coming century, while also keeping away from desirable locations that would antagonize real estate interests and make the cost of municipal acquisition too high. Yet laying out these parks on the map did not automatically make them a reality. The parks were primarily located on private property, and the city would have to purchase the land before these spaces could be realized.[8]

Almost immediately, landowners attacked these penciled-in parks. The Common Council was all too happy to oblige the attackers, as this would save them from having to purchase such pricey lands. In closed-door sessions designed to keep their discussion out of newspapers, the councilmen decided to petition the New York State legislature so they could change the sizes of the public squares. The first order of business was to scale down the Grand Parade. The councilmen decided that the square "might be reduced to one half its present size, if not less, and yet be sufficient in size for all the purposes of the public parade." They also wanted to shrink Hamilton Square in what is now the Upper East Side and "discontinue" Union Place, later known as Union Square, given that these would "doubtless cost a large sum." The city government seemed to see open space as more of a burden than an endowment.[9]

The councilmen were not arguing that the parks were unnecessary, but rather claiming that they were too expensive. Even with the reduction in size of the Parade and Hamilton Square and the deletion of Union Place from the map, the councilmen estimated that the plan would probably cost over a million dollars, a rough number they used to emphasize the prohibitive cost of buying the property in all of the public squares laid out on the Commissioners' Map. The state legislature agreed only to slice up the Grand Parade (they spared Hamilton Square and Union Place) a few years later in 1814, after the city fathers repeated their request. The city and state politicians justified themselves by saying that "the expenses [of purchasing the Parade] will be enormous, and infinitely beyond the advantages which can possibly arise therefrom." The Parade consequently shrank by roughly 60 percent.[10]

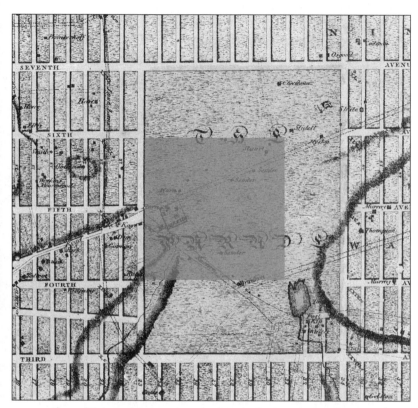

FIGURE 6. The 1814 law significantly shrank the boundaries of the Parade. Author's overlay on detail of the Commissioners' Map of 1811. (Collection of the New-York Historical Society.)

Despite slimming down, the Parade remained a target. While the Common Council appreciated the contribution that parks made to "the future splendour of our growing Metropolis," they also debated scaling down or completely erasing the Parade. Landowners put significant pressure on the aldermen to forget the Parade project and allow them to develop or sell their property as they wished. Their property was in real estate purgatory; unable to sell and unable to develop, they had to wait for the municipal government to decide what its plan would be. One outspoken landowner, Effingham Schieffelin, who served as an assistant alderman, continued to advocate the Parade's demise in council chambers year after year. Given the pressure from landowners, the aldermen felt they had to respond. As they did not have the funds to purchase the park immediately, they felt that the only reasonable alternative would be to whittle down the Parade by shaving off an additional 200 feet on either side. Although the state legislature staved off this encroachment on the Parade, the attacks were far from over.[11]

By 1826, as development inched closer to the park, the campaign to erase it grew stronger. Landowners sent annual petitions to the Common Council, begging the aldermen to take action on the Parade. For two decades their property was "so burthened, fettered and absolutely tied up, as to have debarred them from exercising the common Acts of Ownership over their estates." A real estate speculator appealed to city leaders to abandon their plan to develop the Parade completely and just run streets through it. In 1828, the aldermen finally took action. With property values rising, the council estimated that it would cost over a million dollars to purchase and regulate, or level, the ground. Judging this too high a price for taxpayers, the aldermen decided to rid the city of this proposed park. In a vote of 19 to 5, the council agreed to petition the state legislature to release them from their obligation to purchase the grounds of the Parade and allow them to extend the avenues and streets through it. As far as the city government was concerned, the Parade was as good as gone.[12]

Up until this point, the city's newspapers had made little mention about the future of the Parade. To some extent, this was because the members of the Common Council kept the doors closed during some of their deliberations about the space. Certainly, the fact that the Parade was so distant from the bulk of the citizens made its fate seem less urgent to many New Yorkers. But not everyone was so shortsighted. In June 1828 the front page of the *New-York Evening Post* featured an extensive letter from "Cornelius," who was puzzled by the media's silence, "for surely it cannot be the wish of the majority of our citizens to lose the Parade."

Cornelius's argument in favor of saving the Parade resembled the case that would be made by advocates of Central Park two decades later. His points were threefold: New Yorkers should save the Grand Parade for the health and well-being of the city, for women, who would have a safe place to walk, and for the benefit of future generations. Cornelius wondered how the city could be so callous as to rank wealth over health. Without public spaces, children would be at risk of becoming "puny and debilitated," since they would be unable to "romp and play . . . and inhale the fresh fragrance of the grass and flowers." Previous generations, according to Cornelius, had been wrong not to reserve more open space for its citizens. By neglecting the public's projected needs, they had done the city a disservice. Cornelius called on his fellow New Yorkers and the councilmen to look to the future. He wrote: "I hope that our citizens will be induced to arise . . . in favor of preserving themselves and their children forever so inestimable a treasure." The Parade had the potential to be the pride of the city and the nation.[13]

Bourgeois women, perhaps, had the most to gain from the park. Cornelius called on the city's women to take a stand and "induce their husbands to engage earnestly in the attainment" of the Parade. Cornelius wrote that the Parade should be especially important to women, since "they are less actively employed than we are, and consequently they have much more need of the benefit to be derived from public promenades." New York society accepted that parks and promenades were safe spaces for genteel women, which was not true of all urban spaces. If properly controlled, these spaces protected elite women from the environmental and social impurities of the rest of the city. Just as politicians and authors bemoaned the ways free-roaming animals made the city unsuitable for the gentler sex, carefully calibrated public spaces such as parks might prove a solution. According to Cornelius, if women wanted the freedom to move about in more areas of the city, they would need to champion these spaces.[14]

Unfortunately for Cornelius and other New Yorkers eagerly awaiting the development of the Parade, the letter in the *Evening Post* did little to stop the city and state from erasing the park from the map. Though it took another year, the state legislature sympathized with the city government's position and wrote a law that effectively returned the property to the unrestricted use of the landowners. With the passage of that law, in 1829, New York lost an opportunity to have its first "central park." Without adequate financing and foresight, the Parade was gone. In the 1820s the rights of individual property owners and the chance to limit municipal expenditures trumped the possible benefits of a large, open, public space.[15]

Fashionable Promenades

In the 1830s, New Yorkers' feelings toward parks changed. During that decade, advocates and even politicians came to embrace the arguments previously made by Cornelius as they proposed new spaces in the city. Elite New Yorkers specifically saw new parks as a means for them to retake control of the city's public spaces. Their newfound love of promenading and their insecurity about their status in the rapidly transforming city helped to fuel the park craze of the 1830s.

Promenading, which had been popular for decades, was becoming an increasingly important ritual for elite society in the late 1820s and 1830s, as the city tasted the wealth of the Erie Canal. As they paraded up Broadway or through the Battery, a park at the southern tip of the island, elite, well-dressed New Yorkers would stroll along and greet those they deemed fit to recognize with a graceful tip of their hat or nod of their head. These ritual-filled spectacles would occur at 6:00 P.M. on weekdays, with the most elaborate and extensive promenade right after church on Sunday. Journalist and author George Foster described the promenades in his book *New York in Slices:* "To see Broadway in its glory . . . you must wait till six o'clock, P.M. Then, if you take your stand in the door of a shop on the 'fashionable side,' you will see New York's possible [*sic*] in the way of beautiful women, scrupulously-dressed dandies and pretty children." Foster noted that an individual could risk his or her "fashionable reputation" by walking on the "shilling side" of the street during promenade hours. Rules governed the intricate social interactions on the walks, and knowledge of the rules was as much an indication of one's rightful place in elite society as anything else. While etiquette manuals detailed the standards of refinement, concerned citizens sometimes wrote to the newspapers to alert the public about breaches or about changes that might be necessary. The ideal result was a choreographed uniformity that Foster described: "All dressed in about the same decent habiliments, all carrying heads up, and observing the decorum of the street with due gravity and steadiness." This structured, refined sociability provided a key element of many New Yorkers' days: "their morning's anticipation, their evening's reminiscence."[16]

Yet promenading was not just about displaying fashion. This popular ritual helped to solidify class hierarchy in the intricate performances of acknowledging or ignoring passersby. Recognition legitimated one's acceptance into New York's high society. The complete exclusion and disgust of other pedestrians also solidified this hierarchy. Foster warned his readers, for instance, not to step onto Broadway unless they were in finest form: "If you are in doubt about yourself, if you are under a cloud, if your hat is rusty, or your coat 'going,' if you have been paragraphed as having failed, or as involved in any little unfortunate matter, shun Broadway as you would a fire. You will be shot down on your first appearance like an outlaw." New York's upper class was in a state of transition, as entrepreneurs and real estate speculators cashed in on the economic boom of the Erie Canal era and suddenly rose into the wealthy classes. With a constant flow of newcomers rushing into the city, it was increasingly difficult to keep a handle on the changing ranks of society. The elaborate ritual of promenading helped elite New Yorkers to sift out and shun the nouveaux riches and confidence men in their midst and police the class boundaries they felt slipping from their grasp. Taking place in popular spaces, these spectacles drew crowds of onlookers, who, by setting themselves apart from the promenaders and providing an audience, also reinforced these boundaries and the visual symbols of class formation.[17]

In this carefully calibrated public space, elite women could move freely. As Cornelius had argued in his call to save the Grand Parade, public promenades played a special role in the lives of bourgeois women. Protected from the indecencies of the lower class, as well as from other ethnicities and races, white genteel women could move about freely in a safe and constrained socializing ritual. The promenade was a solution for Victorian New Yorkers who felt that genteel women could not coexist with urban masses. The popularity of promenading and the push for parks in the 1830s was partly a response to the perceived threat that elite New Yorkers felt to their ownership of public space. Reclaiming public space, whether sidewalks or parks, for genteel women and men was one of the few ways they could feel more comfortable about the changing conditions of the city.[18]

Sometimes, however, promenaders found they were nearly powerless to exclude nonelites from their spaces. Asa Greene, author of *A Glance at New York* (1837), described how the working classes went to the Battery on Sundays to "escape . . . from their crowded quarters." He wrote that certain New Yorkers, offended by the intrusion of such people, "would, if it were in their power, banish them from the public walks. They are particularly offended that the common people should presume to appear on that delightful promenade the Battery. 'It is so very vulgar,' say these aristocrats, 'to be seen walking in the same grounds with mechanics, house-servants, and laboring people!'" Greene noted that due to this battle over public space, and the inability of the promenaders to force others out of the park, the Battery was beginning to lose its attractiveness.[19]

Promenades needed to be protected. All types of New Yorkers used the Battery, as Greene described, and making sure its promenade was not trampled or defaced was important to elite New Yorkers. A recurring battle concerned whether the military could practice its drills in the Battery. In 1830, for instance, a writer to the *New-York Spectator* echoed a typical refrain when he asked if there was a law protecting the public promenades of the city. He described a few occasions when he had been taking a walk and witnessed the way "a party of militia, composed of sixteen men, rank and file, accompanied by at least one hundred vagabonds of every age and sex, maneuvered on the Battery, doing more injury in one hour than nature could restore in a month." While protection of the park's landscaping seems to have been a major part of his argument, he was also arguing about which economic classes had true ownership of the park. When detailing another incident, he described the "vagabonds" as "men, women, and children, black and white, with apparently no object other than to wait the return of their officers." Petitioners regularly pleaded with the Common Council, begging the representatives to preserve the Battery from the military. The unspoken implication was that concerned New Yorkers also had to save the park from the militia's lower-class wives and ragamuffin children.[20]

Like social class, race divided those who promenaded from those who did not. In a particularly angry article printed in the *Evening Post* in 1826, the editor requested that the sidewalks on Broadway be segregated. Frustrated that the "mob of Blacks—I beg pardon, *ladies and gentlemen of color,*" were not getting out of the way for those promenading, the author pleaded: "Could not some arrangement, for instance, be made with them by which the street should be given up to them, one part of the Sunday evenings, upon condition they would give it up to us another?" The city's sidewalks, open to all New Yorkers, were too heterogeneous for the author. By advocating for segregated promenades, he was arguing for a way to reclaim the space (albeit temporarily) for certain New Yorkers who preferred not to mingle with the urban masses. New York State was gradually phasing out slavery, and anxiety over race relations and the reordering of the social hierarchy was high. In 1832, when Frances Trollope visited New York to gather material for her book *Domestic Manners of Americans,* she noted with bemusement the presence of African Americans in the promenade: "I have often, particularly on a Sunday, met groups of Negroes elegantly dressed; and have been sometimes amused by observing the very superior air of gallantry assumed by the men, when in attendance on their belles, to that of the whites in similar circumstances. On one occasion we met in Broadway

a young Negress in the extreme of fashion, and accompanied by a black
beau, whose toilet was equally studied; eye-glass, guard-chain, nothing
was omitted; he walked beside his sable goddess uncovered, and with
an air of the most tender devotion." As a theatrical representation of
New York's society, the promenade seemed like the perfect place to make
a statement about how society should be. White working-class New
Yorkers similarly challenged the promenade form, and, when rebuffed
by the elite, developed promenades of their own on the Bowery,
which was in a primarily working-class neighborhood. The reception
of the African American promenaders was cool at best and it inspired
at least some bourgeois white promenaders to find ways to protect their
walks. When elite New Yorkers came out in favor of parks, especially
private parks, certainly a number of the petitioners were looking for a
new space to mark as a promenade, since the Battery and Broadway had
been tainted from their perspective. The genteel New Yorkers who promenaded tried to reclaim urban space from the mixture of classes, ethnicities, and races, the violence and riots, even the pigs and filth endemic to
New York. New parks were a way to secure these refined spaces.[21]

The aldermen who argued in favor of parks also saw the benefits of
refining the city. Parks had the power to raise the value of nearby real
estate and consequently to increase property tax revenue. This allowed
the aldermen to take in more money without needing to make the politically unpopular decision to raise tax rates. While the city government paid for public works projects such as streets, sewers, and parks
with special assessments made on adjacent property owners, they paid
for most other expenses with property tax revenue and various fees. The
aldermen touted a number of benefits that parks might provide in
terms of public health and municipal pride, but the benefit that came
up time and time again was the value they would bring to real estate
and consequently the city's property tax revenue.[22]

It behooved the city aldermen to find ways to benefit from the
canal-inspired real estate boom. As downtown New York became increasingly commercial, wealthy residents moved to chic neighborhoods

uptown. From 1825 to 1830, the Second and Third wards downtown decreased in population by about 11 percent each, while the outer wards saw increases of somewhere between 50 and 108 percent. Throughout the city, property values soared. New York was thriving, and this was a great moment for developers to take advantage of the situation by developing the upper wards in extravagant ways that would lure elite New Yorkers and garner high prices. By going out of their way to support the efforts of developers and by doing everything in their power to bring parks to willing neighborhoods, city officials helped to reshape the urban landscape with their own interests firmly in mind. While their policies led to a city dotted with new green spaces, these spaces were increasingly privatized and far from equally distributed.[23]

The Public Benefit of a Private Park

While private parks were the most exclusive and exclusionary open spaces in a city other than back yards, the city government enthusiastically supported their development in the 1830s. Developers and politicians alike were coming to realize that elite spaces such as private parks had the ability to transform the city and lift property values sky high. Samuel B. Ruggles was one such developer. With the government's avid support, he transformed the marginal land just north of 14th Street into a fashionable, tax revenue–generating neighborhood.

When Ruggles left his law career behind to pursue real estate development in 1831, he first started accumulating farmland in the Twelfth Ward. Using money he inherited and borrowed, Ruggles purchased most of the land from 19th Street to 24th Street, between Bloomingdale Road (later known as Broadway) and Second Avenue. In the course of nine months and twenty-three real estate transactions, he assembled the property for Gramercy Park and its surrounding buildings. He had a plan that he hoped would make him rich.[24]

It took a lot of work on Ruggles's part to turn his property into the blank slate necessary to develop Gramercy into the neighborhood he envisioned. The land was not easy to conquer. The Crommessie Vly, also known as Cedar Creek or Winding Creek, flowed through wetlands and cattails on its way to the East River, cutting a deep gully through the property. Ruggles's friend and Columbia University president Charles King wrote about Ruggles's efforts to tame the land. Realizing that on one side he had morass, or boggy land, and on the other side Bowery Hill, which was twenty feet above sea level, Ruggles acquired both, "and very soon tumbled the one into the other to the amount of some three millions of loads, at a cost of $180,000—squaring the lines as he went along, and regulating the lots." While King had reason to exaggerate the amount of earth moved by Ruggles (the Board of Assistants estimated it was closer to one million cartloads), since he was trying to garner praise for his friend, it was nevertheless an enormous operation. Abiding by the commissioners' 1811 plan for the city, Ruggles leveled the topography of his property and prepared to turn it into an elite neighborhood for wealthy New Yorkers.[25]

Ruggles had plenty of examples to choose from as he dreamed up the plan for his development. New York's real estate developers had taken cues from the elite residential squares and crescents in England's cities, such as London and Bath. Unified in design and spanning at least a block's worth of buildings, these developments made narrow row houses seem almost palatial when combined with their neighbors. Such English squares dated back to the eighteenth century, but were becoming more widespread in smaller towns during Britain's 1820s building boom. By buying large swaths of land and doing some small-scale urban and architectural planning, English developers had found a successful way to design an elite neighborhood and turn a significant profit. New York developers like Ruggles, who could read travelers' accounts of these districts in newspapers and guidebooks, were likely inspired by the work of their British counterparts.[26]

Ruggles also had the benefit of seeing what had succeeded in New York in recent years. In 1827, for instance, Isaac Pearson had designed a set of row houses on either side of Bleecker Street that were intended to

FIGURE 7. Alexander Jackson Davis, *LeRoy Place in 1830*. LeRoy Place was one of the first elite developments in New York City following the real-estate boom sparked by the opening of the Erie Canal. (Collection of the New-York Historical Society.)

attract wealthy buyers to the increasingly popular Bond Street neighborhood. Pearson unofficially renamed the block LeRoy Place and sold the homes for a remarkable $11,000 to $12,000 each. The row houses were set back from the street on either side of the block, giving the sense that LeRoy Place was even more magnificent. The trees planted in front of the homes also helped to signify the refined character of the property. The center two row houses stood out from their surrounding buildings, making the block look like a stately mansion. In a city known for the individuality of its houses, LeRoy Place provided something novel—a planned, unified block—which made it instantly a city landmark. Theodore Fay featured an engraving of LeRoy Place just a few years after it was built in his *Views of New York and Its Environs* (1831), which catalogued New York's most celebrated landmarks.[27]

Perhaps the most relevant example Ruggles could learn from was St. John's Square, also known as Hudson Square. Trinity Church was one of the city's largest landowners, with property spanning a significant portion of lower Manhattan through Greenwich Village. While Trinity had built the celebrated St. John's Chapel in 1807, designed by brothers John and Isaac McComb, the church sold the surrounding lots two decades later, in 1827, during the post–Erie Canal building boom. St. John's Square quickly became one of the most sought-after addresses. One of the park's prime features—perhaps the feature that made it such a draw to New York's wealthiest—was the protection that the iron fence provided. Following the lead of many London developers, the church decided to keep the square private, deeding it to local residents who, for a $10 annual fee, had keys to a park well appointed with catalpa trees, cottonwoods, horse chestnuts, silver birches, plenty of shrubs, flower beds, and an elegant, sparkling fountain. New Yorkers had to pay a steep price in real estate in order to enter this "spot of Eden loveliness and exclusiveness." As the *New-York Evening Post* would swoon years later, "Truly the dwellers here can say *Rus in urbe*," meaning "the country in the city." Residents of St. John's Square could look out onto the gorgeous park, enjoy its shady trees, and bask in the fresh air it afforded them, while also assuring themselves respectable company as they strolled through their park. While New York had a number of private pleasure gardens where visitors paid a steep admission fee to ensure they would mingle with only polite society, St. John's Square took this a step further. Even some of New York's upper crust could not gain access without a connection to the residents. This was the quintessential elite space. Both LeRoy Place and St. John's Square would be short-lived on maps of Manhattan, subsumed after the Civil War by New York's growing commercial districts and the increasing northward push of elite neighborhoods. But in the late 1820s, they were part of the building boom in which Samuel Ruggles hoped to take part.[28]

As Ruggles began to plot out the design for his property located north of the built-up part of the city, much of his work centered on laying out streets. With only 20th Street and 21st Street paved, Ruggles

FIGURE 8. Alexander Jackson Davis, *View of St. John's Chapel, from the Park*. St. John's Square likely served as a model for Samuel Ruggles as he began to imagine what Gramercy could become. (Collection of the New-York Historical Society.)

had to petition the city government to lay out the rest of the grid so that his property would be reachable and salable. During the better part of the nineteenth century, the city government financed the paving and grading of streets with special assessments. Local residents paid for the infrastructure under the assumption that their property values would benefit from the improvements. While city officials could decide to lay out the streets themselves, it was often politically wise to wait until local residents petitioned for the street to be regulated, and in practice that was the usual way streets were laid. The Common Council proceedings were packed with petition after petition for street grading and paving, especially during periods like the 1830s, when the city's footprint was rapidly expanding. Ruggles petitioned for each and every street and sewer in the neighborhood. Since much of his property was on marshy land, sewers, which were used mainly for runoff, were invaluable for keeping basements dry and the property healthy.[29]

Ruggles even went so far as to break with the Commissioners' Map of 1811 and create an additional avenue through his property. Raising real estate values by increasing access to the area, he drew an avenue, seventy-five feet wide, down the center of the blocks he had purchased, between Third and Fourth avenues. Offering up his property to the city at no charge, he extended the avenue from 14th Street to 31st Street. He even jumped through all the necessary bureaucratic hoops, getting the state legislature to pass a statute that would allow the avenue to appear on the official map of the city. Praising him for the work he had done, the municipal government eagerly accepted the street name he suggested, naming a portion of the avenue "Irving Place" after Washington Irving, and agreed to regulate and pave the new street.[30] The Common Council would later agree to name the northern portion of the avenue Lexington Avenue, after the Revolutionary War battle.[31] The changes that Ruggles made to his property would not only affect the local neighborhood, but would also change the face of the east side of Manhattan as the city continued to develop northward up the island.

With all of these streets being laid through his property, Ruggles, as the primary landowner, would have to shell out a significant amount of money for the special assessments. Having become so familiar with the Common Council's procedures, Ruggles devised a way to make some of that money back. He partnered with George A. Furst, a contractor who had helped with the leveling of Ruggles's property, to open a street-regulating business. While Furst handled the physical work, Ruggles was in charge of government relations, such as submitting bids and doing the necessary paperwork to get paid. Ruggles received 40 percent of the company's profits. The majority of the streets that the partners laid were in the Gramercy neighborhood. Even though contractors had to submit sealed bids for each street project, Furst and Ruggles seem to have won most of the contracts in the neighborhood, which held Ruggles's real estate interests. In essence, Ruggles was able

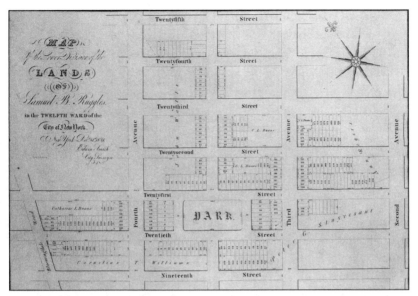

FIGURE 9. Edwin Smith, City Surveyor, *Map of the Lower Division of the Lands of Samuel B. Ruggles, in the Twelfth Ward of the City of New York,* New York, December 31, 1831. Ruggles anchored his real estate development around the private park and new avenue he had laid. (Collection of the New-York Historical Society.)

to make the assessment system work for him by petitioning for the streets, paying the assessments, likely through loans, and then making some of the money back from the city. While proof of government corruption is difficult to unearth, the coincidences point to Ruggles's close ties to the aldermen. In the process, Ruggles got the streets he needed laid out, which was crucial to the development of his neighborhood.[32]

The most notable feature of the Gramercy neighborhood, however, was not the streets but the park, as contemporaries realized. Historians, too, have long praised Ruggles for his work to preserve open space in the neighborhood, rather than cover it entirely in profit-generating buildings. What was portrayed as a farsighted gift or even an act of *noblesse oblige* was actually a strategic move to raise real estate values. In the center of his neighborhood, smack in the middle of Irving Place and Lexington Avenue, Ruggles laid out Gramercy Park—the linchpin for his development. Following the example of what Trinity Church did with St. John's Square, Ruggles deeded the park, which encompassed forty lots, to the purchasers of the land surrounding it. In the deed, dated December 17, 1831, he signed the park over to four trustees, who were charged with surrounding the park with an iron fence and laying it out with walks, trees, and shrubberies. Trustees were responsible for keeping "the said grounds, plantations and decorations in proper order." Following the example of St. John's Square, neighbors paid $10 per year for a key to the gate that kept unwanted visitors out.[33]

In order to ensure that his neighborhood's land values would remain sky high, Ruggles used the deed essentially to zone the neighborhood. He declared that neither he nor any purchasers of the lots could erect "any livery stable, slaughter house, smith shop, forge, furnace, steam engine, brass foundry, nail or other iron factory, or any manufactory of gunpowder, glue, varnish, vitriol, ink, or turpentine, or for the tanning, dressing or preparing skins, hides or leather, or any brewery, distillery, public museum, theatre, circus, place for the exhibition of animals, or any other trade or business dangerous or offensive to the neighbouring inhabitants." In short, the covenant allowed nothing but elite, inoffensive land uses that would not draw excessive crowds to the Gramercy Park neighborhood. Such restrictions would have been helpful in saving St. John's Square. In 1866, Cornelius Vanderbilt purchased St. John's from the surrounding owners so he could build the Hudson Terminal. The residential neighborhood was transformed into warehouses and other commercial properties and lost its open space. Today the area is notable for being the entrance to the Holland Tunnel. Ruggles was able to save his property from such a future, and while theatrical clubs and other banned establishments did eventually surround the park, the residential essence of the neighborhood remained the same and the park is still a prized—and private—city landmark.[34]

The aldermen seemed to love Ruggles. In the eyes of the city government, he had turned a large swath of Manhattan Island's marginal land into "five hundred valuable building lots," thus making it available "for the use of our rapidly increasing population." He seemed to be doing the work of the aldermen, laying roads such as Irving Place and Lexington Avenue, getting the appropriate statutes written at the state level to make that happen, and turning morass into fashionable housing. Most important, in the process of raising the value of his property, Ruggles also increased the city's property tax revenue. The Board of Assistant Aldermen saw the benefit that open space was having on land values, and encouraged Ruggles's work in hopes that others might do something similar. In 1831, they wrote: "It is a fact of material importance to the City Treasury, that the taxable value of lots fronting on squares, is at least double what it would be, if those squares had not been opened; for lots on Fourth-street, now fronting Washington Square, which in the year 1825, were taxed at only $500, are now taxed at $2,100, and a vacant lot on Hudson Square is now taxed at $7,000." These parks that were coming to dot the city, including the private Hudson Square (St. John's Square), and the public Washington Square, were doing wonders for the city's coffers. The city government was slowly coming to learn that they were well worth the investment—certainly a change of pace from the discussion of the Grand Parade. After all the beneficial work that Ruggles had done for the city, the aldermen seemed to bend over backward to help his development plans. In response to his request to open Irving Place and Lexington Avenue, the assistant aldermen not only praised his work but also deemed "it due to the petitioner, that the Common Council should afford every reasonable facility to the extensive and valuable improvements already made and in a state of completion by him." The Common Council had nothing to lose and everything to gain by helping Ruggles move forward with his plans to erect "costly buildings" around his private park.[35]

The council's enthusiasm for private parks was also evident in how they decided to tax them. Ruggles and the owners of lots surrounding

St. John's Square separately brought this topic before the aldermen in the winter of 1831. While public parks as city property were free from taxes, the city government had yet to determine how it would handle private parks. After the 1831 charter revision, the aldermen met as two separate bodies, the Board of Aldermen and the Board of Assistant Aldermen. The split being so new, there was some confusion about what tasks each board would handle, and consequently Ruggles sent his request to the assistant aldermen while the owners around St. John's Square sent theirs to the aldermen. Ruggles's request amounted to having the city government divvy up the property taxes and special assessments for the park among the key holders, so that the trustees of the park would not have to do that bookkeeping themselves. The Board of Assistant Aldermen eagerly passed the measure, agreeing that this minor tweak would encourage others to build more private parks: "[The board] cannot doubt that the city will be financially benefited by granting the prayer of the petitioner."[36]

Before this seemingly innocuous request could be fully enacted, the Board of Aldermen had to approve it. After apparently misreading the Board of Assistants' resolution and assuming that Ruggles wanted the park relieved of all taxes, the Board of Aldermen decided to meet him halfway and offer a relief from property taxes, but not from special assessments. After all, it would be one thing to forgo some of the income they would otherwise get, but quite another to have to pay for improvements out of the city treasury. They had just approved this tax relief for St. John's Square, and although it was far more than Ruggles had actually requested, it provided a consistent policy for all private parks while affirming that the city government was "desirous of promoting the opening of these private parks." Relieved of property taxes, these private parks were essentially publicly subsidized. In making this arrangement, the aldermen were taking a proactive stance toward promoting private parks in the city, while also showing that their primary concern was with the city's coffers.[37]

Private parks were the ultimate elite space in the city. Not even New York's wealthiest and best-connected citizens could gain regular access without having purchased the necessary real estate. Asa Greene described "that charming promenade" St. John's Square as being "as exclusive as the most fastidious could desire." While the steps that the city fathers took toward promoting private parks ultimately proved futile (though other projects were planned, Gramercy and St. John's were the only private parks that reached completion), it does reveal their priorities. The aldermen were most concerned with promoting spaces that would elevate property taxes. Elite neighborhoods were not only a symbol of New York's thriving economy, but also a means to bolster the city treasury. The aldermen therefore did what they could to make developers' lives easier and encourage gated spaces. With an eye on tax revenue, the aldermen were also interested in the ways public parks could positively affect real estate values.[38]

Public Parks, Private Financing

At the same time that Ruggles was developing his private Gramercy Park, he joined other local landowners in petitioning for the city to open a public park: Union Square. One of the few parks that the commissioners set aside in 1811 when they laid out the grid, Union Square, then known briefly as Union Place, had barely survived the chopping block back in 1815, when city and state politicians had their hearts set on rubbing out the commissioners' parks. It had survived, though, and in 1830—twenty years after it had been drawn onto the map—local landowners petitioned the Board of Aldermen in hopes of finally opening the park. Though explicitly public spaces, the public parks that the city government opened during this period were developed within a funding structure that essentially turned them into partly privatized spaces, explicitly benefiting real estate developers, local landowners, and the government's tax revenue. The way the city financed public parks laid the foundation for the unequal distribution of green spaces throughout the urban landscape.[39]

Union Square was almost an afterthought. The commissioners did not reserve the park for idealistic reasons, such as providing a healthy break from the monotony of the built environment, giving children a place to play, or adding to the refinement of the city. Rather, they explained that since so many roads met at this location, formerly called "the Forks," the land would be cut into "morsels . . . of little use or value." The surveyor John Randel, Jr., elaborated that because there was "so small an amount of ground for building purposes, . . . the Commissioners instructed me to lay out the ground, at the *union* of those streets and roads, for a *public square,* which, from that circumstance, they named *Union Place.*" Essentially, this land could hardly accommodate any buildings if the streets sliced through it, so they might as well turn it into a park. The reservation of marginal land for park space was not unusual, and leftover scraps or even economically unattractive property was transformed into both urban and national parks throughout the nineteenth and twentieth centuries.[40]

Though primarily rural and still far on the outskirts of the city, the neighborhood surrounding Union Square held potential. Landowners were eager to prepare it to become an elite neighborhood in advance of the city's expansion. This all came to a head in the 1830s, at the moment when New Yorkers were beginning to appreciate parks for their impact on health, beauty, and, most important, real estate. According to the Board of Assistant Aldermen, prior to its development Union Square presented "to the eye a shapeless and ill-looking place, devoid of symmetry." By inviting the city to open the park, the petitioners hoped the city would grade the parkland and the surrounding streets, making it easier for them to grade their own properties and begin to transform them into an elite residential neighborhood.[41]

Samuel Ruggles, of course, wanted to ensure that the development around Union Square would make it the nucleus of the city. Not only would his property in the nearby Gramercy Park neighborhood benefit, but so too would the property he owned directly abutting the proposed public park. While the municipal government was in the process of acquiring the land for the park itself, Ruggles suggested they go even further. He proposed that the council purchase land on the northern edge of the park, between 17th Street and 19th Street, Fourth Avenue and Bloomingdale Road, for future government buildings. Ruggles even went so far as to engrave maps for each alderman showing all the real estate in the neighborhood, for which he received their praise. Anticipating that the government would grow to meet the needs of the expanding northward-moving population, the aldermen seriously considered Ruggles's suggestion. Ruggles, of course, was hoping to secure Union Square's prominence socially, culturally, and politically. Though this plan eventually died in committee, it was further evidence of the ways the city government and private developers joined together to profit from the island's real estate.[42]

With the state legislature's approval, the city began the work of estimating the special assessments they would need to collect so that they could purchase, regulate, and expand Union Square. By 1833 the aldermen had made plans to remove rocks and buildings on the property and grade the land. After the arduous bureaucratic and physical labor necessary to turn city land into a public space had commenced, the aldermen hit a snag. Though numerous landowners were on board with the park and had even petitioned for its creation, a number of remonstrants from the neighborhood had teamed up to protest the park's creation by looking for a loophole in the legal language surrounding the city's right to regulate public property. They argued that the city had no right to reroute Bloomingdale Road, which ran right through the center of the park. If they were to win their argument, all of the cross streets would also have to remain open, thereby paving over what would have been a verdant open space. The petitioners seem to have been angry because they had paid a special assessment to open and pave Bloomingdale Road, which the city was now going to tear up and reroute. In rebutting their argument, the Board of Assistant Aldermen essentially had to clarify the rights of landowners to public space. They wrote that although the landowners had paid a special assessment "to defray a portion of the expense, they did not thereby acquire any right, privilege or legal interest in the highway superior to that of any and every other inhabitant of the city,—and certainly did not become vested with any legal title in the land itself covered by the highway, paramount to that of the Corporation." Laying out their legal right to reroute Bloomingdale Road and open the park, the assistant aldermen successfully argued against the petitioners. Still, the resistance that the petitioners posed shows the brewing distaste for special assessments among some of the city's landowners.[43]

Work on the park continued. The Board of Aldermen and the Board of Assistant Aldermen decided to make the square an oval (a joke not lost on countless writers of the time), enclose it with an iron fence, and landscape it with shrubbery, grass, and trees. Having collected the special assessments and conquered the legal hurdles, the city ornamented the park "for the embellishment of the city, and the common use, benefit, and enjoyment of its inhabitants, in such mode as is in the reasonable discretion of the Common Council." The language of the aldermen and assistant aldermen made it clear that they had begun to appreciate parks as more than just spaces to circulate air; they were embellishments, ornaments, and spaces for beauty.[44]

As with their enthusiasm for private parks, the aldermen were elated that "the *pecuniary interest* of the public will be promoted by the liberal embellishment of Union Place." In other words, the city fathers believed it was their duty to foster elite spaces in the city in order to raise tax revenues. With property taxes accounting for two-thirds of the city's tax revenue, the aldermen saw that it was in their best interest to hasten "the erection of valuable houses on the square." Opening Union Square, the assistant aldermen calculated, would result in an annual increase of $16,200 into the city treasury. In addition, the city government owned a large quantity of real estate in the outer wards known as "the Common Lands," real estate which they intended to sell to individuals. Having an elite neighborhood in the proximity of these lands would raise their values accordingly. Finally, the city fathers hoped that by establishing desirable residential neighborhoods, they would stop losing New York's wealthiest to Brooklyn suburbs. They wrote: "We are also admonished by the rapid growth of a rival city, lying on the very borders of our city, and seeking to share largely in its prosperity and wealth, that we shall most effectually retain within our reach that portion of our population which contributes most largely towards the public burthens, by increasing the attractions of our own city." Wealthy New Yorkers were beginning to move to Brooklyn Heights and commute to their jobs in Manhattan via ferry. Worried about losing their tax base, the city fathers thought one way to combat this was to promote projects like public parks. Everything about Union Square seemed to benefit the city and its tax revenue.[45]

By the end of the decade, Union Square was thriving. In 1834 petitioners asking the aldermen to open Union Square said that they intended "to erect expensive houses upon the square, and its immediate vicinity" as soon as the Common Council finished enclosing and decorating the park. Just five years later, the *New-York Mirror* proclaimed that "around Union-Place new blocks of houses, capacious and stately, are springing up with surprising celerity." Having just survived the Panic of 1837, the *Mirror* saw this development as evidence of "the renewed prosperity of our noble city." Union Square would be a focal point in the celebration of the city's water works a few years later, after acquiring a fantastic fountain, and would also become a center for civic action and political rallies. While the city intended it as an embellishment and a promenade, New Yorkers gave it other meanings and uses. Still, the city achieved what it was after. The neighborhood, at least for the time being, was an elite residential area that drew in some of the city's wealthiest residents. While Union Square would not become the seat of the city government, the new park and its neighborhood, in conjunction with the adjoining Gramercy Park neighborhood, helped to secure the area's real estate values and the city's property tax revenue. However, the aldermen did not have such an easy time with all proposed parks.[46]

At the same time that the aldermen were working on Union Square, they were also considering another park to its south in the Eleventh Ward, in what is now known as the Lower East Side. The neighborhood, which was a mile south of Union Square, was already densely developed. In 1833, a group of sixty-nine residents from the Tenth and Eleventh wards proposed that the city open a park on a block that had no buildings, bound by Stanton, Orchard, Rivington, and Allen streets. With buildings continuing to go up, the local residents had good reason to try to preserve this bit of open space. The petitioners argued that keeping the block undeveloped would benefit the neighborhood by maintaining public health. The city had been hit by cholera during the previous two summers, yet there were few cases in the immediate neighborhood of this block—something the petitioners attributed to open space. In addition, they contended that "public squares are the great enduring ornaments of large cities," an argument very familiar to the aldermen. The neighborhood was not far away from chic Bond Street and other fancy real estate developments, and the petitioners were likely trying to secure a similar tony character for their properties.[47]

Not all of the local residents were enthusiastic about the proposed park. Two petitions, holding the signatures of 230 people total, argued against it. A group of five widows who owned houses and lots along the proposed park claimed that whatever special assessment the city declared appropriate for their properties would be devastating for them. They were "entirely dependent on the rents" for their livelihoods, and the assessments would be ruinous, forcing them to sell their buildings and lose the meager income that supported their families. The rest of the remonstrants made several arguments that likewise focused on the burdens of the special assessment system. For instance, they "set forth that although they admit that the public squares are an ornament, . . . they think the advantages of them are less extensive in their operation than the assessment which they occasion." Many of the remonstrants were in fact lessees of property who would have been responsible for paying the assessment, likely due to the nature of their contracts, without reaping any benefits in the long term. Like the widows, they claimed that if they proved unable to pay, they would have to relinquish their leases before their terms were up. It was not atypical to purchase a lease for

FIGURE 10. James Smillie, *View of Union Park, New York, from the Head of Broadway*. By 1849, Union Square had become what Ruggles and the city fathers had hoped: an elite neighborhood filled with expensive housing and high property values. (Collection of the New-York Historical Society.)

ten, twenty-five, or even a hundred years in New York. Often, these lessees were responsible for building homes and other improvements, as well as for handling the taxes during their term. The remonstrants claimed that while the park would benefit some, it would be disastrous for them. In addition to these complaints about the assessment system, the landowners of the targeted block did "not wish to part with their property at the present time for any purpose."[48]

The Street Committee considered the perspectives of both the petitioners advocating for the park and those protesting against it. Since the aldermen were considering the park only because they had received a petition, they had a hard time continuing to support it with just 69 petitioners for it, and 230 opposed. The committee did not agree with the remonstrants' claim that the value of the park did not outweigh the cost of the assessments, maintaining: "The effect which large squares have in bringing a good population into the vicinity of them is not to be overlooked, and the Committee have no doubt but that if the proposed measure was carried into effect, it would change the aspect of that beautifully situated section of the City, and give it a propriety and a value not only heretofore wholly unprecedented, but also greatly outweighing the expense of the square." However, as so many people would be inconvenienced by the expense of establishing the park, the committee could not recommend that the city pursue its development. And with that, the plans for the Eleventh Ward park evaporated.[49]

The battles over parks such as these were not nearly as heated as the battles over loose animals. While both cases involved unequal control and distribution of urban resources, the citywide nature of hog and dog laws led to much more furor than the localized creation of parks. Parks were an addition to the city and no one was visibly or dramatically losing something, as was the case with the hogs and dogs. The protests of those like the widows and lessees near the Eleventh Ward park never got much newspaper coverage, because the issues were so localized and lacked the drama of a hog riot. The city handled these complaints on a case-by-case basis, making sure the majority of a neighborhood wanted to fund the park. At the same time, the piecemeal, grassroots creation of parks obscured the unequal access they would provide New Yorkers and diverted blame to residents if they wanted but did not have a park.

The way the city government financed these parks played an important role in determining their fate. Special assessments had been legal in New York City since the late seventeenth century, but they gained widespread use only in the 1830s, when the city needed to finance the extensive grading and paving of streets in the quickly expanding city. This taxation arrangement was not unique to New York, though New

York pioneered its use and provided a model for other cities and states considering various methods of financing public works. As with streets, while New York's aldermen had the legal right to initiate their own projects, in practice the Common Council waited for the petitions of private individuals, preferably landowners in the area affected by the improvement, before they took action and assigned a committee to report back on the proposal. With support from a number of citizens, the Commissioners of Estimate and Assessment would determine what properties would benefit from the improvement. They would then determine how much money to assess the landowners, based on the estimated price of the improvement and the cost of whatever property might need to be purchased. Public improvements were therefore funded locally, by the landowners who were most likely to see a rise in the property value and desirability of their holdings.[50]

Special assessment fans saw this form of taxation as an equitable and rational way to pay for public improvements that would, by their very nature, benefit those closest geographically. Those who owned property around a park, for instance, would see an immediate jump in their property values once the government opened the park. Special assessments were designed to avoid the redistribution of wealth that would have occurred if the city paid for improvements out of the general budget from taxes collected citywide. To those who lived across the city from a new park, this might have seemed like a fair arrangement, as they might not visit it regularly, let alone see any monetary benefit to their property. In a sense, special assessments could also be seen as satisfying an older tradition that held property owners responsible for social goods, including parks. Yet those who benefited from these parks were so localized that it really served little more than their interests.[51]

This ad hoc form of taxation certainly had its critics, though. When the city assessors could not locate a property owner or if the city's bookkeeping was askew, the city would confiscate and sell the property in question to pay for the delinquent (or at least supposedly delinquent) assessments. Opposition to special assessments mounted in the 1840s, at a moment when public works expenses were rising while property values were declining. A group of anti-assessment New Yorkers began publishing the *New-York Municipal Gazette* in 1841, declaring that their goal was to reveal the abuses of the assessment system. In their inaugural issue, they claimed that the source of these abuses was a combination of the "extravagant anticipations of those engaged in real estate speculations" and the excessive powers of the municipal government. They wrote: "The exercise of this power is dangerous to civil liberty and destructive to the welfare and prosperity of the city. The partial, oppressive and excessive assessing of private property, under the pretext of making public improvement, has been carried to great extremes, and such has been the effect, that in very many instances estates have been by these means actually confiscated." To those unable or unwilling to pay for the improvements, it certainly felt as though speculators had hijacked the government for their own interests and as though the government, in turn, was exercising far too much power over private property. The aldermen extensively assisted speculators and developers in the 1830s, since their interests in raising property values tended to intersect. As is evident from how Ruggles finagled a way to benefit from the special assessment system by starting a street-paving business, there was also plenty of room for corruption and mismanagement. The system certainly had its faults.[52]

Yet in other ways, by paying for improvements like parks with special assessments, the city government had essentially limited its own power. While government officials were able to trumpet that they had not paid for the park with a dime of public funds, thereby avoiding the politically unpopular step of raising taxes, they also handed over a good deal of power to local residents. In the 1830s, public parks like Union Square or the Eleventh Ward park were essentially created or destroyed by the will of the people. The funding structure helped to give local residents a powerful voice in the process. In 1834, when residents in the Twelfth Ward petitioned for a park, the Common Council ended up not pursuing the project, because the residents could not agree on where they wanted to locate it. "Unhesitatingly" supportive of parks, the aldermen were frustrated that the inability of the owners to decide on a plan had left them powerless. If the government was truly omnipotent, as many assessment critics contended, they could have made a declaration about where they wanted the park and assessed residents accordingly. Instead, at least with regard to the parks, they typically deferred to the wishes, or in this case the indecision, of the local residents.[53]

Funding parks by special assessment led to an unequal distribution of green spaces throughout the city. When private citizens had to initiate public works projects such as parks, this inevitably meant that wealthier areas of the city were favored with more parks than others. Neighborhoods where residents or, more likely, speculators hoped to exact expensive change and reap the benefits in resale often found the government eager to develop parks. However, there was little incentive for landlords in poorer neighborhoods to push for expensive improvements like parks, especially if they had little chance in recouping the costs of the assessments from the rents. The placement of parks in the urban landscape, then, became an expression of social and political inequity. The government made few efforts to place parks where landowners were inclined to resist, as was seen with the proposed Eleventh Ward park. While property holders certainly paid handsomely for these public works projects, the cost for the propertyless was perhaps even steeper. They were left voiceless in the city government when it came to parks and other public works paid for by assessments. Renters had little sway over whether their neighborhoods had accessible open space. With few exceptions, you had to own property, and your community had to have sufficient wealth to pay for special assessments in order to get a neighborhood park. While promenaders certainly did their best to make their spaces exclusive, the city's funding structure helped as well. Few, if any, petitions from renters exist because of this structure. By funding parks with special assessments, the Common Council essentially represented the interests of developers, speculators, and landowners, and the conversations about the existence of certain parks happened between these parties. Public goods were in private hands.[54]

While the 1830s park boom led to the creation of many green spaces in wealthy neighborhoods, there was one exception to that pattern. The city opened a tiny park in a thoroughly working-class neighborhood, though not at the behest of its renters. In 1831, the city government decided that it ought to address the blighted Five Points neighborhood, home to some of the city's poorest residents, as well as taverns, gambling dens, and brothels. The neighborhood had been built on the poorly filled-in Fresh Water Pond that continued to fill basements with stagnant, contaminated water. In a prime location near City Hall but built on some of the worst land in the city, the tenements housed countless African American and Irish families. Residents in nearby communities petitioned the city to have the area, which "has long been notorious in the annals of the Police Department," cleaned up. In an early attempt at urban renewal, the city government proposed widening several streets and knocking down the buildings in the triangle where the streets met (giving the neighborhood its name) to make a park. The petitioners and the city seemed to believe that a park would help to solve some of the issues facing this neighborhood. The *New-York Spectator* predicted that, through the demolition of a section of Five Points, "the miserable rookeries which are now chapels of ease to the Penitentiary, and reservoirs for the vilest moral filth of a not over-moral metropolis, will disappear altogether, and give place to decent stores and dwellings." Like many twentieth-century urban renewal attempts, however, the destruction of buildings and the insertion of a small park hardly solved the larger issues facing Five Points and its residents. Though leaseholders were able to block the widening of the streets, the Common Council successfully cleared the triangle in 1833. George G. Foster, chronicler of New York's underworld, wrote disdainfully in 1850 that the park, frequented by "couples chattering and carrying on their infamous bar-

FIGURE 11. *The Five Points in 1859.* The Five Points Park was evidence of the hopes 1830s New Yorkers had for the change that parks could bring to neighborhoods. Engraving from D. T. Valentine, *Manual of the Corporation of the City of New York,* 1860. (Collection of the New-York Historical Society.)

gains," reminded him "of the reverse of rural life with all its innocent blandishments and moonlight love-walks beneath the whispering trees." He seemed almost baffled that the park had not transformed the neighborhood into something more refined, full of "virtue" and "innocence." The 1830s had been filled with hope that parks could work magic for neighborhoods.[55]

By the mid 1830s, while both Union Square and the park in Five Points were underway, New York City was at a peak in its fervor for public parks. Just six blocks north of Union Square on Broadway stood a prime location for yet another public park. It was halfway between the rivers, at the juncture of many streets, and, lo and behold, it was part of the old Grand Parade grounds. Though the aldermen had essentially erased the park from the map and laid streets through much of the property, the city government continued to own a small section.

The city's House of Refuge, an institution for juvenile delinquents, was located at the intersection of Broadway, Fifth Avenue, and 24th Street. Though the reformatory was run privately by the Society for the Prevention of Pauperism, it was funded partly by city and state monies and situated on city-owned land. The House of Refuge had been built only in 1824, but by 1835 the city government was already considering pushing the institution farther north and out of development's way. Juvenile delinquents and large institutional buildings, after all, did little for property values. The Common Council's Committee on Lands and Places, which ruminated over the future of that site, wrote quite bluntly that "the presence of its prison like buildings and its massive and gloomy walls, operates with material force in depreciating the value of the surrounding property." They decided, therefore, that the public authorities should find a more suitable location. It would be in the city's best interest, the committee argued, to build a park in its place: "[Parks] beautify and embellish those particular sections where they have been formed, and by the rapid appreciation in value of the surrounding property, most abundantly remunerate the cost of forming them. Public opinion is so universally in affirmation of this point, the Committee believe it wholly unnecessary to dwell upon it." Given that local residents had proved willing to pay special assessments to build a public park in place of the House of Refuge, the Committee endorsed the plan. With that, the Grand Parade was reborn in a much smaller form. Following the state's approval in 1837, the city opened a small public park a decade later and named it Madison Square.[56]

Speculators and landowners had killed the Grand Parade in the 1810s and 1820s, but they helped to revive it, in part, in the 1830s. In 1837, Asa Greene wrote: "Happy are we to say—nay, thrice happy—that, in this land-speculating age, we have any public squares, whatever, to set our feet upon. Why, the temptation to sell them is so great, that we marvel exceedingly that the fathers of the city have not, ere this, cut the

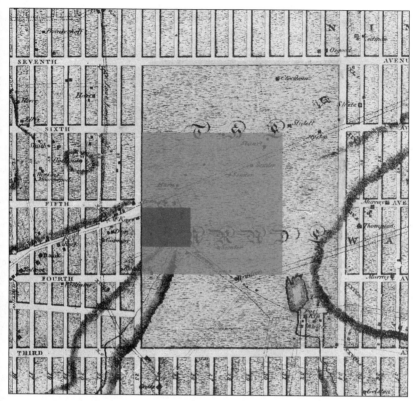

FIGURE 12. Following passage of a state law in 1837, New York City obtained the authority to open Madison Square Park, the last remnant of the Grand Parade. Detail of the Commissioners' Map of 1811, with author's overlays. (Collection of the New-York Historical Society.)

Park and Battery into building lots and set them to sale at the auction room of Bleecker and Sons." Greene gave the aldermen too much credit. They had hardly shed their ties to real estate interests. Instead, the city fathers and real estate developers who had once seen parks as wasted space had come to appreciate the way green spaces could improve property values. In the long history of the Grand Parade and Madison Square, real estate interests played a central role in shaping both municipal policy and the urban landscape.[57]

Private Trees in Public Spaces

Parks were not the only privatized green spaces in antebellum New York. Street trees—the popular ornaments shading sidewalks and row houses alike—were yet another symbol of privatized nature in New York. Trees planted along the sidewalks were an unspoken way to communicate that the neighborhood was primarily residential, refined, and likely expensive. By providing shade, trees helped to make the streets hospitable for promenading, especially in the hot summer months, when people avoided staying indoors. As with parks, the city government did not really come to appreciate the effect trees had on the urban environment until the 1830s.[58]

The Common Council had a complicated relationship with street trees. In the early nineteenth century, street trees, though on public property, were not planted by the city government. Individuals had to take the initiative to purchase and plant the trees outside their homes. At times, the city government actively discouraged street trees, as they had the potential to pose traffic problems. In 1791, the Common Council banned all street trees and even required the removal of existing trees, considering them to be a downright nuisance. The aldermen perpetually battled crates, building materials, and other items that encumbered sidewalks and blocked traffic; trees were just another one of these obstacles. Angry citizens who desired "cool and shaded walks . . . without being exposed to all the inconveniences of the summer sun" quickly petitioned the city to express their opposition to the ordinance. Responding in kind, the aldermen amended their ordinance to forbid only those trees that obstructed the sidewalks. In the following years, though the Common Council banned trees on streets less than forty feet wide, they would typically grant special permits to influential New Yorkers, such as the large property owner John Watts or Mayor Richard Varick, to plant trees in front of their houses. It seems that wealthy and influential residents who wanted to plant a street tree and had appropriate connections were having exceptions made for them.[59]

Despite making these exceptions, the city government's policies were often at odds with the wishes of New Yorkers, who were coming to prize street trees. In 1822, when Thomas Hodgkinson, an actor, theatrical manager, and owner of the Shakespearean Tavern, planted two horse chestnut trees on Nassau Street outside his home and business, the city immediately acted to have the trees removed. Apparently Hodgkinson was unaware that he was violating the law that banned trees on narrow streets. The Street Committee of the Common Council visited the site and determined that the trees would remain pretty small and would not obstruct traffic. They recommended that the aldermen make an exception to the law and permit the trees to stay. The Common Council disagreed, however, and voted to remove the trees. While Hodgkinson was not as influential as John Watts or Mayor Varick, he was a leading figure among the New York literati, a fact that probably helped him garner support from the media. The *New-York Evening Post* featured an editorial calling on the council to "reconsider this ungracious, and, I assure you, this unpopular vote." Convinced that their move was truly unpopular, the aldermen rescinded their vote and allowed the trees to stay. Public outcry saved those two saplings. At least in the opinion of people who championed the trees, the city's beautification ought to have trumped the law.[60]

Even when street trees were completely legal, aldermen did not actively promote them. Without a government-led movement, local newspapers took charge, publishing articles in the spring and fall alerting readers that it was an appropriate time to plant their shade trees. The *Evening Post,* former champion of Hodgkinson's trees, tried to pressure New Yorkers to do their part and beautify the city's streets. Without government support, however, the editors were pessimistic about the fate of the project: "It is a just remark, that what is every body's business is nobody's, and though it is admitted to be very desirable by every body,

yet we have reason to fear it will not be undertaken by any body." Trying to design a community project without the help of the government
proved difficult. Every six months, the paper published these reminders
and pleas championing the benefits of street trees, the low cost of purchasing a sapling, and the dramatic and positive change it would provide for both the homeowner and the city. The papers had to appeal to
citizens to purchase a public good for the city.[61]

While aldermen of the early nineteenth century typically saw street
trees as encumbrances, by the 1830s the tide had shifted. As with their
newfound love of public parks in the decade that saw an enormous real
estate boom, the aldermen also came to appreciate the impact trees had
on the beauty and value of city property. In September 1833, right before homeowners would typically consider planting saplings, Alderman
Palmer presented a resolution to the council, calling for a government-
sponsored program to encourage street trees. He contended that since
"our City is much ornamented and beautified by having trees planted
in front of our houses, and the shade they give, adds much to the comfort and health of the inhabitants," the city should pay a premium to
"all persons who shall plant forest trees before their respective lots." He
specified that residents had to plant their trees twenty-five feet apart,
which would have brought a certain amount of uniformity to the otherwise individualized streetscape. Unfortunately for lovers of street
trees, the resolution got lost in committee and never resurfaced. Other
moments show the Common Council acting on this newfound appreciation of urban trees. Earlier that year, the aldermen took action to
protect two trees that stood "partly in the street" in front of Saint Mark's
Church. The aldermen considered them "large and elegant," and determined that since there was ample room for carriages to pass around
them, they should remain. Much had changed since the council's 1791
edict to remove all of the city's trees.[62]

The *Evening Post*'s advocacy and the Common Council's eventual
protection and occasional encouragement of street trees were not just
about ensuring shade for pedestrians. They aimed at beautifying the

city. Trees provided "relief to the eye by their grateful verdure." Street trees helped to visually separate residential neighborhoods from business areas. Trees also decorated larger avenues, helping to indicate their grandness. The *Evening Post* regularly rhapsodized about how wonderful Broadway would look decked out in trees. Broadway was one of the most frequently rendered, most often visited, and most beloved streets in New York. It was also where refined New York men and women promenaded. Trees feminized these spaces. Authors remarked on the feminine grace and beauty of urban trees. These trees also demarcated spaces where elite women could safely exist in public space. In addition to promenades, trees lined fashionable residential streets—a visual, if perhaps unconscious, symbol of the boundaries of elite female space in the city.[63]

Trees were also relics of the city's history. Trees that outlasted human lifespans seemed to reach back in time. In view of how rapidly New York was being torn down and rebuilt, they probably seemed like one of the few remnants of the city's past. Perhaps the most famous and revered street tree was a pear tree at the corner of Third Avenue and 13th Street. The story goes that Peter Stuyvesant planted the tree in 1647 after bringing it from Holland. Once a part of his farm, the tree was in the middle of a busy sidewalk by the nineteenth century. In 1837, as the neighborhood began to encroach, the city erected a wood paling around the tree to protect it from traffic. By the 1830s, the Common Council believed that venerable old trees, especially those as symbolic to the city's history as Stuyvesant's tree, clearly deserved the protection of the city government. Unfortunately an 1867 carriage accident knocked the tree down, but a piece of the tree was sent to the New-York Historical Society, and by 1890 the Holland Society had installed a plaque on the building.[64]

New Yorkers also lamented the loss of old but far less famous trees. For instance, in 1831 when city leaders altered the old jail, officials had to remove "two noble trees, which for a century have shaded the front of that building." The *Evening Post* regretted that "even their venerable appearance could not save them." The mere fact that they received

FIGURE 13. *Stuyvesant Pear Tree, N.E. Corner, 13th & 3rd Ave., NY City.*
The Stuyvesant pear tree was New York City's most famous street tree in
the nineteenth century. This photograph was taken before 1867 and published as a stereoscope image around 1900. (Robert N. Dennis Collection of
Stereoscopic Views, Miriam and Ira D. Wallach Division of Arts, Prints and Photographs, The New York Public Library, Astor, Lenox and Tilden Foundations.)

something close to obituaries shows the growing importance of trees in
the urban landscape.[65]

Regardless of their fame or even the appreciation they were accorded,
street trees continued to be a privatized part of the urban landscape. In

1845, Horace Greeley, in his *New-York Daily Tribune,* wrote a plea to private citizens for street trees—an appeal that resembled the ones published in the *Evening Post* decades before. In addition to the usual argument that trees add "largely to the beauty of a street and to the value of property located upon it," Greeley argued that trees might even slow down speeders. On the drive up Third Avenue to Yorkville (a small suburb located around 86th Street), children and chickens hardly had time to get out of the way of speeding carriages. Greeley understood why people sped through the neighborhood, marked as it was by "the horrible stench of that massive Hog-Yard at 40th-st." Trees could change that, however. Greeley called on the landowners to rise up and plant trees, so that travelers would instead enjoy the pleasure of a ride "well shaded and freed from nasal abominations." He even went so far as to call on "Young Men and citizens of slender pecuniary means" to buy up land and transform the uptown neighborhood into something worthy of pride. The first step in this transformation, of course, was "Tree-Planting." Trees had the power to refine spaces and raise property values, and, as with parks, New Yorkers had truly come to appreciate the value these green additions had in transforming the urban landscape.[66]

Trees straddled the boundary between private and public. They were private trees on public property, subject to and protected by city ordinances, yet financed completely by private funds. They were certainly a benefit to private real estate values, but they were also a public good, improving the city's image and the public's health. Still, they served as another example of the city government's dispersed power. The government was not looking to control this part of the public landscape, other than to keep trees out of traffic's way. With the exception of the unsuccessful resolution to encourage residents to plant trees, city officials did very little to encourage this kind of refinement. Instead, they passively waited until residents (with the aid of newspapers) took the initiative and transformed the urban landscape. As a result, trees were planted only in wealthy neighborhoods, where residents had the time, funds, and inclination. Pedestrians who spotted trees on a sidewalk could immediately know they were entering an elite residential neighborhood. Like parks, trees marked the social inequities of the urban landscape.

In many ways, the commissioners who laid the gridiron over Manhattan Island in 1811 were looking to take control of the city's growth. The grid anticipated dramatic expansion and tried to ensure that it would occur in an orderly way. When New Yorkers eventually came to appreciate and embrace green spaces and their range of benefits, park creators and funders were still trying to exert environmental and social control in a city whose population seemed increasingly uncontrollable.

Parks and promenades show one way that elite New Yorkers pushed back against democratic society in the 1830s. They used these spaces to foster an urban aristocracy, and in the process they necessarily affected the physical landscape of the city. The city government had a direct incentive to assist real estate developers and landowners in this refinement process. Not only would these spaces beautify the city and trumpet its commercial dominance and prosperity, they would aid the city treasury by raising property values and keeping New York's wealthiest from leaving for Brooklyn or other locations. It seemed like everybody would win from the development of parks.

Yet not all New Yorkers had equal access to open space. Promenaders could even bully non-elites off of Broadway's sidewalks if such people dared to take a walk during the promenading hours. Private parks were obviously off limits, and public parks could be found only in wealthier neighborhoods where residents petitioned and paid for them. If the city introduced a park to a neighborhood that had a mix of social classes, poorer New Yorkers would soon be priced out of their rentals as real estate values rose. By funding these parks with special assessments and remaining passive in the planting of street trees, the aldermen not only set the stage for an urban landscape that reflected class inequalities, they also abdicated a significant amount of power to their constituents. In short, the municipal government privatized the creation of green spaces, putting the power to create public goods directly in private hands.

In the city government's quest for refinement and higher property tax revenues, they disregarded the needs of the urban masses, who lacked equal access to these spaces. In report after report where the aldermen celebrated the reasons they should adopt parks, not once did they mention the benefits that open spaces would give to the working class. Even in the case of the Five Points park, it seemed that the Common Council was more interested in using the park as a way to clear the neighborhood than it was in providing any real benefit for the current residents. It would take a few more decades until reformers, such as those who argued for Central Park, began to champion truly democratic spaces that would give tenement dwellers room to breathe. In the meantime, elite New Yorkers fiercely protected these parks in hopes of keeping them refined, and safe from the mobs of immigrants, African Americans, and even nouveaux riches who hoped to join their ranks. New York's urban landscape of the 1830s reflected not only the wealth of the post–Erie Canal city, but also the nervousness of elite New Yorkers about the changes occurring around them. They felt an almost desperate desire to hold fast to their rank and their space, and the new parks were a product of this combination of excitement and anxiety. In short, the parks of the 1830s were born of a combination of private enterprise, government cooperation, and class fears, with the idea that they would also enhance the city's health and beauty.[67]

The Panic of 1837, followed by the subsequent business recession and the crash of the real estate market, dampened park enthusiasm for a few years. Many of the neighborhoods surrounding Union Square, Gramercy Park, and Madison Square would finally be realized in the mid-1840s, once the market rebounded. By 1849, New York writer E. Porter Belden declared that Union Square was "surrounded by splendid private mansions, some of which are of costly magnificence, and its vicinity is the most fashionable portion of the city." The city government finally got to reap the benefits of its enlarged tax base, and elite New Yorkers could celebrate their "fashionable" spaces. It was increasingly difficult, however, to call New York fashionable or even refined when the streets were filled with garbage and manure.[68]

3

The Dung Heap of the Universe

New York City left quite an impression on Charles Dickens during his visit in 1842, and not because of the plethora of new parks. On Broadway, amid "ladies in bright colours, walking to and fro," he found two portly sows "trotting up behind this carriage, and a select party of half a-dozen gentlemen-hogs" turning the corner. Referring to one porcine acquaintance, Dickens declared: "He is in every respect a republican pig, going wherever he pleases, and mingling with the best society, on an equal, if not superior footing." Despite the park boom of the 1830s, pigs continued to rule the dirty streets of New York, "turning up the news and small-talk of the city, in the shape of cabbage-stalks and offal."[1] They were able to do this because the city's streets remained filthy.

While Dickens declared that Manhattan was the "beautiful metropolis of America," he quickly qualified that it was "by no means as clean a city as Boston." This was an era when a number of U.S. cities, including

San Francisco and New Orleans, were striving to improve sanitation. New Yorkers believed filth was a major blemish on their city's reputation. The notorious pig population was a symbol not only of the city's grime, but also of the municipal government's impotence. It must have been an amusing juxtaposition to see ladies promenading alongside mud-splattered swine on Broadway, the most glamorous street in the city. New Yorkers had long been struggling with this combination. In 1817, "A Citizen" wrote to the *New-York Evening Post* commenting that "there is a mixture of meanness and magnificence that seems to have entered the character of our city, as well as its appearance." Despite its wealth and standing, New York was the "*filthiest* city in the United States, if not the world."[2]

Without an efficient sanitation program or adequate infrastructure, the city provided a welcome environment for pigs, disease, and ridicule. Trying desperately to keep up with New York's burgeoning population, the Common Council passed ordinance after ordinance in an attempt to legislate its way out of the muck. The city government grappled with several major sanitation issues from the 1820s through the 1840s, including how best to sweep the streets, gather horse manure, and remove the city's human waste. Since aldermen routinely chose arrangements that saved or made them money over those that might have been more efficient and effective, the management of filth during the antebellum period was largely a private enterprise. While Manhattan's enduring problems with filth had a lot to do with crowding, loose animals, and rudimentary infrastructure, the value of garbage for private industry remained a central part of that equation. Removing waste was a moneymaking venture for local entrepreneurs. The municipal government's uneven involvement in sanitation, though, had severe repercussions. While epidemics affected all New Yorkers regardless of people's wealth, the poor felt the greatest impact.

The Common Council fielded a constant din of complaints from frustrated New Yorkers, but the panic became deafening when cholera seeped into the city's water system in 1832 and 1849. Public health crises would serve as a tool for the growth of municipal power, though this growth was ultimately incremental and uneven. Pressure to reform the city eventually brought massive changes, but New York's notorious piles of filth were a mighty foe even for a determined city government.

Lost in the Mud

New York suffered from serious sanitation problems during the second quarter of the nineteenth century. As the city's population grew, so too did its garbage heaps. Householders dumped their trash onto the streets in anticipation of its collection by scavengers. Rotten food such as corn cobs, watermelon rinds, oyster shells, and fish heads joined with dead cats, dogs, rats, and pigs, as well as enormous piles of manure, to create a stench particularly offensive in the heat of the summer. Between the piles of odoriferous waste, deep mud puddles, and sauntering hogs, New Yorkers had much to complain about. One grumbled, "No one can cross Broadway but on tiptoe; ladies can only wishfully cast their eyes from one side to the other; if they have any regard for their clothes, will not venture further; indeed no pleasure carriage can drive the length of the street without being covered with mud so as to require washing before it can be used a second time." It was hard for elite New Yorkers to maintain a modicum of respectability under such conditions.[3]

In newspapers and books, elite New Yorkers alternated between chiding politicians and poking fun at the city's dire situation, or indulged in some combination of the two. An 1829 article, for example, lampooned Manhattan's situation. According to the story, a pedestrian came across a woman poking a stick into the mud on one of New York's main streets, saying, "Ah me! I'm sure he's here about some where, the dear cratur, and if I ounly had a longer stick, so that I could poke down a little grain deeper, I should find the darling!" The bystander asked, "What have you lost, good woman?" (offering to assist in the search with his cane), to which the woman replied, "Och, bless your kind sole! It's my swate little child, my darling Jemmy, that's lost in the mud." After a fair amount of struggle, the bystander successfully pulled Jemmy out of the mud with his cane. The mother gently scolded her five-year-old son: "Jemmy, my dear Jemmy, listen to your mother, and never try again to cross the streets of this blessed city, till you're big enough to hilp yourself out o' the mud, jist, my darling." While this parody likely had New Yorkers chuckling about the accents or ridiculousness of the situation as they read their morning newspapers, the touch of reality in the tale gave everyone something to relate to. The filth in New York's streets made traveling through the city difficult for pedestrians, both young and old. Not only was it unpleasant to live with, but it was a handicap as New York strove to compete with other cities.[4]

New Yorkers fretted about their standing as the "filthiest city in the United States." Even though New York had developed one of the strongest commercial markets in the country by the 1820s, the city's inhabitants still felt uneasy about how it compared to the other metropolitan centers. Boston, for instance, was known for its cleanliness and, time and again, critics of New York turned their eyes to Boston as a standard for comparison. Referencing the city-versus-city competitive fever of the era, the editors of the *New-York Evening Post* chided the Common Council: "Are we too proud to take a leaf from [Boston's] books?" To the chagrin of New Yorkers, Boston prided itself on its superior and efficient street cleaning. New York's Board of Assistant Aldermen declared, "The city of New York, the commercial emporium of the western world, with her ample means, should never be behind her sister cities in the arrangement of her domestic comforts." New York needed to polish its image.[5]

New Yorkers also worried about how international tourists, such as Dickens, saw their city. If New York was ever to compete with London or Paris, tourists would have to be impressed when they visited. Dirty streets, however, obscured the civility and economic strength that New Yorkers hoped to exhibit. After the Glasgow printer Robert Hedderwick visited the city in 1823, he returned to Scotland with a scathing review of what he had found: "The streets of New York are not to be perambulated with impunity by either the lame, or the blind, or the exquisitely sensitive in their olfactory nerves; to use an American phrase, a person must be 'wide awake,' not to dislocate his ankles by the inequalities and gaps in the side-pavements, or break his legs by running foul of the numberless moveable and immoveable incumbrances with which they are occupied." The *Evening Post* reprinted Hedderwick's article for local readers, as they typically did with published reviews about the city. New Yorkers were accustomed to such comments, and in their eyes the condition of the streets marred the city's identity as a growing metropolis.[6]

The councilmen were keenly aware of this issue and reevaluated the street cleaning system almost annually. Since garbage and manure were typically scattered all over the streets and sidewalks, "street cleaning" and "garbage collection" were two aspects of the same problem. In an attempt to improve the city's system, the councilmen called on grand juries to assess the state of the city's streets and suggest ways in which the council might improve conditions.[7] Despite these efforts, citizens regularly complained that the Common Council rarely enforced its multitude of laws. Politics often interfered with efficiency. After the election of a new set of politicians to the Common Council in 1823, the *Evening Post* expressed the hope that the street-cleaning department would no longer be weakened by "party patronage and party jobs." Ineffective sweepers with political connections kept their jobs and their "good round salaries" despite the horrible state of the streets. Unfortunately, politics and general inefficiency continued to hamper street-cleaning efforts.[8]

New York wavered between running its own street-cleaning system and hiring contractors to fill that role. Every few years, the city switched between private and public solutions, convinced that one or the other would be more efficient or less expensive. The public/private debate involved both sweeping and collecting—two tasks typically separated in Manhattan's waste removal. Historically, garbage was a private affair. New York's property owners were responsible for sweeping the street and sidewalk right in front of their home or business. Twice a week they would brush the waste into a pile for the cartmen to come and collect. While wealthier New Yorkers were able to assign this task to their servants or slaves, poorer New Yorkers had to take care of this arduous job before their workday began. In addition, landlords often neglected their rental properties. Consequently, working-class neighborhoods were even filthier than their wealthy but still grimy counterparts. The councilmen thought they could solve this inequity by hiring sweepers. In the best scenario, the sweepers would coordinate with collectors and sweep just before the carts came through. Unfortunately, their work was irregular and caused enough of a ruckus to annoy residents. According to the *Evening Post,* "When these gangs entered a street, there was a cry set up, lo! A troop cometh, and the windows and doors were shut, every aperture throughout the house was closed as soon as possible, the clothes-lines were stripped of the linen, &c., and every crevice was shut against the clouds of dust that filled the air and choked and blinded those who were so unfortunate as to be caught in the street." Critics recommended that homeowners should be responsible for their streets, given their stake in the outcome. Regardless of who swept the streets, there were problems with both private and public collection of the piles. The public-run system was riddled with patronage and the pressures of partisan politics, and lacked effective oversight. Frustrated with high costs and subpar work, the Common Council reverted to paying private contractors, but these, too, typically fell off schedule or failed to collect the trash. Neither the public nor the private system seemed to work.[9]

One of the repeated complaints leveled against street cleaning, both public and private, was that the trash collectors—or "scavengers," as they were commonly called—would pick and choose among the rubbish, leaving much of it behind. Collectors frequently passed over dead cats and rats, to the dismay of many New Yorkers. Scavengers were so selective because there was a huge market among regional farmers for the city's street manure. The very fact that the city could profit from its waste convinced critics that the publicly run option might not be as much of a drain on the city's coffers as many feared. In the eyes of both politicians and entrepreneurs, the piles of horse waste might as well have been piles of gold.[10]

The Value of Manure

The average horse left behind thirty-five to forty pounds of manure each day, a good portion of which ended up on the city's streets. In 1835, with over 10,000 horses in New York, the city was a veritable manure factory. Horses pulled carriages, street cars, and fire equipment, hauled freight, and even powered industrial machinery. In short, horses made the city run. The number of horses would increase dramatically throughout the century, as the population boomed and the city's dependence on them persisted.[11]

The enormous piles of dung were both a challenge and an opportunity for the city government. While the Common Council had to pay for the removal of residential and commercial refuse, manure provided a chance for the city to rake in a profit. The same farmers in the region who produced hay, vegetables, and grain for urban markets eagerly purchased the manure left on the streets. This large-scale regional recycling system helped to defray some of the city's sanitation costs while also servicing the farmers' need for fertilizer. Though the term "recycling" had yet to be coined, agriculturists used phrases like "nature's reciprocity system" to describe the reuse of waste to nourish farmland. As the agricultural journal the *Cultivator* put it, "What consummate folly to throw away the raw materials which form our daily bread!" With city residents and their animals consuming most of the produce from the hinterland, it seemed only natural that the city's waste should be returned to a farm, where it could benefit the next round of crops. Farmers who might otherwise have headed upstate or out west to find more arable land stayed near New York, in part because of the city's demand for their perishable or bulky products. Urban waste made it possible for them to stay. In its ideal form, the waste-recycling system would allow the city and the country to develop and expand in tandem. City aldermen, entrepreneurs, and farmers each had reasons for embracing this system.[12]

Many of the farmers in New York's hinterland found it lucrative and efficient to use their land solely for the hay, grain, or vegetables they would sell to city residents. Until the invention of hay balers later in the nineteenth century, it was not profitable to transport the bulky material over long distances. Regional farmers, therefore, seized the opportunity to fill that niche. Hay was crucial for the city, after all, as it was the primary fuel for its transportation system: horses. In 1843 William Ketchum, a Long Island farmer, observed that in order to fully capitalize on this market, "farmers generally keep as little [live]stock to consume the produce of their farms as possible, selling their hay and grain at New York and Brooklyn, and buying their manure in return." Since there was little topsoil on Long Island, farmers needed significant amounts of fertilizer in order to produce high yields. Many Long Island farmers had been supplementing or replacing their barnyard manure with imported stable and street manure from regional cities (New York, Brooklyn, Albany, and Boston) since at least the beginning of the nineteenth century. The urban/rural recycling system allowed farmers to intensify their practices and devote most, if not all, of their land to cash crops.[13]

Farmers were not the only ones benefiting from this relationship. In 1830 the New York City government raked in $19,033.45 for its street scrapings, which amounted to nearly 75 percent of the entire cost of cleaning the streets. During a time when street cleaning accounted for one of the city government's largest expenses, the ability to offset a major portion of the costs was not only good for the budget but also good for politics. While citizens complained endlessly about the dirtiness of the streets, they were suspicious about the high price of removing it. Contractors were notoriously corrupt and inefficient. By keeping the net cost down, the city tempered some of the criticism thrown its way. Manure ranked as one of the city's most profitable ventures, alongside taxes, tavern licenses, and the sale of public property. It was so important to the city that the municipal government even appointed collection agents to visit farmers who had outstanding bills.[14]

City officials alternated between selling the manure themselves and selling that right to private contractors. Contractors submitted sealed bids to remove all of the city's trash, including its manure, and the lowest bidder typically won. The sale of manure helped to lower the costs of the bidders' estimates by offsetting their other expenses, sometimes even resulting in a profit for the city, if the value of manure was higher than the cost of removing the rest of the garbage. This system, while convenient and profitable for the city's coffers, was not without its faults. When, in 1825, the Common Council's Street Committee met to reform the system, they remarked that since only one or two contractors held the right to collect the entire city's manure and clean its streets, the system was inherently inefficient. "Those few having the monopoly, and paying a large sum for the privelege, their interest only was consulted by them, and the filth and dirt removed, only when the interest was best subserved." Citizens and reformers alike criticized the contractors for neglecting general sanitation in favor of collecting valuable dung. Less profitable refuse remained on the streets for weeks or months at a time, creating odors and providing the roaming pigs with fodder. Without sufficient public oversight, the private solution was unsustainable. It is easy to romanticize the filthy, "organic city" as a moment when cities were more in tune with their environments and where waste was not wasted, but the realities were not so ideal.[15]

From the perspective of farmers, however, the system seemed to work fine. As of 1842, the going price for street dirt purchased in Manhattan was a reasonable 30 cents per cartload. They could also purchase it more locally on Long Island or Staten Island for an additional 20 cents per load at the docks, though farmers would then need to arrange to have oxcarts deliver it to their farms. A typical oxcart could hold two city cart loads, or approximately twenty-eight bushels. Another option was to transport the waste via rail. By the 1840s, the Long Island Railroad provided a crucial artery for the development of the Island's agriculture from Brooklyn out to North Fork. Milk, potatoes, blackberries, peaches, and fish went west to the city, while urban waste went east. In 1860, the Long Island Railroad transported more than 100,000 cart-loads, or 1.4 million bushels, of horse manure. Since the railroad ran down the center of the island, it became easier for inland farmers to access supplies of urban manure. By 1849, New York's Commissioner of Streets and Lamps was looking to gain access to other railroads as well, notably the Harlem and New Haven lines, which would expand the city's fertilizer market by taking it into Westchester and Connecticut.[16]

Maintaining the quality of New York's street manure was a chal-lenge for the municipal government. The New York State Agricultural Society generally considered street dirt to be "a great fertilizer but . . . not uniformly good." Farmers had to accept manure blended with a mess of garbage, including sand and remnants of building construc-tion, as well as "brick-bats, paving stones, sticks, old shoes, iron and other refuse material." In an attempt to prevent such issues, the aldermen regularly appointed manure inspectors to monitor its quality. Even so, nonorganic rubbish still made its way into the bushels that farmers pur-chased. Despite these drawbacks, street dirt was an excellent fertilizer. Some of the city's accidental ingredients actually made the quality bet-ter. The Agricultural Society described it as "a compost of earthy sub-stances ground fine by the constant attrition of carts and carriages, with lime from new and old buildings, ashes occasionally thrown into the streets, the droppings of horses and other animals driven about the city, and many animal and vegetable substances from the markets and houses, &c. All these, when mixed together, form a fermentative mass containing all the elements which nourish vegetation." For the better part of the nineteenth century, farmers continued to buy this bulky but accessible and relatively inexpensive manure to fertilize their crops.[17]

The municipal government was protective of its manure. Legally, whatever was left on the public streets was theirs. While private citizens were responsible for sweeping in front of their homes, they were forbid-den to use or sell the street manure. As early as 1817, offenders would be charged a fine of $25 every time they tried to remove the odorous heaps—regardless of whether they were doing this for profit or for cleanliness. This provision in the manure laws points to the fact that independent entrepreneurs attempted to edge their way into the profitable fertilizer market by harvesting wealth from the city's public spaces. The Common Council felt compelled to protect its street manure monopoly. The city streets were public spaces, not common spaces, and city officials essentially declared that the manure was *theirs*.[18]

The municipal government had plenty of competition in the manure market. While horses deposited a significant amount of manure on the streets, they also left their valuable waste in stables, and stable owners used this to their advantage. Some farmers favored stable manure, since they thought it was likely to be free of impurities such as random rubbish, and they considered it to be in a separate category from street manure. Other farmers continued to worry about the purity of the product, however, especially as many middlemen were involved with the process. Stable owners sold their stores of manure to dealers, who then processed it and sold it directly to farmers. Unlike street dirt, which was pulverized and mixed by city traffic, the stable manure, though purer, had to be fermented before it was suitable for use by farmers. Sometimes this process was handled by the farmers themselves, but dealers could get a higher price for their product if they took the trouble to ferment it. Manure dealers deposited cartloads of waste on empty or abandoned lots near the wharves, so that they could easily ship their product after it had matured.

Quality control was also an issue for stable manure. Many dealers added in a number of materials in order to bulk up their product, compromising its effectiveness. The Long Island farmer William Ketcham reported that the "dealers and collectors are at great pains to increase its bulk by adding saw-dust, shavings, tan-bark, &c. giving the whole a rich dark color by a liberal use of the leaves of the sumack." The purest product, he advised fellow farmers, was sold in Albany, where "there is not the same inducements to so liberal use of the above ingredients as at New-York." With demand high in New York, dealers had an incentive to do what they could to increase quantity at the expense of quality. Farmers also complained about the number of seeds found in stable manure. Horses could not completely digest certain foods, such as radishes, and as a result farmers had to deal with unwanted weeds in their fields. The same complaint, however, could be made about street dirt, "particularly in summer, when ever[y] kind of garden, fruit and flower seeds, thrown into the streets from the houses and markets, abound to it."[19] One way or another, horse-produced urban waste was bound to cause the growth of weeds.

The location and storage of both street dirt and stable manure was a constant source of debate and complaint among New Yorkers. While urban waste was a definite asset for both the city treasury and private entrepreneurs, it was also a source of foul smells and, potentially, disease. The "mountains and pyramids of earth, which lie in huge cones and heaps," crowded sidewalks and streets, causing malodorous winds to greet the noses of residents and passersby. The manure dealers' process of raking the piles also angered urban residents who lived nearby, as it caused foul odors to rise and penetrate the surrounding neighborhood. The miasma theory of disease, which remained popular for much of the nineteenth century, held that diseases were transmitted through tainted air, indicated by odors. Sense of smell, then, was integral to the way nineteenth-century urban residents understood and shaped their environment. Critics of the city's hogs often used their horrid smell as an argument to get rid of them. The smell of decomposing matter and pungent manure triggered even greater fears of illness and danger. To make matters worse, manure heaps also attracted flies, especially in the warm summer months, which helped to spread the fear that disease was imminent.[20]

The city government had to carefully balance the health of its residents with its own budgetary needs. Inspectors targeted the deposits of privately owned stable manure, especially as the dealers often fermented their product illegally on vacant lots. The City Inspector regularly required that street inspectors fence off unoccupied property to keep out

FIGURE 14. *North Battery, Foot of Hubert St., New York,* engraving by James Smillie, 1833, after a painting by Robert W. Weir. In 1831, the Common Council proposed using the dilapidated North Battery, on the Hudson River just west of Greenwich Village, to store the city's street manure. Nearby residents were outraged. (Emmet Collection, Miriam and Ira D. Wallach Division of Art, Prints, and Photographs, The New York Public Library, Astor, Lenox, and Tilden Foundations.)

trespassers who might dump manure or other waste. While the city government punished private manure dealers, they also tried to manage the municipal piles. The aldermen recognized that piles of manure left for long periods of time were "not only extremely offensive but injurious to the health of the Citizens." The main issue, then, involved finding an unobtrusive place to deposit and store manure and arranging ways to remove it swiftly. The storage place for street dirt needed to be "removed far from the dwellings of man" but also close enough that carters could reach it easily. After the city established specific wharves where scows and other boats could dock to receive and remove the manure, nearby residents lodged complaints about the choice of docks.[21]

For a brief moment in 1831, the Common Council considered transforming the old North Battery, built as a fort for the War of 1812, into a manure storage facility (see Figure 14). The Common Council's Committee on Wharves, Piers, and Slips that came up with this proposal had been facing complaints from residents living near the manure docks. Whereas Castle Clinton, formerly known as the West Battery, or Fort Clinton, had opened as a fashionable resort in the heart of Battery Park in 1824, the city had left the North Battery vacant. The fort was in poor condition and would require significant renovations in order to turn it into an entertainment center similar to Castle Clinton. The committee boasted that the site was surrounded by nothing but a few vacant buildings, so there were "no Inhabitants to be annoyed" by manure boats docked at the basin. The structure itself could hold 20,000 loads of manure, and the space outside it even more. Manure boats could easily dock at the long wharf attached to the fort and ship the material elsewhere. The aldermen quickly approved the measure.[22]

The proposal was hardly as popular with the public. The *New-York Spectator* called the plan "preposterous"—an abomination that would be "morally, as well as physically, a stench in the nostrils of the community." Angry citizens sent remonstrances to the Board of Aldermen until the measure was eventually dropped. Though the residents of that part of the city preferred a plan for a promenade and entertainment center, in the end the city demolished the structure. While the city government found manure to be a gold mine, city residents were none too pleased to have it stored in their neighborhoods.[23]

Urban fertilizer certainly had its supporters, but it also left many complaining. While regional farmers used it as a means to transform their farms and focus on market crops, the benefits for the city were less obvious. The government and manure dealers profited, but the city streets remained filthy. Residents had to step clear of the piles of what, to them, was valueless waste on the pavement and deal with the unpleasant odors produced by all of the manure stored on nearby docks and lots. The countless manure piles would seem even more threatening once cholera arrived on the city's shores.

Cholera's First Visit

Cholera found a welcome home in New York City, due to the burgeoning population and ramshackle infrastructure. Immigration outpaced the housing supply, forcing high-density living in neighborhoods ill-equipped to handle the needs of their new residents. High real estate values compounded this issue, forcing poor families to squeeze into as little space as possible. With an inadequate water supply, badly managed waste removal, and a privy system better suited to a smaller population, Manhattan offered some of the best conditions for cholera to thrive.[24]

Cholera is a bacterial disease that typically spreads through contaminated water, as well as uncooked fruits and vegetables. People infected with the bacterium *Vibrio cholerae* suffered from diarrhea that led to severe dehydration. About half of all people infected with cholera died, often within hours of showing the first symptoms. When the sick used their privies or cesspools and the waste overflowed into the nearby water wells and basements, cholera spread rapidly through the neighborhood. By 1832, only the poorest classes of New York used the pumps for drinking water, as many who could afford to bought water imported from elsewhere in the local region. Still, pump water was commonly used for washing clothing and for other household needs.[25]

Since the water-borne nature of the disease was not yet known, scientists, doctors, and the general public had several theories about how cholera spread. Many believed, for instance, that miasmas, or odors, spread the disease. Poor sanitation and bad drainage—typical in nineteenth-century cities like New York—were responsible for such smells. When severe outbreaks of cholera hit neighborhoods built over swampy land, such as Five Points, the miasma theory seemed to have proven correct. This theory also helped to justify complaints against storing manure in dense neighborhoods. New Yorkers fretted about these smells and conditions. In 1832, with cholera threatening to visit New York following its European tour, a committee of doctors guided the Common Council on preventive measures. They warned that "the destroying angel, should he visit our city, would walk unseen in the midst of us, enveloped in a pestilential vapour." Some doctors argued that the seemingly atmospheric qualities of cholera explained not only how the disease moved from country to country, but also how it could affect New Yorkers from a wide range of neighborhoods and social classes. Quarantines had been the go-to method of preventing public health disasters during past yellow fever outbreaks, and though the city still instituted them, people were beginning to question their value. Cholera seemed to defy such barriers.[26]

Panic pervaded the city in the summer of 1832. Without a solid grasp on how to stave off the epidemic, people took solace where they could. Former mayor John Pintard found comfort in the fact that cholera seemed to favor the poor and depraved. He wrote, "At present it is almost exclusively confined to the lower classes of intemperate dissolute & filthy people huddled together like swine in their polluted habitations. A visitation like the present may work beneficially to promote Temperance, proving a blessing instead of a curse." In retrospect, it certainly seems perverse that Pintard found a silver lining amid the horrors that cholera was spreading in the city. Yet his perspective was far from uncommon. As someone who felt righteous, Pintard must have been reassured by the idea that the afflicted had somehow brought cholera upon themselves through their own bad behavior. He hoped this would scare sinners into a more virtuous life. Other temperance advocates pleaded with New Yorkers to abandon alcohol in order to keep their constitutions strong. Handbills and newspaper articles warned readers to avoid specific foods, such as shellfish, cucumbers, and watermelons, to cook all foods, drink milk, bathe regularly, dress in warm clothing, and, most of all, stay calm. In other words, New Yorkers should embrace

"TEMPERANCE, CLEANLINESS, FORTITUDE, and FEARLESS-
NESS" if they had any hope of remaining alive.[27]

Having visited ailing Montreal and corresponded with European officials, New York's Board of Health declared that good sanitation was
the key to saving the city. According to its report, New Yorkers had to
keep their bodies and homes clean, as well as their city. The city had a
handful of public baths set up for residents, though little could be done
to force New Yorkers to use them. The Board of Health, which consisted of aldermen as well as medical professionals, instituted a policy
in mid-June 1832 giving aldermen and anyone in their employ the right
to inspect the "dwellings, yards, and premises" in their wards, to make
sure that their constituents were doing their part to keep the disease at
bay. The board designated the aldermen "Health Wardens" responsible
for making sure residents followed all public health laws. The city was
desperate to enforce such laws in the face of a potential crisis, and putting responsibility in the hands of the most public figures in the wards
seemed to be the best way. Several aldermen informed the Board of
Health that they had employed teams of laborers and carts to go through
and purify private property in their desperately dirty wards. They were
happy to report that the laborers had been "aided by the uniform vol-
untary and cheerful cooperation of the Inhabitants who appeared to be
actuated by one general sentiment of submitting to private inconvenience
for Public good." It seems unlikely that every poor family was eager to
have their home whitewashed and covered in lime by government officials, but among middle-class and wealthy New Yorkers there was plenty
of support for these intrusive measures. The *New-York Spectator* com-
mended city officials for their efforts and encouraged them to go further: "Let . . . the inhabitations of the poor be well white-washed, and
all filth removed from them, and let them be inspected daily, that no
offal matter be collected. If the houses of the poor be found crowded,
let their inhabitants be dispersed at the expense of the corporation, and
provisions made for them without the bounds of the city. Especially let

those be removed who live in cellars and damp situations." Cholera gave the city government the power not only to intrude on private residences in order to purify them, but also to remove residents from their homes. The public health crisis aided an increase in municipal power for the sake of public good. Private spaces were now a public concern.[28]

Unlike private residences, streets were more typically under the jurisdiction of city agencies. Yet the streets seemed wildly out of control. Waste removal continued to be an issue. When the Board of Assistant Aldermen formed a committee to review the city's street-cleaning policies early in the summer of 1832 before cholera struck New York, they noted: "That terrible disease, the *cholera,* which has caused so much alarm throughout Europe, has as yet prevailed extensively only in the most dirty and filthy districts, and among such classes as neglect a proper degree of cleanliness." The committee was well aware that New York's filth could rival that of most other cities, and they would therefore need to make drastic changes in order to prevent a cholera outbreak. They proposed abandoning the use of private contractors and instituting reforms that expanded bureaucratic control of the streets— hiring professional street sweepers and multiple street inspectors who would supervise sweeping and collecting in the morning, between sunrise and the start of business. Though neither of these proposals was particularly novel given that the Common Council had already attempted them in one form or another, there was a new sense of urgency. In the past, the aldermen had shied away from public control because of the taxes that would be necessary to finance the effort, but they now felt that there was a worthy cause. At a cost of about $1.25 per householder for the year—the equivalent of what families annually spent on brooms—not only could the public spaces be thoroughly cleaned and many lives saved, but men who would otherwise depend on public welfare could find employment. The city instituted the new street-cleaning policies on June 13, 1832, less than two weeks before cholera struck the city. One resident remarked how shocked he and other New Yorkers were to see the streets clean. An elderly woman who had lived in the city all her life purportedly declared, "I never knew that the streets were covered with stones before." It seemed that the Common Council was taking bold, definitive steps toward true reform. The public health crisis trumped the earlier political debates that had hampered full reform.[29]

Yet when cholera finally arrived on June 26, New Yorkers did not place all their faith in sanitation. New York State governor Enos Throop wrote in a statement to the state legislature that an "infinitely wise and just God has seen fit to employ pestilence as one of the means of scourging the human race for their sins." A solution, of course, was to declare a citywide day of "fasting, humiliation and prayer." Alderman Cebra, who introduced the measure in the Common Council, contended that a great number of the city's "respectable citizens" had petitioned them to do so. The city designated August 3 as a day in which "all the people may unite in imploring the mercy of Heaven, that the plague may be stayed, and our city restored to its wonted state of industry and health." With the clergymen unable to coordinate their efforts, the aldermen took it upon themselves to take care of the city's spiritual health. The city had to prepare in whatever way it could.[30]

Spirituality, however, was just one mode of defense. Even in 1832, a number of people in the medical and political communities, as well as in the general population, embraced the idea that diseases might result from environmental conditions, such as filthy streets and homes. Though they might cite God's will, they also emphasized the importance of sanitation. The aldermen still had to grapple with the city's sanitary conditions, despite vigorous measures taken before the outbreak. Hogs, for instance, continued to roam the streets. With a public health crisis at hand, the aldermen were reenergized to tackle this political minefield, and they passed a new version of the anti-hog law just as cholera struck the city. Owners were fined $5 per loose hog and had to collect their animals at the local pound after paying for their room and board. If the hogs were not claimed by their owners, they would be sold at a city auction. Despite these efforts, the hogs remained. In August, a month after the law was officially on the books, an "Indignant Citizen" wrote to the *New-York Mercury* complaining about the number of hogs on the streets. He blamed the hogs for his family's ailments: "Two inmates of my family have been carried to the grave within the last year, and I verily believe that the existence of two hog-pens hard by me, and the effluvia created by swine running in the streets, may have had an influence in hurrying these people out of life." The writer implored the aldermen to enforce both the law against swine and the street-cleaning law, which (as usual) had not been enforced. He reasoned that if the law indeed kept people from throwing garbage in the streets, the hogs would have nothing left to subsist on. While the city had high hopes for reform and even touted its improvements in official documents and meetings, the reality was less than stellar.[31]

Hogs were a saving grace for the city's poor during the cholera epidemic. Most of the businesses in the city closed their doors when New Yorkers with resources escaped to their summer homes to avoid the epidemic. Those who relied on "their daily labor for their daily bread" were at a particular disadvantage. Lacking the means to leave town and unable to work, they were left at the hands of charity. Committees and benevolent organizations formed to gather donations and food for the poor, but they could not solve the entire problem. Hogs provided an inexpensive food source for their owners. The aldermen renewed their efforts in August to sweep the city clean of hogs, but were met with resistance. The mostly Irish owners came out in force, as they had during the earlier hog riots, to protect their livestock from collection. In the end, the hogs remained, as did the city's larger sanitation issues, despite the renewed push to clean the city for the sake of preventing cholera. After several decades of unsuccessful attempts to establish a workable sanitation program while also pursuing the sale of manure, the city government's last-minute attempts to reform the streets came far too late. Too much needed to be done to effect real change that could save the city from devastating epidemics.[32]

Panic did not cease with the waning of the 1832 epidemic, despite the return of most New Yorkers and the reopening of businesses. Though the epidemic receded, it did not disappear. For the next two summers, cholera returned, reminding New Yorkers of the need to persist with their sanitation efforts. Following each outbreak, New Yorkers grew even more enraged about filthy streets now that their lives were so clearly at stake and cholera was fresh in their memories. By May 1833, the *New-York Spectator* reported: "[It] is a remark in the mouth of everybody, that our streets were never in a more filthy condition than at present." The *Spectator* as well as other newspapers saw this as ominous. While other cities were actively looking to improve their public spaces, New York's aldermen appeared to be idle. The *Morning Courier and New-York Enquirer* railed that the municipal government practically invited the disease back onto Manhattan's shores by neglecting the "precautions which guard against it."[33]

New York's filth was closely bound up with politics. By the spring of 1834, months before cholera's final appearance in the city during that decade, Andrew Jackson's controversial Bank War was brewing. National political debates over the fate of the powerful, federally charted Bank of the United States played out in the local politics of the city. The Whig Party formed on both a local and national level in response to Jackson's attack on the bank. Despite the centrality of national issues in the election of 1834, local issues, including the city's filth, also played a role. The city's Whigs used the sanitation problems as a way to jab at their Democratic foes, who ran city government. Critics referred to street manure as "Jackson mud," pilloried the city leadership as the "Jackson dy-*nasty*," and criticized the Democratic street inspectors as "too busy just now, in patriotic labors to keep their offices, to leave much time for the discharge of their duties." In the first election that allowed New Yorkers to vote directly for their mayor, the anti-bank Jacksonian Democrat Cornelius Lawrence won by a slim margin. The newly formed Whig Party, however, celebrated its success against the more established local Democratic organization, Tammany Hall, in winning a majority on the Common Council that April, though the city streets hardly benefited in the years that followed.[34]

Not only did the 1832 cholera epidemic inspire political rancor, but it also led to political action on a long-debated topic: the city's water. For decades, New York had suffered from an inadequate supply of fresh water. Large-scale fires that destroyed hundreds of thousands of dollars' worth of property were common enough to inspire committees of aldermen to consider ways to reform New York's shoddy infrastructure, but cholera was the impetus for more decisive action. The Manhattan Company, founded by Aaron Burr, had had a monopoly on the city's water supply since the turn of the century. Though it laid pipes, the company had more interest in establishing its profitable banking arm than bringing long-lasting change to New York's water supply. In addition to the Manhattan Company's water, which was drawn mainly from the swampy and tainted former Collect Pond waters under Five Points, a few hundred wooden pumps could be found on street corners, though the free water they spouted was the most contaminated in the city. With quantity and quality lacking, reformers argued that it was time to bring in water from beyond salt-water-ringed Manhattan. In 1831, before cholera hit, the New York Lyceum of Natural History reported that New York's water supply was filled with organic matter leaching from the privies and the streets. They estimated that more than a hundred tons seeped into the city's water each day. While the Common Council discussed the failures of the Manhattan Company and the ways to release themselves from the company's monopoly, they could not agree on whether the city should fund a large public works project. Newspapers, however, continued to push for municipal action.[35]

Finally, with the fear of cholera fresh on their minds and the need for clean water imperative, the Common Council, the mayor, and the state legislature agreed in early 1833 to appoint a commission to handle supplying the city of New York with pure water. Though it still was not clear to New Yorkers or anyone else that cholera stemmed from contaminated water, what was clear was that clean water was a fundamental ingredient for good sanitation and healthy people. When the commissioners presented a report to the Common Council in the spring of 1835, they recommended a $5.5 million public works project that would bring water from the Croton River in Westchester via an aqueduct into Manhattan. The Common Council's Committees on Fire and Water supported this project and asserted that the *"public health requires it."* They argued that "Bad air and bad water are leading causes of sickness in all populous towns. With a river at our command the causes of the noxious vapours which our gutters now supply, and which contaminate our air, will be removed." Tainted water also cost the city commerce. During the recent cholera epidemics, businesses had closed and laborers as well as capitalists had lost money. New York needed reliable sanitation and quality drinking water in order to be a functioning and competitive city.[36]

New Yorkers came out in support of the grand public works project in mid-April 1835, voting three-to-one in favor of the measure, with the most support coming from the wealthier wards downtown. The "Great Fire" that struck the city's business district that December further underscored the need to establish a reliable and extensive source of water. Since the current reservoir was depleted and the pipes and pumps were frozen, firefighters had a difficult time subduing the fire, which ripped through twenty blocks downtown. They tried in vain to chop through ice in the East River and shuttle water to the flames. Raging for three days, the Great Fire destroyed roughly 700 buildings and at least $20 million worth of property, more than three times the cost of the Erie Canal. This disaster had many repercussions, including the bankruptcy of most of the city's fire insurance companies, the unemployment of thousands who worked downtown, and the rise of the penny press to meet New Yorkers' demand for information. It was also increasingly difficult to argue against the need for Croton water.[37]

After seven years of budget negotiations, engineering puzzles, labor disputes, and difficulties with Westchester landowners, Croton water finally reached Manhattan in 1842. On October 14, the whole city came out to celebrate its arrival downtown with a parade and several speeches. One hundred guns were fired at the start of the day, followed by the ringing of all the church bells. Engineers, city officials, firemen, temperance societies, and a slew of mechanics and other citizens joined in the seven-mile-long parade. The *New-York Tribune* declared the occasion to be one of the most significant in the city's history—second only to the opening of the Erie Canal.[38]

With the promise of a steady supply of water from the Croton Aqueduct, washing the streets was finally feasible. Good sanitation seemed likewise attainable. The fountains in Union Square and City Hall Park jetted far into the air, celebrating the abundance of water that the city's new infrastructure could deliver. During the celebration, the New York Sacred Music Society, as well as New Yorkers who received freshly printed copies, sang "The Croton Ode" by poet George P. Morris. Together, they chanted:

> Water leaps as if delighted,
> While her conquered foe retire!
> Pale Contagion flies affrighted
> With the baffled demon, Fire!
> Safety dwells in her dominions,
> Health and Beauty with her move,
> And entwine their circling pinions
> In a sisterhood of love.

Hopes ran high that Croton water would improve public health through a combination of clean streets, pure drinking water, and a decreased dependency on alcohol. The panic over epidemics and fires, paired with pressure from business interests, helped the city take control of this public amenity that had so long been in private hands. Water meant

FIGURE 15. J. F. Atwill, *Croton Water Celebration*, 1842. With the fountain squarely in front of City Hall, this lithograph, which was distributed
during the celebration on October 14, 1842, on the cover of sheet music for
the "Croton Ode," celebrated the power of New York's municipal government to bring about great public works. (Collection of the New-York Historical
Society.)

survival for the expanding city. Unfortunately, the aqueduct could
not solve all of the city's ills. New York's privy system left much to be
desired.[39]

Privy Profits

In 1844, the Board of Aldermen estimated that the residents of Manhattan were producing somewhere between 700,000 and 800,000 cubic
feet of "excrementitious matter" each year. As a point of comparison, this
amounted to roughly half the amount of horse manure being shipped
on the Long Island Railroad in 1860. Humans were not as prolific as
horses, but their waste still posed problems for a city with a rudimentary

infrastructure. Property owners had to hire night scavengers to empty their privies at least once a year, to keep the containers from overflowing. In the best scenario, the night scavengers carted the material away in closed containers and dumped it in the slips between the docks of either the Hudson or the East River, while their clients slept soundly. In reality, though, the containers were inadequately sealed, allowing odors and a slimy trail of liquids to escape while horses pulled the carts down bumpy streets.[40]

While the city government had gained significant power to control the urban environment as a result of the cholera outbreak, it remained unable or unwilling to tackle issues relating to "night soil" (a contemporary euphemism for human waste). The most visible of these issues involved its disposal. The material that made it to the rivers settled into the slips, making it difficult for ships to dock. The City Inspector's office had to pay to have the slips dredged on a regular basis—a costly and temporary solution. Two private companies approached the city, however, with a proposal they claimed could save the municipal government money and headaches. These companies—the New-York Poudrette Company and the Lodi Manufacturing Company—turned human waste into fertilizer for East Coast farmers. For exclusive rights to the material, the companies pledged to pay the night scavengers 25 cents per cartload, giving the scavengers an incentive not to dump their material at a more convenient dock. While the city would not profit in the same way it did with street manure, since it was not directly selling the waste, the companies' proposals seemed likely not only to save the city the cost of dredging slips, but also to solve some of the city's smelliest sanitation issues. This was yet another private solution for a public issue.[41]

Though the New-York Poudrette Company and the Lodi Manufacturing Company, established in 1837 and 1840, respectively, were at the forefront of a new industry in the United States, they were hardly novel in terms of European and Asian developments. Most famously, Parisians had long been tinkering with ways to use human waste as fertilizer on local farms. At the turn of the nineteenth century, the French chemist M. Bridet had patented a deodorized and dried fertilizer called "poudrette" (from the French word *poudre,* meaning "powder") made from the human waste of Parisian cesspools. The Montfaucon waste-processing center outside Paris was legendary in the minds of American agriculturists and entrepreneurs keen on turning urban waste into profits and produce.[42]

Looking to revolutionize fertilizers and make money from a ne-glected resource, businesses popped up around American cities, where human waste was plentiful and relatively convenient to collect. Both the New-York Poudrette Company and the Lodi Manufacturing Com-pany wanted local farmers to be their stockholders, since farmers would be the main consumers. They offered benefits such as guaranteed pou-drette for five years, in return for each share a farmer purchased. The processing of poudrette required enough equipment, facilities, and la-bor to make the business much more capital-intensive than the processing of street manure. Through the intensive French process that turned waste into fertilizer, the companies were able to do away with "the disgusting, offensive character" of the night soil. Marketed as a concentrated fer-tilizer, poudrette required extensive labor and specialized equipment to reduce its bulk and transform it into a less offensive form. The New-York Poudrette Company, founded by Daniel K. Minor, had its offices and factory in Manhattan. Minor expanded the company's activities to include emptying privies and transporting the contents directly to its factory. New-York Poudrette did not survive more than a handful of years, but the Lodi Manufacturing Company had better luck. Es-tablished by Anthony Dey, Jacob C. Dey, and Peter Barthelemy, a for-mer colleague of Minor's, the Lodi Company shipped Manhattan's waste to its facilities in Lodi, New Jersey. The company had its eye on large-scale distribution, posting agents throughout the Northeast so that farmers distant from New York could place orders. To farmers ac-customed to purchasing other urban-waste fertilizers, poudrette seemed to be an easy substitute for the more typical street scrapings and stable manure.[43]

The long process of creating poudrette began when barges pulled up to the company's wharf from New York, ready to deposit their cargo.[44] The Lodi factories were located on 400 acres of salt marsh and meadowland along the Hackensack River. Most of the property was used to produce hay for the New York City market, while six acres were devoted to the factories. The barges would arrive with approximately 8,000 bushels of New York City's night soil, and workers would transfer the material with buckets into canal-like reservoirs. The privies' contents passed through a large sieve as they entered the reservoir, separating all other types of refuse commonly discarded in the outhouses. The *American Agriculturist,* a monthly journal, remarked on the wide range of refuse found and repurposed. Workers recovered jewelry and money accidentally lost, "perhaps one incentive to the following of a business at best unpleasant." Female workers collected the glassware and animal bones and sold them to various merchants and dealers. Other refuse ranged from toys and shoes to kitchen pots. The poudrette companies had to be careful to remove this refuse if they wanted their product to be valuable and reliable.[45]

After Lodi's employees sifted the manure, they shoveled it onto drying beds consisting of a combination of wood planks and naked, smooth ground. They then spread the night soil thickly over a thin layer either of muck from the surrounding marsh or of alluvial soil from the Hackensack and Passaic rivers. Early in the company's history, it seems that the night soil was also combined with peat moss ground in horse-powered machines. While it all dried, Lodi employees shoveled it several times to mix the night soil thoroughly with the muck. Once the mixture was dry and blended, the men carted it to the screening buildings, where they piled the fertilizer into large heaps and mixed it further to make the product as uniform as possible. The men then beat the piles through box sieves with a shovel in order to pulverize the dried manure as finely as possible. Packed in barrels, the poudrette was finally ready for market.[46]

Proponents of poudrette were especially enthusiastic about reclaiming the nutrients otherwise being lost in the rivers. Poudrette fit firmly

FIGURE 16. Men shovel sifted night soil onto drying beds, at left, while ships on the right deliver more from Manhattan. Engraving by Lossing-Barritt from Lodi Manufacturing Company, *Circular* (New York, 1852), 4. (Courtesy of the American Antiquarian Society.)

in the urban/rural recycling system that had matured over the previous few decades. To many farmers, entrepreneurs, and city leaders, it seemed only logical that New York's human waste should be utilized like its animal waste. The exchange between the city and the country had the potential to solve the city's problems with human waste while also benefiting the country. In the Lodi Company's incorporation papers, the founders celebrated the role that the firm would play in this reciprocal relationship. "It is difficult to conceive of any improvement combining more directly the interest and convenience of the city and country. The Docks have been made offensive and unhealthy, and must often be cleared out by mud machines—the fish in the cars rendered objectionable, and thousands who live on shipboard, offended by the state of the docks. If all these evils can be remedied, and the grand nuisance of the cities be required and demanded by the country, it will form a combination of benefits most devoutly to be wished." Lodi claimed that property values would rise and public health would improve. The city's gain would be the country's gain. While the Lodi Company was eager to emphasize this idyllic urban/rural relationship, the reality was murkier. The company, firmly rooted in the emergent industrial economy, had much to gain from the city's human waste.[47]

Yet not everyone was enthusiastic about poudrette. An editor of the *Cultivator,* an agricultural journal, noted that "its use has always been limited, owing to prejudices arising from its disagreeable nature, and its offensive odor." Some shied away from using the manure because of its human source. While the odor of horse manure was familiar in the cities and countryside of the nineteenth century, human waste had a more pungent smell that held taboos for many. The Lodi Company repeatedly attempted to assure potential customers that their "chemical process" removed all smell from their product. A good number of farmers were so interested in experimenting with urban-waste fertilizers during this period that they found it possible to move beyond cultural taboos.[48]

Poudrette companies advertised that their product was twelve to fifteen times more potent than other urban fertilizers, such as street dirt. In 1840, the Lodi Company guaranteed shareholders fifty bushels of poudrette annually for five years. At $100 per share, this made poudrette over eleven times more expensive than local street manure. For $100, a farmer could have purchased roughly 2,800 bushels of street manure in 1842. To make its price reasonable, poudrette would have to live up to the company's claims that a little would go a long way.[49]

The reviews were mixed. While some farmers reported success, many more believed that poudrette was not nearly as effective as advertised. Farmers wrote letters to agricultural journals describing their results. For example, H. B. Glover of Newtown, Connecticut, reported that poudrette provided no visible benefit to the corn he planted. Fertilizers high in nitrogen, like poudrette, typically produced greener leaves that grew quickly at first, but eventually growth would slow and plants would mature at the same rate as did plants nourished with other manures.[50]

Farmers also accused the poudrette companies of adding extra ingredients that impaired the quality and effectiveness of the manure. As early as 1842, the New York State Agricultural Society contended that while poudrette was advertised as stronger than stable manure, "it has been found otherwise in practice, the article being so diluted with peat or other earthy substance as to reduce its strength and value." Some of the waste the poudrette companies tried so diligently to sift out of their product likely still remained. Coal ashes, for instance, would have been almost impossible to separate out using their rudimentary methods. The Lodi Company responded by claiming that they stood behind the quality of their product. They also advertised extensive improvements to their poudrette that made it the "cheapest and best Manure now known," relying on such claims to persuade skeptical consumers and attract those hesitant to work with human waste. Yet when Yale agricultural chemist Samuel W. Johnson analyzed Lodi's fertilizer in his *Essays on Peat, Muck, and Commercial Manures* in 1859, he found that "all manner of city refuse, old nails, apple-seeds, &c., &c., are found in it." In addition, the value of poudrette depended on how much was needed, compared to other fertilizers, in order to produce similar results. Many farmers found they needed much more than Lodi advertised was necessary, making poudrette less cost-effective than the company claimed.[51]

Poudrette never caught on as a long-term solution for most American farmers. Most poudrette companies based in American cities lost out to competition with cheaper urban-waste fertilizers, Peruvian guano that came from bird waste, and eventually chemical fertilizers toward the end of the nineteenth century. The Lodi Manufacturing Company lasted into the 1870s, surviving as long as it did by reformulating its product and combining it with popular fertilizers such as guano to attract new or skeptical customers. Even so, the Lodi factory was able to produce only a small amount of fertilizer. In 1853, for instance, the company produced just 10,157 barrels of poudrette, which could at best fertilize about 5,000 acres. By the time the city had introduced an extensive sewer system at the end of the nineteenth century, any hopes for revisiting poudrette were flushed away. The poudrette market declined even in France, where the reliability and ease of using commercial fertilizers made the repurposing of human waste less and less attractive.[52]

Poudrette also failed to solve urban woes. Poudrette or no poudrette, New York's infrastructure was unable to handle the volume of human waste it produced, and the consequences were dire. When waste was stored in unreliable privies and cesspools, it seeped into the local water wells, which in turn fueled cholera epidemics. The poudrette companies could hardly solve these larger, systemic problems. If anything, the solutions provided by the private poudrette companies may have delayed the city's adoption of new publicly funded infrastructure that might have helped to prevent future epidemics.[53]

Cholera Returns

Cholera revisited New York in 1849, despite the new supply of water and attempts to control the city's waste. On May 15, an Irish-American family living at 20 Orange Street, in the heart of Five Points, was struck by the disease. The City Inspector and local physicians visited their home to verify, and were horrified by the conditions they found in the neighborhood. Not only were the streets a mess, but so were the apartments. The *Tribune* noted that the families had no bedding, while the *Herald* went further: the inhabitants "were in regular debauch—without food, and subsisting only on the diluted and poisonous liquid sold in that vicinity." As with the 1832 outbreak, anxious citizens took solace in their supposed moral and financial superiority to the cholera victims. Repeatedly, newspapers and health officials noted that those most affected were not only poor but had bad hygiene, dirty homes, and intemperate habits. Cholera once again found a favorable setting in the marshy areas, such as Five Points, where bad drainage combined with dense housing. It was no coincidence that the poorest New Yorkers lived in these unattractive environments. The greatest victims of the uneven municipal response to sanitation were in these neighborhoods. Still, those from other neighborhoods wagged their fingers at the immigrants and African Americans who called these blighted communities home, finding the source of their downfall in their lifestyles.[54]

The city government again mobilized to calm the fears of its citizens. Despite having months to prepare—cholera had been spotted on the quarantine grounds six months earlier but had not spread—city officials only belatedly took steps to institute public health measures after doctors confirmed the cases on Orange Street. The Board of Health's "Sanatory Committee" appointed the aldermen and assistant aldermen of each ward as health wardens to increase effectiveness, since the representatives knew their neighborhoods well. Some politicians likely used this increased power for their ward's benefit, while others used it as a political tool to benefit favorites by overlooking noxious industries or residences of the politically powerful.[55]

Based on their past experience in 1832, members of the Sanatory Committee immediately knew that they had to focus on sanitation. The newspapers reinforced this awareness. The *New-York Tribune* chided the city government for not having achieved better sanitation. Although New York was located between two rivers and had "the whole volume of the Croton flowing through our streets to wash us clean," it was still the dirtiest city in the country. "Dirt and garbage of all varieties accumulate in our thoroughfares, and in the poorer quarters, such as Elm-st. Orange-st. Mulberry-st. The heaps of matter thus collected sometimes cause the streets to resemble a Western bog-road rather than the avenues of the American metropolis, while the stench from decaying substances is overpowering, except to the habit or the resolution of a native. Now, this is shameful at all times, and at all times a source of danger." Despite the rush to clean the city after the 1832 outbreak, and despite the hubbub surrounding the introduction of Croton water, New York's streets remained a mess. As one New Yorker put it, the city, though improved, was "still quite too much of a slattern." After the previous decade's panic had subsided, the aldermen had not continued to allocate the necessary funds for street cleaning, and familiar problems had returned.

Piles of manure and other waste persisted on the streets and docks. City Inspector Alfred W. White assured the government that he had enlisted "gangs of men" to clean the city's streets that May, in order to make up for the city's transgressions. These gangs went through the "infectious district," whitewashing and purifying what they could with chloride of lime. The Croton water supply was not sufficient, however, to flush the streets of the city. Just three days after the first case of cholera was confirmed, City Inspector White contacted the president of the Croton Board, hoping to get full access to the supply of water in the reservoirs. The board denied the request, claiming that the reservoir levels were too low. Inspector White disregarded this and used the water to flush out Five Points. While the better supply of water in 1849 perhaps lessened the severity of the cholera outbreak, it was still insufficient to protect or even fully cleanse the city.[56]

In a hurried attempt to rectify the city's health issues, the City Inspector and Sanatory Committee targeted the "nuisances" that had long been politically thorny: pigs, manure, noisome industries, and cemeteries. City Inspector White had been struggling with these "nuisances" for years, but the cholera epidemic of 1849 gave him the power to truly take control of the city's public spaces. Just two days after the first death was confirmed, the Sanatory Committee called on the police to demand that all hog owners remove their swine within twenty-four hours. On Orange Street alone there were pens containing 160 hogs, "the stench from which in so confined a locality is enough to produce a plague of deadly form," according to the *New York Herald*. After decades of struggling to gain control of the city's notorious hogs, the government was finally acquiring the political support necessary to get the job done. Not everyone was thrilled, however. While the press did not report on any riots or protests from hog owners, objections came from residents on the outskirts of the city, where owners and police deposited the refugee swine. The citizens of the Twelfth Ward, along with their representatives, fought to extend the anti-hog law to their neighborhood. When cholera struck that area particularly hard later in the summer, calls for change grew louder. Horace Greeley, editor of the *New-York Daily Tribune*, who had recently lost his son to cholera, erroneously blamed the epidemic on the arrival uptown of "twenty thousand hogs." While hogs would temporarily remain in the outer reaches of the city in large, penned properties known as "piggeries," they would no longer roam the streets of New York in the same way they had for centuries. Cholera had sealed the hogs' fate.[57]

The city also targeted the manure heaps that had long graced the docks and vacant lots of the city. Worried about the miasmas rising from these piles, City Inspector White sought to dump the material in the rivers or remove it by boat. The *Herald* railed against the city government for not arresting the manure dealers who stored their product in vacant lots. Police had a hard time identifying who owned the manure, a failing that the paper found unacceptable: "If ever there was a confession of imbecility in a city government, this is. What are the police good for, if they cannot find out the names of the parties guilty of accumulating such a huge plague spot as that under their nose?" The city also ran into trouble when, on one occasion, the officers in charge of removing the manure "were assaulted, the carts seized and driven off, and a scene of riot produced." Apparently, the manure dealers came out to resist the government's attempt to remove their property. Despite the outcry against manure and in defense of public health, it would continue to be a difficult issue for the government to tackle because of the extensive monetary benefit to manure contractors as well as the government.[58]

The City Inspector and the Sanatory Committee also had their eye on noisome industries and practices that were long assumed to be dangerous to public health, especially those that created offensive smells or waste. Inspector White closed the various bone- and flesh-boiling establishments in the upper wards, where poorer residents boiled all types of animal matter as well as edible garbage found on the streets so that they could feed their hogs or sell the products to various industries such as soapmakers, tallow chandlers, and sugar refiners. The fact that these industries were located in the low-density outer wards, where cholera hit unexpectedly hard, led to their demise. Reformers blamed them, along with refugee pigs, for all of the wards' problems. Finally, Inspector White also targeted cemeteries as a source of pestilential disease. While the city government was able to close the urban cemeteries during the epidemic, White believed that permanent closure was the only solution for avoiding further epidemics. He complained that the urban cemeteries were so full that it was impossible to bury anyone without disturbing someone else's decaying remains—a sure way to spread pestilence through the neighborhood.[59]

The panic that cholera caused among New Yorkers allowed sweeping changes to take place. The municipal government boldly flexed its power to remove the malodorous industries and pests they had had difficulty dealing with in the past. Their motivation for these structural changes to the city government was not a fear of immigrants and newcomers, as some scholars have argued. Rather, vast urbanization, relatively frequent, devastating epidemics, and the fear that resulted gave cities the tools and infrastructure necessary to tame the urban environment. Yet they did not do so without hesitation. That July, in the midst of the outbreak, the Board of Health's Sanatory Committee defended itself against critics who claimed it was too slow in closing down noxious industries. Defining exactly what constituted a nuisance was tricky. The committee wrote: "It is not every thing that is offensive to the sight or smell that is really a nuisance. What is looked upon as such by one class of persons, is not so by another. It is not always so easy therefore to decide at once what is a nuisance, and how far the authorities are justified in removing or suppressing it." In addition, some of the most noisome factories employed hundreds of New Yorkers who depended on those wages for their "daily subsistence." The Sanatory Committee, the Board of Health, and the City Inspector were therefore not exerting their power without some thought, often to the dismay of wealthier, panicked New Yorkers who wanted the city reformed immediately. The aldermen also considered financially assisting business owners whose soap factories or tanneries were closed during the epidemic, although they often decided against this.[60]

The 1849 cholera crisis highlighted the disastrous impact of the city's uncontrolled development. As the City Inspector wrote, "Our city is growing so rapidly that no portion can be said to be 'outside the wall,' and, in removing a nuisance from our own doors, we have no right to throw it before our neighbors." Extending the laws to allow nuisances only above a seemingly distant street would inevitably present problems for future generations as long as the city continued to expand up the island. In this period before the city had adopted and enforced zoning laws, officials struggled with how to achieve a fair and effective balance between the needs of the changing city and the uses of its land. At the very least, the laws needed to keep up with the city's growth. The *New York Herald* perhaps said it best: "The population has extended in that direction, but the Common Council are not keeping pace, either with the population or progressive spirit of the age." While it would have been almost impossible for the aldermen to prevent cholera's arrival on the city's shores, they certainly could have tamed its fury with better sanitation and infrastructure. Unfortunately, they tried to catch up in a moment of crisis when even their best efforts proved to be too little, too late.[61]

Though city officials attempted to exert more control over public space during the 1830s and 1840s, their grasp was only fleeting. By 1852, the city's newspapers were already complaining about the state of the streets. That January, the *Tribune* teased: "Some of the workmen engaged in turning up the ice in Broadway yesterday came across a sort of fossil which seems to prove a fact which has been much disputed of late. The fossil was that of a brush broom, and apparently settles the point that at some past age the streets of New-York had been swept. The custom has, however, been obsolete for some years." Whatever momentum had been gained by the cholera outbreak had dissipated. The reform that was so promising in 1849 seemed a distant memory once New York City's streets returned to their usual disorder.[62]

Managing the city's waste required grander and more sustained efforts. The mix of public and private solutions to the city's issues caused ancillary problems that frustrated efforts to clean the city thoroughly. Private waste-management enterprises delayed the creation of necessary infrastructure. In retrospect, it is easy to look back on antebellum cities and romanticize arrangements that involved the remarkably efficient recycling of human and animal waste. But the reality was more complicated. The "organic city," with its privatized removal of waste, was a filthy, disease-ridden place. These early forms of recycling had serious consequences that were clearly recognized by New Yorkers of the era.

The cholera epidemics marked a turning point for the municipal government. Though reform and control were often fleeting, they did give the city government a sense of what was possible. Truly taming the city's filth required public solutions, not the cobbling together of private contractors who lacked proper oversight. Rather than just writing ordinance after ordinance in an attempt to control the urban environment, the government actively ensured the laws' enforcement. Out of necessity and panic, the city government extended and strengthened its power. Garbage disposal, traditionally a private affair, was increasingly becoming a public concern. City officials entered properties, whitewashed homes, and removed families and their livestock, all for the sake of public health. Protecting public health required controlling private as well as public spaces. Following a long history of passively managing streets, parks, and sanitation, the municipal government was beginning to take a strong hand in the public control of these public goods. With some effort and a touch of political maneuvering, perhaps New York could rise from its infamy as "the filthiest city in the United States" and even "the dung heap of the universe." Such progress, however, came with a price. The anxiety that pushed the city to clean the streets and make the city healthier also drowned out the voices of hog owners and other New Yorkers who used urban space in a way that seemed to threaten public health and "progress." Yet, the economy of turning waste into valuable property did not end with the 1849 cholera epidemic. Political corruption allowed it to thrive, to the chagrin of many who hoped to transform New York into a healthier environment.[63]

4

Hog Wash and Swill Milk

Journalist George "Gaslight" Foster, upon entering one of the corner groceries that were common in poor neighborhoods, was struck by the "inferior and often positively unwholesome" food it sold, ranging from overpriced spoiled butter to rancid meat. The milk that the grocer kept in a tub was "ready to curdle from the loathsome diseases with which every particle is rife." Though the grocery claimed it was "Orange County Milk"—the gold standard—Foster was confident that it was "swill milk": milk from cows fed distillery waste. The food sold at these groceries, Foster contended, was "unfit to sustain life, . . . highly conducive to disease," and one of the reasons poor neighborhoods were struck particularly hard during epidemics. In the 1850s, corrupt food production and the associated industries that recycled food waste inspired public health hysteria and left the city reeling.[1]

Food processing and food waste, such as offal, bones, swill, vegetable scraps, and even carcasses, seemed to encourage more fraudulent dealings and public outcry than any other of New York's informal waste recycling programs. In the midst of the heated debates and newspaper exposés over food regulation, politicians and city officials would decide alternately to destroy or to ignore parts of the waste-recycling industry. Several events in the 1850s, including the development of a corrupt partnership to buy and process offal, the newspaper campaign against swill milk, and the dramatic Piggery War of 1859 reveal the deep-seated corruption of local politics and the way that corruption exacerbated environmental injustices.

After the 1849 cholera outbreak, the city government decided to confront the uptown food waste industries that not only put public health at risk but also brought down real estate prices. Yet the inconsistent actions taken by city officials to solve public health issues surrounding waste recycling and urban food production show how corruption complicated the government's responsiveness to its constituents. Media pressure to address the city's corrupt food production and urban-waste industries grew especially strong through the 1850s, allowing the municipal government to take unprecedented control of the urban environment and private spaces.

Politicians exercised this power by declaring industries to be "nuisances" under the law. Those who wanted hogs and dogs off the streets deemed them nuisances. Promenaders considered ragpickers sorting through garbage heaps to be nuisances. Neighbors called manure piles and overflowing privies nuisances. The City Inspector judged unimproved, vacant lots with standing water to be nuisances. Nuisances were everywhere in the city, and the food waste industries were no exception. When specific land uses seemed incompatible with residential neighborhoods, threatened public health, and lowered real estate values, those campaigning to remove them labeled them "nuisances." Used as an early form of zoning, nuisance laws pushed objectionable industries, such as bone boilers and piggeries, to the outer limits of the city, only to evict them again once development crept farther north. Yet in rationalizing who and what belonged where, those who deployed nuisance laws effectively helped to segregate the city by race and class, whether wittingly or unwittingly. While courts typically favored newer industries such as mills, coal yards, and railroads over more traditional industries such as Manhattan's waste recycling operations, the municipal treatment of even the latter type of business was notably inconsistent. The everyday use of nuisance laws to categorize and condemn urban industries and land uses demonstrates how these designations were socially charged and embedded in politics. The selective targeting of specific food waste industries over others reveals how political kickbacks, real estate interests, and racial and ethnic prejudices led to inconsistent protection of consumers and the regulation of the urban environment.[2]

The Offal Contract

Offal was not particularly prized in nineteenth-century New York's cuisine. Butchers dumped offal into rivers or gave it to scavengers. Offal typically refers to organ meat and viscera, though journalists, politicians, and others from this era occasionally lumped it together with bones, blood, and other parts of animals not typically consumed. The recycling of food waste was an enormous industry in the mid-nineteenth century. Given the number of animals the city depended on for work and food, there was certainly a lot of material to recycle. Besides the thousands of horses that clogged the city's streets transporting people and goods to and from their destinations, countless livestock were herded into the city's slaughterhouses and markets. Meat was a major component of New Yorkers' diets. By 1850, butchers were slaughtering approximately 2,500 cattle, 5,000 sheep, 1,200 calves, and 1,200 hogs each week to serve the city's needs. The amount of offal left over far surpassed the city's ability to dispose of it. While many New Yorkers considered this surfeit to be a repulsive nuisance and public health threat, others saw it as a business opportunity.[3]

FIGURE 17. *General View of the Piggery District, Situated on Fifty-Sixth and Fifty-Seventh Streets, between Sixth and Eighth Avenues.* The image shows a mix of shanties, offal-boiling establishments, and piggeries in 1859. Though these land uses were on the outskirts of the city, they faced repeated threats in the 1850s. From *Frank Leslie's Illustrated Newspaper,* August 13, 1859. (Sterling Memorial Library, Yale University.)

Establishments for fattening pigs, boiling and grinding bones, melting fat, and skinning and rendering dead animals popped up all over the city, especially in the uptown "rural" wards. Unlike the poudrette-producing Lodi Manufacturing Company that was based in New Jersey, these establishments were neither out of sight nor out of mind. Scattered amid the clusters of wooden shanties north of the city, they recycled materials that many considered waste—restaurant scraps, carcasses, offal, bones, and blood—by refining them for other industries and feeding them to hogs. These entrepreneurs were mainly recent immigrants from Ireland and Germany, as well as a handful of African Americans. On unwanted land, using unwanted materials, these New Yorkers scraped together a living.

Gathering the waste was an occupation in and of itself. The owners of the piggeries and boiling establishments either sent their children or

hired middlemen to collect materials from around the city. They con-
tracted with hotels, butcher shops, and slaughterhouses for the right to
remove the waste from these establishments for six months or a year,
paying somewhere in the range of $50 to $200 for the privilege. The
middlemen also sought out the thousands of Irish and German ragpickers who gathered bones, offal, and kitchen scraps from the gutters
and garbage receptacles on the streets. These men and women lived all
over the city, in the poorest tenements and shanties, and derived a significant part of their income from selling recycled waste. When reformer Charles Loring Brace toured New York's poorest neighborhoods
in the early 1850s, he routinely found women and children pulling home
their loot after they had spent a long day digging through the piles of
garbage. Brace described a "colony" of 300 German immigrants, all living together in a basement, who hoped to move west and buy farms. To
earn the money they needed, they collected bones during the day and
heaped them together in an enormous pile in the middle of the floor
before selling it to middlemen. Even official, city-employed waste collectors would occasionally moonlight in the offal-collecting business.
Instead of dumping their carts' contents at the approved docks, they
would veer uptown and sell the contents to the boiling establishments
for a profit. Thousands were involved in collecting these valuable materials that were deemed a nuisance by so many.[4]

Nothing was wasted. The proprietors of the boiling establishments
collected or purchased these materials and then processed them until
they were useful for manufacturers or could be fed to their own hogs.
The owners set up cauldrons on their property to render down the
bones, offal, or fat by boiling or melting. Soap boilers and tallow chandlers bought rendered fat; button and toothbrush makers used bones;
builders used horsehair to bind plaster; and sugar refiners used a combination of butcher-shop blood and charred ground bones for sugar
purification. Farmers purchased whatever ash was left over in the sugar-
refining process to use as fertilizer. The offal boilers fed the edible remains to the hogs kept in large pens nearby. Some very large-scale es-

tablishments skinned horses' and other animals' carcasses that were found on the streets, though offal processing seems to have been the more dominant industry. Collecting thousand-pound carcasses off the streets was more labor intensive and required more expensive equipment than most small-scale boilers could afford.[5]

The cholera outbreaks that inspired so many new environmental controls had a particularly strong impact on offal boilers. In an attempt to explain the prolonged presence of cholera in the upper wards of the city in 1849, Dr. Seth Geer, a member of the Sanatory Committee, blamed the "many filthy localities" such as the bone-boiling establishments, which had "immense piles of bones scattered around, while heaps of the same were found with meat attached, and all in an advanced state of decomposition, and exhaling a stench which was horrible in the extreme." Those nervous about smells emanating from the cauldrons petitioned their aldermen and the Sanatory Committee to shut down the businesses for the sake of the city's health, and the Board of Health complied.[6]

The citywide panic over cholera justified this increase in power, but it also created a number of problems, especially involving the management of all the now unused offal. With the offal-boiling industries closed, the city had an unmanageable amount of offal to dispose of, yet lacked the necessary infrastructure to do so effectively. To ensure that the bone-boiling establishments would remain closed until the epidemic passed, the Board of Aldermen proposed that butchers and garbage collectors dump all offal into the East and Hudson rivers so that boiling establishments could not use it. After they began this task, however, city officials realized that the waste was not being swept out into the ocean, as they had intended. It lingered, floating "around the city with the tide," washing up on the shores of Long Island and New Jersey, and clogging the port. The buoyant material was visible from the docks. Disappointed with this outcome, the Board of Aldermen complained that "strangers, visiting our city, were presented, at its very threshold, with sights, not only of the most disgusting character, but reflecting disgrace upon the internal government of the city." The City Inspector desperately tried to sink the carcasses by attaching stones and other weights to them. The city's offal problem seemed to have become worse.[7]

Despite these issues, City Inspector Alfred W. White was determined to close the working-class bone-boiling establishments in the upper wards once and for all. In his annual report to the Common Council at the end of 1849, he pleaded with the aldermen to bring a permanent end to the establishments. He contended that the business was "an exceedingly lucrative and profitable one" and that even the scavengers who "scrape the filthy material from the gutters and streets" had the ability to amass a fortune. While he certainly exaggerated, there was some validity to his statement. This waste was valuable to many industries in the city. He suggested that the city would do well to force paupers out of this business and find wealthier people who could afford to carry on the business wherever the aldermen deemed it acceptable, far from the center of the city. White had nothing good to say about the current bone boilers. He referred to them as a "class of persons, of the lowest dregs of the city" who "could not speak the English language, and were irresponsible, reckless, filthy, and ignorant; incapable of understanding or obeying any system of police regulations." How could such people be trusted with a "business so intimately affecting the public health"? It was necessary, in White's opinion, to exert control over the lower-class New Yorkers who seemed to blatantly disregard the health and safety of the rest of the city. In other words, the city government needed more power over both public and private space in order to ensure its citizens' well-being.[8]

The same power that allowed White to shut down the nuisance industries during the epidemic opened up room for corruption. The following spring, after the epidemic had passed and the waste-processing businesses reopened, White had a revelation. Not only could he get rid of the despised piggeries and boiling establishments for good, but he could also personally profit from their removal. During a meeting with a manure contractor who had been ordered to stop piling manure at the corner of 33rd Street and Tenth Avenue, the contractor complained that the municipal government needed to determine a suitable place where manure and other waste could be stored and processed. White "reflected for a moment" and then exclaimed that it was "the greatest chance for a fortune" he had ever seen. Inspired by the idea of relocating nuisances in distant locations, he began conjuring up a way to establish boiling and rendering facilities far from the city. With the aid of his political position, he could secretly set up a business and eventually achieve a monopoly. White's plan involved shutting down the immigrants' boiling and piggery businesses in order to open his own. Not only would he personally profit from the business, but he would also be seen as a hero for getting rid of a major public health nuisance.[9]

White needed a company to make this work. He cobbled together a firm that included the manure contractor William C. Lent; a building contractor, John Brady; William L. Baxter, a farmer and manure freighter from Long Island; James D. Morgan, who had the funds to purchase materials and land; and Heman W. Childs, the Commissioner of Streets and Lamps, who controlled the city's markets and their wastes. In late May 1850, the six men formalized their partnership by establishing the firm of Baxter, Brady, Lent & Co., with White and Childs as silent partners. As city officials, White and Childs had to disguise their inappropriate involvement. The firm searched for a spot where they could set up their business and eventually purchased South Brother Island, otherwise known as Eaton's Island, on the East River.[10]

While private companies fought for contracts to collect garbage and manure, no such contracts existed yet for collecting offal. Without a contract-based monopoly, White and his partners were on equal footing with every other independent offal collector. They competed daily to purchase carcasses, offal, and bones from collectors, slaughterhouses, and institutions around the city. Using their own carts and boats, they removed the waste to South Brother Island. The firm used a steamboat to tow several sloops and barges back and forth from the docks to the island, which they outfitted with bone-boiling cauldrons, shacks, and a

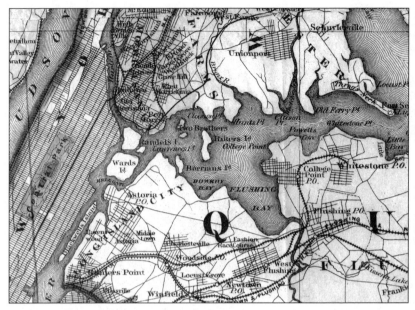

FIGURE 18. While South Brother Island, the more southerly of the two islands labeled "Two Brothers," was located far from most residents on Manhattan Island, it was close enough to Queens County and Westchester County (now the Bronx) for offal-boiling odors to bother the farmers living there. Detail from *Colton's New Map of Long Island,* 1873. (Collection of the New-York Historical Society.)

few thousand pigs. The pigs ate on the beaches of the island so that their leftovers could be washed away during high tide.[11]

Almost immediately, the company faced several serious challenges. One partner, Baxter, took advantage of his control of the steamboat for personal gain. A manure freighter, he had a background in shipping, and the group therefore put him in charge of the boats. Even though the partners had hired a "careful pilot" to man the steamboat and tow the barges filled with offal to South Brother, Baxter insisted on acting as its captain. His partners accused him of living on the boat, as well as using it for parties with friends and a "number of loose women and common prostitutes." They claimed that their boat had become known as the "North River Brothel" because of his exploits. While Baxter was making these pleasure excursions, he left the reeking barges tied up at the Manhattan docks. Frustrated, his partners confronted him and severed his connection with the business.[12]

Ironically, though Inspector White had started the company as a way to get the bone-boiling nuisances out of Manhattan, their operations on South Brother Island had become an affront to their neighbors. First, the Newtown Board of Health in Queens County declared the business a nuisance. Soon afterward a group of farmers from West Farms (in what is now the Bronx) took the issue to the Queens County Supreme Court, complaining about the smells wafting into their homes and fields. Little did they know that New York's own City Inspector was actually the source of the problem. Of course, though White denounced boiling establishments as nuisances in Manhattan, his partners argued that their operation should not qualify as a nuisance. To their chagrin, the court issued an injunction and the firm ultimately had to cease operations on the island. To make matters worse, around the same time Baxter retaliated against his firing by filing an injunction in the Queens County Supreme Court, claiming that his erstwhile business was a public health nuisance. The company, forced to leave South Brother Island and facing issues with a vindictive former partner, regrouped. The partners began to make plans to reestablish their operations elsewhere.[13]

Though his business was falling apart, White was finally able to push legislation through the Common Council that would allow the city to contract with an individual company to remove all of the carcasses, blood, bones, and offal to a location distant from Manhattan. This would have essentially allowed him to establish the monopoly he had long hoped for. The New York State Senate and Assembly, as well as the city's Common Council, had passed legislation that spring and summer increasing the power of the City Inspector's office. With public health reform on their minds, the Whig-dominated Committee of the Board of Health met in August to discuss the bone-boiling issue. White himself was a Whig, and he likely used this political connection to his benefit. The committee encouraged the City Inspector to draft an ordinance that the council passed after just a week. White then strengthened it further by getting the boards to ban the grinding and burning of bones, as well. Under the ordinance, anyone who carried on offal-rendering businesses within city limits would be fined $500 and charged with a misdemeanor—a huge punishment for the relatively poor owners of boiling establishments.[14]

The city was serious about closing down these businesses, and the steep fine certainly sent a message to boilers while also conveniently elbowing out White's competition. Once the legislation was in place, White and the health wardens immediately attacked his competitors' property, including the rendering facilities owned by John Green at 41st Street and Tenth Avenue. Green owned $10,000 worth of equipment and buildings, including boilers, steamers, stables, and a glue factory— operations far more extensive than those of typical boilers and piggery owners. Jumping at the chance to use the government's new powers for his personal benefit, White had his employees tear everything down. Green kept what was left of his property but moved temporarily across the Hudson River to the New Jersey Palisades to continue his work in peace.[15]

With the legislation in place, the city needed a contractor to take care of all the waste that small-scale bone boilers and their associates were no longer collecting. White suggested that his firm put in a bid low enough to win the contract. They did just that, sending in several bids, including one deceptively submitted under the name of one of the partner's nephews. That bid won with the lowest price: $19 per day to remove all of the city's offal. The firm began to collect materials from the butchers, but after a mere ten days the contract would no longer be theirs.[16]

Likely concerned that his corrupt dealings would be revealed, White secretly transferred the contract to a new firm, where he probably continued to be a silent partner. With all of the trouble caused by the steamboat-turned-brothel, a vindictive partner, and the nuisance accusations from irritated neighbors, White cut his losses. Morgan, the part-

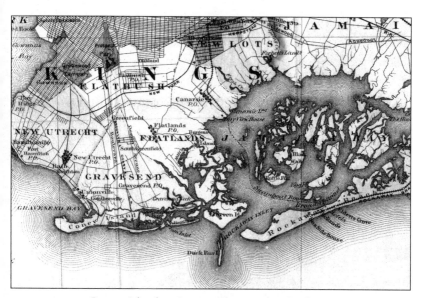

FIGURE 19. Barren Island in Jamaica Bay, just south of Brooklyn, where the new offal-boiling operations opened in 1851. For decades afterward, the area would be infamous for processing animal carcasses and waste, even after the operations changed hands. Detail from *Colton's New Map of Long Island,* 1873. (Collection of the New-York Historical Society.)

ner who owned most of the company's assets, surreptitiously transferred the contract to William B. Reynolds, a hardware store owner with no background in waste management. The spurned partners were furious. Reynolds of course jumped at the chance to get in on this lucrative contract. By February 1851 he had leased Barren Island, a marshy island in Jamaica Bay, just south of Brooklyn. It was distant enough from the city to make it an ideal spot for the odoriferous processing of offal and bones. Following the model of the Manhattan offal boilers, Reynolds brought somewhere between 2,000 and 3,000 hogs to the island to fatten them with the city's offal.[17]

While Reynolds's ties to city officials were much less clear than was the case with Brady, Baxter, Lent & Co., they certainly existed. City

Inspector White worked hard to protect Reynolds's monopoly and the anti-offal legislation by diligently fining and jailing boilers and skinners. The city was intent on closing down these businesses and making Reynolds's contract work. Though no smoking gun, the sudden successful enforcement of the anti-offal laws was unusual. Additionally, Reynolds and his company had amazing luck when the time came to renew their contract in April 1852. Despite the fact that several bidders pledged to *pay* the city for the right to take all of the city's offal, Reynolds won a contract that paid him $63,000 for the honor. Besides that, many of the competitors thought the aldermen in charge of making the decision had already chosen Reynolds before all parties had a chance to present their bids. Something was fishy. Through all of this, Alderman Oscar Sturtevant seemed to be acting as Reynolds's guardian angel, or, at the very least, as White's accomplice. He had been on the Sanatory Committee during the cholera outbreak of 1849 when the city banned offal boiling uptown; he had been there to recommend the legislation completely banning it when he was an assistant alderman in 1850; and as an alderman, he had helped to usher through Reynolds's scandalous contract in 1852. Perhaps he, too, had his hands in the offal fortune.[18]

Corruption like White's was not completely tolerated in 1850s New York. By 1853, government watchdogs such as the comptroller, Azariah C. Flagg, sensed that something was not quite right with the offal contract. Coming to the city after an extensive career in Albany as New York secretary of state and comptroller, Flagg was on a mission to reform the city's out-of-control spending and corruption. The district attorney and city clerk took affidavits from men who knew something about the contract, including disgruntled former partners and competitors whose property had been demolished by White and his employees. The men they interviewed testified about City Inspector White and Street Commissioner Childs: their corrupt involvement, their abuse of power, and the suspicious bidding procedures that had landed Reynolds the handsome offal contract. Beyond all of this, Flagg heard stories about how Reynolds had been caught violating his contract, dumping the offal and blood into the rivers instead of transporting it away from the city.[19]

Looking to combat the corruption, Flagg fought with the aldermen over whether they should continue to pay Reynolds. In April, while Flagg was in the midst of his investigations, the new City Inspector, Thomas K. Downing, tried to pay Reynolds but Flagg blocked the funds. With Reynolds threatening to stop work, Downing panicked about what this would mean for the city's public health and image. Envisioning tourists encountering a city overrun with carcasses and the revived offal-boiling industry, Downing pleaded with the Board of Aldermen to force Flagg's hand. Unsurprisingly, Downing had another reason to support Reynolds's contract so fiercely: his hand was also in the offal fortune. Reynolds had bribed Downing with $500 for his support, and Downing worked hard to hold up his end of the deal. His pleas were certainly heard by the aldermen. By controlling the city's offal, Reynolds essentially controlled the city's image. The Board of Aldermen's Committee on Public Health, headed by the always supportive Oscar Sturtevant, grew furious with Flagg. After reviewing Flagg's reasons, perusing the affidavits, and hearing the district attorney's opinion on the contract, the committee decided to disregard those points and continue paying Reynolds.[20]

While the aldermen were still under Reynolds's spell, city residents were growing increasingly frustrated with his inefficiency. Those who lived near the offal docks had special reason to complain, as they suffered from the smells of waste left for extended periods of time. Residents and dockworkers complained that they had to keep their windows closed because the odors made them sick. Landowners were frustrated by declining property values and unrented apartments, and the city was doing very little to correct the issue. Thirty-five rioters rallied together that summer and set fire to Reynolds's scow, derrick, and crates. With the police unable to find or prosecute any of the rioters, the aldermen decided to pay Reynolds generously for his loss.[21]

The corruption surrounding the offal contract ran deep. Even after elections that ousted Sturtevant and brought in fresh faces to the Board of Aldermen, the board's support for Reynolds continued. Flagg unveiled the results of his investigation to the aldermen, but that hardly seemed to sway their loyalties. To teach Flagg and his other opponents a lesson, Reynolds and his employees deliberately positioned dead dogs and horses at the doors of their homes and offices during the summer of 1854. The *New-York Daily Tribune* reported that the comptroller, "whose scent for corruption was supposed to be blunted by constant collision with it, was favored for a number of days, in the hot days of 1854, with a full view of a dead horse from the windows of his dwelling and another from his office window." Yet Flagg stood his ground and the "jaws of the Treasury remained clenched."[22]

Finally, after a year of battle, Flagg was able to destroy the corrupt offal contract. Reynolds gave up the fight. He had pleaded with the aldermen and councilmen, bribed city officials, and even taken the issue to court, but the city was still not paying him. Reynolds offered to end his contract if the city would purchase his buildings, boats, equipment, and lease on Barren Island. The Common Council was in no hurry to decide on the best way to handle this. All of the overt municipal corruption led to heated debates where aldermen interrupted one another and threatened to expose the corruption of their fellow aldermen. With the reputation of the Whig Party in New York City at stake, they would not go down without a fight. Yet it was not easy to just pay Reynolds for his property to make the issue go away. The scandal by now was public, and few aldermen wanted to be caught giving any favors to Reynolds after he had taken so much money from increasingly outraged taxpayers. So they deferred, as the aldermen often did, and sent it to committees for further review.[23]

In 1856, while the municipal government struggled to clean up after the offal contract, they managed to hire a new offal contractor for just $5,000—a much cheaper rate than Reynolds's $65,000. Even with the outright corruption swept away, complaints rolled in that the new contractor was not removing offal quickly enough, leaving it to rot in slaughterhouses and on the streets. The piggery businesses uptown that had waned with Reynolds's monopoly began to crop up again. While newspapers eventually stopped reporting on the fallout of the offal contract controversies, the story remained a lesson to lawmakers. When seemingly excessive and suspiciously corrupt contracts came before the Common Council, the aldermen often spent a little more time determining the fairness of the cost, reminding themselves that they did not want to see another "offal contract."[24]

In an attempt to establish their authority over the urban environment and in so doing ensure the city's health and well-being, municipal officials such as the City Inspector became increasingly powerful. This power, however, also opened up opportunities for officials such as White and his accomplices to use it for their personal profit. Politicians who one minute condemned the industry benefited from it the next. They forced the entrepreneurial poor out of business ostensibly for the sake of the public health, but it was also for their own pecuniary gain. White used public power to create a private business through which he could profit. The government's role was more complicated than simply acting in the public's best interest.

In the case of the offal contract, corruption created few winners. While White's personal motivations resulted in the government's effectively closing industries that annoyed many, the losses were ultimately greater than the gains. Reformers, speculators, and landowners who had campaigned for the city to take care of the uptown nuisance industries may have seen them close, but only temporarily. Those who worried about the quality and safety of meat from pigs fed on offal still had offal-fed ham entering the markets. This time, however, the ham, rather than coming from immigrant-owned piggeries, was supported through government contracts. The shanty dwellers who no longer had to smell the boiling offal, bones, and fat likely saw their quality of life improve during the brief period when City Inspector White shut down the industries, but those who either owned the operations or collected waste for them lost their livelihoods. In a sense, by limiting access to resources and land, this corruption had essentially exacerbated environmental

injustices. The only true winners were the corrupt politicians and contractors who found a gold mine amid the city's waste.[25]

Lost in the shuffle of political corruption and debates, the city's offal
piled higher. Subsequent offal contracts proved ineffective, creating an
opportunity for boilers to reopen their businesses and even thrive for the
time being. However, a scandal involving cows' milk would soon turn
the spotlight back on their industry.

Swill Milk

Corrupt politicians were also tied to corrupt food. While the offal-
recycling controversies were festering, another recycling program—
turning distillery swill into milk and meat—also made headlines. Swill
was a combination of processed corn, barley, and rye malt left over from
the distilling of liquors such as whiskey. Americans consumed massive
amounts of alcohol in the nineteenth century for a combination of cultural and sanitary reasons, given the poor quality of water in most towns
and cities. Cities like New York consequently had a wealth of swill. By
feeding this slop to cows, the distilleries helped to turn the remnants of
an adult beverage, often seen as corrupted and corruptible, into what
was seen as the purest of foods, suitable for the youngest babies: milk.
Yet the purity of this milk was exactly what was most troublesome.[26]

Though the swill milk crisis came to a head in 1858, New York had
been struggling with the quality of its cows' milk for decades. By the
late 1830s, several distillery owners in Manhattan, Brooklyn, Williams-
burg, Jersey City, and Hoboken—New York's milk shed—had begun
to dabble in the milk business. They built cow stables next to their
buildings so they could pipe their leftover swill into the cows' troughs.
London distilleries had already been doing this with some success, perhaps inspiring these New York entrepreneurs. The production of swill
milk was an easy way to turn waste into profit. Just as bone boiling
turned offal into salable materials and pig meat, distillery cowsheds
helped to turn food waste into milk and beef. The cows' owners rented

stalls from the distillery and paid a few dollars each week for space and swill. According to the calculations of the *New York Times,* cows fed on swill produced somewhere between five and twenty-five more quarts of milk per day than hay-fed cows, resulting in much higher profits.[27]

Dairy production for large cities like New York was complicated in the mid-nineteenth century. Farmers had to locate their dairies close enough to the city center so that they could transport their milk before it spoiled, but far enough away that they could afford extensive meadows to feed the animals. In the days before refrigeration and pasteurization, this was a challenge. Dairy owners in nearby New Jersey, Westchester, and Long Island dealt with long transportation times as they relied on a combination of horse- or ox-drawn carts and ferries, with some lucky enough to have access to the railroads. A growing population of New Yorkers meant an increasing demand for fresh milk, but it also meant higher real estate costs. Without the technology to enable the transport of milk from a distance, swill milk seemed like an amazing opportunity. Cows could live right in the heart of the city, consuming food that would have otherwise been wasted, without even needing meadows. To distillery owners, this must have seemed like a perfect solution to meet the needs of the growing market. In fact, it proved too good to be true.[28]

Swill was hardly a nutritious meal for cows. When introduced to the boiling liquid, cows typically refused to eat for a few days, until desperation drove them to consume the slop. A diet consisting exclusively of swill made the cows sick, led to ulcerated sores all over their bodies, and caused their tails to fall off. New Yorkers nicknamed these animals "Stump-Tail Cows" because of their tell-tale condition. The milk that such cows produced was watery with a bluish tint, so venders would mix in chalk and other ingredients such as eggs, flour, and plaster-of-Paris before it reached consumers. This was hardly an attractive, let alone healthy beverage.[29]

On top of feeding the city swill milk, distillery owners also sold beef to the city's butchers. In a map of Johnson & Sons' operations, a butcher

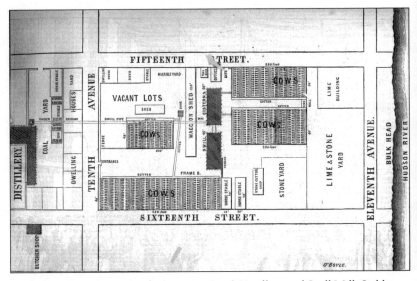

FIGURE 20. This map of Johnson & Sons' Distillery and Swill Milk Stables illustrates the way swill was piped across Tenth Avenue into the cowsheds. From *Frank Leslie's Illustrated Newspaper,* May 22, 1858. (Sterling Memorial Library, Yale University.)

shop is located in the bottom right-hand corner of the map, mere feet from the distillery and cowsheds. One observer remarked that the meat of swill-fed cows was easily distinguishable from that of their country cousins. Critics described the meat as having a "peculiar bluish appearance," and spoiling faster. Butchers sold the meat in poorer neighborhoods, where the low price perhaps made up for the funny smell and appearance. Despite an assortment of market laws controlling the way food was sold within city limits, inspectors barely enforced such regulations during this period.[30]

If the cowshed proprietors had fed the cows a combination of oats and hay along with their swill, the cow's health, milk, and meat might not have been nearly so compromised. When cornered about their business practices, many owners claimed that their cows consumed more than the boiled liquid, but evidence proved otherwise. A doctor who had examined a stable found that although the cows there were fed the occasional "wisp of hay," they often could not eat it, since their teeth had fallen out as a result of the swill. Distillery swill hardly compared to the hay, grass, and oats typical in a cow's diet, but it was an inexpensive feed readily available in the densest urban environments, where pastures were rare and animals were no longer permitted to roam the streets and parks freely.[31]

Swill milk helped to satisfy a burgeoning market for cheap milk in a city whose population was growing astronomically. The poorest New Yorkers could afford only the lowest-quality milk that the venders offered, and at around 6 cents a quart, swill milk was a bargain. Even the rich were swindled into purchasing swill or adulterated milk that was deceptively advertised as pure country milk. It was difficult for New Yorkers to tell if they were buying swill milk or something more pure. The vendors' carts and the groceries that advertised "Orange County Milk," "Westchester Milk," or "Pure Country Milk" might actually have been selling milk from the distilleries on 16th Street or 39th Street, or from sister cities across the rivers. Poor regulation and enforcement kept the business of dirty milk profitable and viable.[32]

Disaster seemed imminent to reformers who saw New York's population continuing to grow and cows' milk as an increasingly popular staple in most infants' and children's diets. Year after year, doctors attributed high infant mortality rates to several digestive and nutritional diseases such as *cholera infantum* and *marasmas,* which likely had roots in babies' consumption of swill milk or other contaminated or spoiled foods. One 1853 estimate placed the annual number of infant deaths caused by swill milk at 8,000 to 9,000. Reformers claimed that the children of the working class were disproportionately represented in these death tolls, as many of their mothers who worked outside the home were forced to wean them early and rely on cheap cow's milk for their food. By the mid-nineteenth century, wealthier women were also beginning to wean their children after a few months and rely

FIGURE 21. Woodcut of an Irish "milkmaid" milking a nearly dead cow suffering from "disease and ulceration." While images like this may have evoked sympathy for the cows and their condition, the primary focus of the media was not on animal cruelty but rather on the threat posed to New Yorkers who drank the milk. From *Frank Leslie's Illustrated Newspaper,* May 15, 1858. (Sterling Memorial Library, Yale University.)

more on cow's milk and artificial mixes to feed them. Overall, this left more children vulnerable to the dangers of the unregulated milk market.[33]

Doctors, reformers, and journalists had been calling for an end to the tainted-milk trade since the 1840s. After each lecture or article, there would be a small uproar about the issue but it would quickly wither away. City politicians ignored the newspapers' continued pleas until 1858, when Frank Leslie and his artists took on the subject. Frank Leslie, born Henry Carter in 1821, was the son of a glove manufacturer in England. Fascinated by engraving at an early age, he defied his father's hopes that he would follow in the family business. He found success submitting engravings under the untraceable name "Frank Leslie" to publications in London. In 1848, after working in the engraving department at the *Illustrated London News,* Leslie moved to New York with the ambition of starting his own illustrated newspaper. After accumulating some savings, he did just that, publishing the first issue of *Frank Leslie's Illustrated Newspaper* in 1855.[34]

After struggling for a few years, Leslie's newspaper made its mark with its fresh exposure of the swill milk dairies in New York and Brooklyn. Leslie advertised heavily in competing newspapers to alert readers about his series exposing the corrupt industry. He lured readers in by causing them to panic about the purity of their milk. In an advertisement in the *New York Times,* he asked readers: "Are you aware what kind of milk you are drinking? Are you aware that over seven thousand children die every year in New-York and Brooklyn from drinking swill milk? . . . If these facts are not known to you, if you are still blindly confident that the milk you use is pure, the exposure which I have prepared will reveal the horrible extent of your delusion, and awaken you to the danger you and your infants hourly incur by partaking of that abomination—distillery swill milk." Leslie must have seen a huge jump in his circulation rates, as all of the other newspapers began to report on his campaign. Somewhere around 80,000 people purchased issues of Leslie's newspaper in 1858. Special editions, such as the swill milk exposé, drew readerships closer to 130,000. Leslie's sensational writing and graphic images not only brought in new readers, but also convinced them that reform was necessary.[35]

Unlike the previous exposés in the *New York Times, New York Herald,* and *New-York Daily Tribune,* Leslie's articles were filled with woodcut images that would come to ignite the public and pressure previously reluctant politicians to address the issue. The owners of the distilleries recognized the power of these images immediately. The Irish dairy hands physically attacked Leslie's artists who had set themselves up outside the stables. One Irish "milkmaid," as newspaper reporters usually referred to these men, even mistook an average citizen curiously examining the stables to be an artist and dealt the unsuspecting man a severe "blow between his peepers." The men working at the dairies recognized the threat that these images posed to their livelihoods. The images fed into the growing public disdain for their work. The situation was simply not good for business.[36]

Frank Leslie presented images to the public that not only opened the eyes of readers to the sickly appearance of the cows and their horrid living conditions, but also emphasized the "otherness" of the men working in the industry. While the distillery owners were wealthy, powerful, native-born New Yorkers, Leslie's artists strategically focused on the laborers. The artists made the social class and ethnicity of these laborers easy to decipher visually. This is particularly evident in the illustration where Leslie's artist, on the right-hand side of the image, is confronted by a rowdy group of Irishmen looking to protect their Brooklyn cowsheds from further publicity. The Irishmen wear sloppy, patched-up clothing, misshapen hats, and ill-fitting boots; some throw wood and stones, while others wave clubs in the air. Their roughly drawn features stand in contrast to those of Leslie's artist, which are crisp and distinct. The milkmaids resemble something closer to animals—their apish and swinish features shine through. Leslie was sending a message to readers by depicting the milkmaids this way: brutish, untrustworthy, and violent outsiders had control of the city's food. Something needed to be done.[37]

When Leslie's exposé inspired the Committee of the Board of Health to investigate, New Yorkers might have assumed that swill milk's days were numbered. The public was enraged, bad press was inescapable, and pressure to close down the businesses seemed to be coming from all types of constituents. Left and right, experts insisted that turning swill into milk was not good for public health and that the lives of the city's

FIGURE 22. Irish "milkmaids" in Brooklyn confront one of Leslie's artists. From *Frank Leslie's Illustrated Newspaper,* May 15, 1858. (Sterling Memorial Library, Yale University.)

most vulnerable residents—babies—were at stake. This was a perfect opportunity for the municipal government to exercise its power for the sake of public health.

Politics, however, had long been on the side of the swill milk proprietors. In 1854, four years before Leslie's exposé, the *New-York Daily Tribune* had railed at the continued existence of the cowsheds. During a period when the City Inspector and the Board of Health were targeting the piggeries far from the city center, they left the distilleries' cowsheds in the heart of the city untouched. The *Tribune* ridiculed the situation: "All the bone-boiling establishments, hog-pens and slaughterhouses combined are beneath notice, compared with this diabolical milk business." In contrast to the case of the uptown bone-boiling establishments and piggeries, the "wealth and influence" of the swill milk proprietors kept lawmakers at bay. The city government was selective in choosing its targets.[38]

The same remained true in 1858. In response to the growing outrage over the city's milk supply, the Common Council sent a committee of aldermen and councilmen to investigate the cowsheds on 16th Street and 39th Street. The committee was made up of Michael Tuomey, William Tucker, E. Harrison Reed, Charles H. Haswell, and James M. Cross. On May 27, 1858, these men, along with two clerks and a couple of representatives from the City Inspector's office, filed into carriages at City Hall and went straight to Johnson & Son's cowsheds and distillery at 16th Street and Tenth Avenue. Behind them were two carriages full of newspaper reporters. This was hardly a surprise visit. The distillery owners had had more than a week to clean up their stables, put diseased cattle out to pasture, and tear down unfit buildings. The journalists along for the tour commented on how much things had changed since Leslie had published his images. The tours included opportunities to sip milk, collect samples for testing, and watch the slaughtering of a cow. After hearings and inconclusive chemical analyses, the majority of the committee voted in favor of keeping swill milk, recommending only that the sheds have better ventilation.[39]

The committee's decision was far from unanimous. It was notable that its members did not divide along partisan lines, as might have been expected. The swill milk supporters included a Democrat and two Republicans, and the opposition was a Democrat. If there was any tie joining the seemingly disparate group, it might have been social class. The majority report was written by artisan-politicians, notably two butchers and a mason. This illustrated a change that had been taking place since the early nineteenth century in many American cities: professional politicians with artisanal backgrounds were increasingly replacing merchants and lawyers on the Common Council. Perhaps the butchers felt ties to the city's livestock industry. Yet a professional—an engineer—wrote the minority report. Those who signed the majority report were also exclusively aldermen, rather than councilmen from the lower legislative house. Regardless of how they formed their coalitions, the politicians continued to allow the swill milk dairies to operate, unfettered by government regulation.[40]

Frank Leslie was livid. Three days after the Board of Health's meeting, he published an illustration alluding to the corruption of Tucker,

FIGURE 23. When Frank Leslie depicted William Tucker, Harrison Reed, and Michael Tuomey whitewashing swill milk stables, he implied that corruption had led to the swill milk decision. The moneybags are labeled "Rec'd $5,000 for whitewashing." From *Frank Leslie's Illustrated Newspaper,* July 17, 1858. (Sterling Memorial Library, Yale University.)

Reed, and Tuomey, the pro–swill milk contingency. In the image, the three aldermen are whitewashing the stable hand, the stable, and the cows in an attempt to cover up the actual conditions threatening the city's public health. Meanwhile, the superintendent of the stables appears to be slipping a bag containing $5,000 into Tuomey's pocket. Reed had already won his booty. Leslie implied that the bipartisan supporters of swill milk were perhaps most united by their willingness to profit at the expense of the public good. As with the offal contract, government corruption swayed politicians from representing the interests of anyone but themselves and those willing to bribe them.[41]

Despite the exposé and the proposed solutions, distilleries would continue to produce swill milk and milkmen would continue to sell it on the streets of New York for years to come. Though the stables and the products they produced were legitimate nuisances, the power of the proprietors to sway politicians helped to keep them in business. While Leslie was ultimately unsuccessful, he directed the public's attention to the political entanglements of food regulation, changing the way New Yorkers viewed food produced within city limits.

The Piggery War

With all the attention given to the conversion of waste into food, it seemed that it would be only a matter of time before reformers' attention returned to the offal-boiling piggeries uptown. The *New York Times* declared that the "recent developments concerning the swill-milk business have opened the eyes of our citizens so completely to some of the causes of ill-health that we have, in our midst and around us, that people have begun to inquire anxiously concerning the various other articles which are brought to the New-York market for home consumption." Throughout the swill milk fiasco, petitioners continued to beg the city to close down the offal-boiling establishments that produced so much of the city's pork. News that butchers were slaughtering New Jersey's diseased and swill-fed hogs and selling the meat in New York's markets struck fear among many. Regulation was desperately needed.[42]

The offal boilers and piggery owners played a specific role in Manhattan. As in the dairy industry, the market for cheap meat benefited from having a local source of hogs to draw from. With food waste plentiful and the infrastructure and public services to remove it lacking, the piggeries turned waste into protein. The proprietors essentially collected something that would otherwise be considered a nuisance and turned it into something useful. Of course, critics would have argued that they turned one nuisance into an even larger and more threatening nuisance.

Complaints about the uptown piggeries mounted as the city's footprint extended farther north. Wealthy downtown neighbors referred to the area, mainly centered in the Fifties between Sixth and Seventh avenues as "Hogtown," "Pigtown," or "Stinktown." Their disdain for the piggery smells clearly extended to the proprietors. A writer from the *New York Times* described the neighborhood as a group of "shanties in which the pigs and the Patricks lie down together while little ones of Celtic and swinish origin lie miscellaneously, with billy-goats here and there interspersed." German proprietors, or "Dutchmen" as they were often called, were not immune to such criticism. The increasing ties between the proprietors' ethnicities and the piggeries cemented the threat that these people and their hogs posed for consumers, and emphasized the inappropriateness of their place in the city.[43]

When politicians debated the future of Hogtown, real estate values tended to come up repeatedly in their arguments. The two wards that had the majority of the piggeries were the Nineteenth and the Twenty-Second. Yet the representatives of each ward saw the matter quite differently. The councilman representing the Nineteenth Ward criticized those who were calling for the removal of the piggeries for being aristocrats who had once been happy to live near a pigsty, but once they became wealthy "their refined noses couldn't stand the smell." He claimed that pigs or no pigs, the Nineteenth Ward was one of the healthiest wards in the city. On the other side of the argument was the councilman representing the Twenty-Second Ward, who considered the pigsties nuisances. He argued that "the Twenty-second ward was improving rapidly, and the people there wished to make it a pleasant residence for those doing business down town." As the uptown neighborhoods around the developing Central Park were rising in value, the piggeries were becoming not only more visible but also more of a liability.[44]

Central Park itself directly threatened the piggeries. When Frederick Law Olmsted took his first tour of the park in 1856, he complained that "the low grounds were steeped in [the] overflow and mash of pig sties, slaughterhouses and bone boiling works and the stench was sickening." The swine and their odors would have to go. The Board of Commissioners of Central Park removed the piggeries from the park in 1857,

but that only increased the density of the establishments in the surrounding areas to its south and east.[45]

Most of the complaints lodged against the piggeries had to do with
the smells those operations produced. Frank Leslie reported that the
"steam from the bone-boiling kettles is sometimes so intensely pene-
trating that the passengers in the Sixth avenue cars are obliged to stop
their breath with their handkerchiefs while passing." Like deciphering
beauty, deciphering what smells particularly good or bad can be subjective, and critics' disdain for the proprietors mixed with their disdain for
the smells. Critics linked the inappropriate smells and occupations to
the proprietors' ethnicities. Many, though, fully believed that the smells
were not just offensive but actually dangerous. Critics blamed the fumes
for "scattering the seeds of disease and death."[46]

Ignoring the continued agitation and complaints from nearby residents and visitors, city inspectors and politicians "neglected to abate
the nuisance, from a fear of disturbing their political equilibrium." The
issue was just too contentious. Mayor Daniel Tiemann certainly found
this to be the case. Despite being a Tammany Democrat, Tiemann had
been elected in 1857 as an Independent candidate facing off against the
popular but politically controversial Democrat Fernando Wood. Wood
had alienated many Tammany Democrats by vying for the governor-
ship when he had not gotten the party's backing, and Tiemann found
support among these reform-minded foes, as well as from a combination of Nativists (who rallied behind an anti-immigration platform)
and Republicans. Politics in 1850s New York City was as tumultuous as
politics on the national stage. The newly formed Republican Party, with
a "free-soil" agenda opposing the expansion of slavery into the Western
territories, had gained the support of antislavery Whigs and Democrats,
including prominent ministers, journalists, reformers, African Americans, and merchants whose fortunes were tied to the transcontinental
railroad. Manhattan's Democrats typically included members of the
white working class, immigrants, and a mix of merchants and bankers

closely tied to the Southern slave economy. Yet Tammany Hall, which had been the leading political machine of the city's Democrats, found itself splitting when Fernando Wood opened Mozart Hall to rival Tammany in 1858. National political divisions were replicated on the streets of New York and would leave Tiemann in a tough spot, especially on the issue of controlling the piggeries and other nuisances around the city.[47]

After admitting frustration over his inability to control the City Inspector's office in 1859, Tiemann tried to reform the office by appointing someone with a medical background to the position rather than a politician or lawyer, as had long been the practice. Mozart Hall and hardline Tammany Hall Democrats stymied Tiemann's efforts by blocking nomination after nomination. The aldermen were unwilling to support this reform, as it would cause them to lose their political control and likely the financial perks they enjoyed from having a corruptible politician rather than a medical doctor in the position. After six months of battles and nine unsuccessful nominations, the mayor and aldermen finally compromised on Daniel E. Delavan, a high-ranking Tammany insider who had been serving as the city's chief tax assessor for the previous two years. All signs seemed to indicate that this man would avoid politically contentious reform.[48]

Oh, how wrong they were. Though he was not a medical doctor, Delavan had his eye on dramatic reform. He immediately got to work on the outer wards, filling in sunken and marshy lots and removing refuse—typical City Inspector tasks. By early July, however, he was focusing on a much bigger target: the uptown piggeries. He pressed the health commissioners to pass an ordinance banning piggeries as well as bone- and offal-boiling establishments south of 86th Street. As soon as the commissioners approved the resolution, the "Piggery War" began. Delavan seemingly ignored the political strife that had kept previous City Inspectors from acting on the piggeries, and in the process "stirred up a hornet's nest" of politicians who warned him to postpone action lest they lose the votes of Irish Democrats in the upper wards. With widespread support for the piggeries' removal, Delavan disregarded the politically cautious naysayers, moved forward with his agenda, and began the process of full-scale hog removal.[49]

The troops, made up of sanitary and health inspectors as well as members of the newly formed Metropolitan Police force, visited each piggery, ready to confront the notoriously vicious guard dogs and their potentially riotous owners. Instead, they met with a "good deal of loud talk and grumbling . . . accompanied by the deepest bass grunting of the hogs." The inspectors and police gave the owners three days to get rid of their hogs and remove the associated structures (cauldrons, pens, sheds, etc.), after which they would return to tear everything down and drive the hogs to the pound. The piggery owners had to act quickly to sell or relocate their animals. The new glut of pork on the market likely hurt their profit, but many of the piggery owners were successful in clearing out their property.[50]

When the police and health inspectors returned three days later, they came armed with guns, clubs, pickaxes, crowbars, and a team of reporters. The visitors complained of the smells and conditions in the piggeries. A typical piggery was described as "a most disgusting, abhorrent hole, surrounded by high rocks, with dilapidated sheds on all sides, forming a hollow square more formidable to a sensitive human being than the bristling bayonets of a thousand Zouaves" (i.e., French infantrymen). The more sensitive invaders held handkerchiefs to their noses and mouths as they adjusted to the industry's odors. Once they got their hands dirty chasing pigs and tearing apart pens, any attempt to protect themselves from the fumes was futile. Despite the "barking of dogs, the jabbering of Hibernian [Irish] females, the noise of falling rubbish and the grunting and squeaking of swine," the police and inspectors persisted in dismantling pens and carting away hogs and cauldrons.[51]

While residents did what they could to hide the remaining hogs—sometimes concealing them under beds and linens—the police were determined and successful. The newspapers reveled in the stories of the Irish "biddies" hiding plump porkers in their homes. The *New York Herald* reported: "One of the invading force approached, lifted a corner of the blanket, and came very near receiving a hearty salute from the snout of as bouncing a pig as ever eat [*sic*] swill. In several other cases pigs were hid under beds, (it is a pity the ladies in the locality do not dress in the prevailing fashion), and perhaps many a porker was snugly stowed away in a ricketty bureau drawer." During a time when womanhood was intricately tied to domesticity, the idea that these women would welcome dirty barnyard animals into their sacred refuges reinforced the idea that the Irish immigrants were brutish and completely different from typical middle-class New Yorkers. They were so unfashionable they could not even use the hoopskirts then in fashion to hide their illegal pigs.[52]

It was no wonder that the women and their families did what they could to hide their hogs. This was their business and their livelihood. They were already losing most of their property, so they desperately tried to hold on to what was left of their livestock. Butchers could make anywhere from $13 to $17 per barrel of pork in 1859, even more than they would with beef. While the piggery owners probably got only a small portion of that profit, especially given that their hogs were offal-fed, they still must have made a fair amount of money. Demand remained high throughout the year, since pork was a staple in the American diet during this period. The piggery owners had a lot to lose when the police threatened to haul away their hogs.[53]

While piggery owners often threatened the police, little violence actually occurred. One of the most vocal members of the so-called "pork army" was James McCormick, an assistant foreman at a local fire company, who was seen as a leader in the area. The *New York Times* ridiculed him as "king of the offal-boilers," and the *New York Herald* called him "Gen. McCormick, of the pork gentry." McCormick had threatened the police and inspectors, claiming that he would shoot any man who laid a hand on his property. In the end, though, he removed his

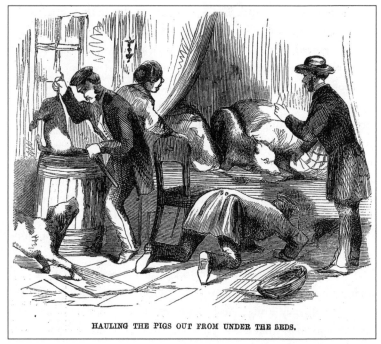

HAULING THE PIGS OUT FROM UNDER THE BEDS.

FIGURE 24. *Hauling the Pigs Out from Under the Beds.* Leslie and other journalists poked fun at Irish domesticity when they showed how closely the immigrants lived with livestock. From *Frank Leslie's Illustrated Newspaper,* August 13, 1859. (Sterling Memorial Library, Yale University.)

hogs, dismantled his pens, and pulled down his sheds before the police had their chance. It was reported that instead of fighting the city for the right to keep his animals, McCormick, like many of his neighbors, planned to move his business to New Jersey. McCormick likely continued to supply New York with cheap pork and ham, only with higher transportation costs.[54]

Women actually played the most violent role in resisting the police. Perhaps because the officers were less likely to treat a female attack seriously or to assault a woman, the piggery owners' wives chose to take up clubs and other weapons and defend their property. In one case, after a policeman seized a hog by the ears, he was confronted by a "large squarely built German woman" with an enormous tin pot. She whacked the officer with the pot "in a way that made him see stars." The *New York Herald* reporter described what he saw as a comic encounter: "The battle field at this moment presented a thrilling scene, and the spouting of the German, the screams of his frau, the banging of the tin kettle, the shouts of the beleaguered official for aid, and the shrill squealing of the captured porker, struggling to free his tail from the vice-like grasp which held it, altogether sent a combination of sounds which could hardly have been surpassed on any battle field in Italy." Aside from the occasional female assault on a police officer, the only other reported act of rebellion occurred at the pound. After the first night of hog collecting, some of the male owners broke into the temporary pound on 50th Street and drove the squealing fugitives back to their pens. Police quickly located the hogs, however, and took them into custody again. These attempts at resistance did little to prevent or even stall the Piggery War.[55]

The city seemed to have gained the upper hand. During the earlier hog riots of the 1820s and 1830s the municipal government had been fairly weak, but now it held far more control of the urban environment in terms of both public and private space. The absence of a riot surprised the media and the police. Perhaps the large number of heavily armed police and inspectors kept resistance at bay. Such strict enforcement of public health laws was rare, and the owners were likely unprepared for the city's committed response. Police power was a novelty in the city during this era.

The tables had certainly turned. In 1857, two years prior to the Piggery War, the New York State legislature passed the Metropolitan Police Act. Funded largely by the counties and under the governance of state-appointed commissioners, it combined the forces of New York, Kings, Richmond, and Westchester counties. The act declared that the Metropolitan Police were responsible for enforcing *all* of the city's laws, an issue the city had struggled with for decades, as was evident from the hog and dog riots, public health violations, and the city's uneven control of public space. Challenged unsuccessfully by Mayor Fernando Wood, the Metropolitan Police were a part of the state legislature's attempt to take charge of the unruly city and its corrupt politicians. The novelty of this better-organized police force helped to fuel public interest in the Piggery War and the ways that the government was suddenly able to control New York's public and private spaces.[56]

Despite the power of the police, or perhaps because of it, the press reveled in moments when they lost control over the hogs and chaos ensued. Journalists highlighted scenes where the hogs ran between officers' legs and knocked the men over, or where the police desperately tried to hold on to a pig's tail slipping through their fingers. Some of this chaos is visible in Leslie's depiction of the police driving the hogs to the pound. The police ran in all directions, only partly in control of their leaping and darting captives. Still, this was more control than the city had exhibited in previous battles with these animals.

The novelty of the city government's power was also evident in journalists' extensive use of dramatic war metaphors to describe the events. Reporters portrayed the police and sanitary officers as an "army of expulsion" or an "invading force," and their opponents as members of the "pork army." Hogtown was often referred to as the "seat of war." The writers even drew parallels to the recent Crimean War in Europe. For instance, toward the end of the Piggery War, a journalist interviewed the Superintendent of Sanitary Inspection and reported that "notwithstanding the example set by one Napoleon III in Italy, he intends to fight to the last, and that until the whole porcine race are driven from the island he will not consent to peace."[57] Frank Leslie published an image showing the superintendent giving directions to "his forces" of policemen and health inspectors the morning they attacked the piggeries (see Figure 26). With the men lined up in near-military style and the American flag flying above the tavern where they gathered, the image is reminiscent of

DRIVING THE CAPTURED PIGS TO THE POUND—SCENE OF GREAT CONFUSION AND RIOT.

FIGURE 25. *Driving the Captured Pigs to the Pound—Scene of Great Confusion and Riot.* The newspapers delighted in describing moments when swine overwhelmed the newly professional police. From *Frank Leslie's Illustrated Newspaper,* August 13, 1859. (Sterling Memorial Library, Yale University.)

what one would expect of a scene depicted before a battle. Undoubtedly this comparison was partly tongue-in-cheek, but it also celebrated the expanded power of reform and the discipline of the police.

The drama was good for selling papers, but it was also indicative of the way the public viewed the piggeries. The issue was much more black-and-white to people who believed that public health was at stake. The newspapers portrayed the Piggery War as a battle for the city's health and prosperity. Similarly, journalists described the mostly Irish proprietors as outsiders who threatened the city's health and challenged its civility. How could a city be the nation's metropolis yet have no control over its public health, its food supply, its land, or the practices of its residents? In almost every article, authors painted the Piggery War in triumphant terms. They equated the police and the health inspectors with war heroes, while describing the piggery owners as ridiculous,

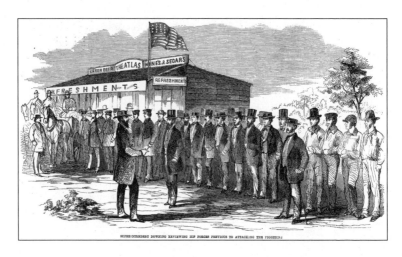

FIGURE 26. *Superintendent Downing Reviewing His Forces Previous to Attacking the Piggeries.* The newspapers used military comparisons both to celebrate the new power of the police and to express amusement about the amazing efforts needed to remove urban pigs. From *Frank Leslie's Illustrated Newspaper,* August 13, 1859. (Sterling Memorial Library, Yale University.)

backward, stubborn, and defiant. During the swill milk crisis, corrupt politicians had stood in the way of active change; during the Piggery War, in contrast, reformers were victorious in closing down the piggeries. New Yorkers must have been shocked to see their government act so efficiently.[58]

By September, the Piggery War was largely over. Delavan proudly reported that the police had removed 9,000 hogs, whether by force or threat, demolished 3,000 pens, and confiscated 100 boilers. As one newspaper put it, Delavan and his men had done a "fearful amount of laudable depredation." Delavan emerged from the "war" a hero to reformers. While police had driven a number of those hogs to the pound, the owners had removed most of them to New Jersey, Westchester, and Brooklyn. The transplantations only increased problems in these areas, where local governments struggled to control their own livestock populations. Hogs brought controversy wherever they went.[59]

Reflecting back on the Piggery War and its success, a writer for the *New York Herald* wrote that it was "hardly possible to conceive that so much abomination could have existed in a city like this as that represented as found in the neighborhood of the beautiful Central Park. It is hardly credible, and the recital of it is positively sickening." The city was transforming itself, and the movement of wealthier residents and speculators uptown meant that the piggeries and their proprietors were elbowed out of the way. The smells, the public health threats, the unsightliness, and the fact that the proprietors were less than respectable in the eyes of bourgeois and elite New Yorkers left the piggeries with little political footing.[60]

While offal-boiling piggeries and swill milk stables arguably produced similar, traditionally recognized nuisances that threatened New Yorkers' health and well-being, the city government's treatment of these two types of nuisances was anything but consistent, for several reasons. For one thing, the swill milk stables did not have the same physical presence that piggeries did. They were scattered, in less desirable areas. The cows were out of sight, housed in stables, and development pressure did not threaten these as greatly as it did the uptown piggeries. Leslie even had to publish maps to explain where the swill milk stables were located; this was unnecessary for the more visible, outdoor piggeries.

The very public nature of offal also contributed to its undoing. While the waste produced by large-scale distilleries seemed relatively private, especially since the same owners that produced it ultimately recycled it, offal was more publicly visible. The need for public intervention and control encouraged City Inspector White to turn his attention to the business, and the public nature of the waste and smells later in the decade helped to justify the interventions of Delavan and the police during the Piggery War.

Many were surprised that political corruption had not weakened the Piggery War, as had been the case with swill milk regulation. The *New-York Tribune* expressed shock that the piggery owners were unable to muster more support. Perhaps their inability to bribe the politicians and inspectors was their main problem. Frank Leslie, fuming about the persistence of swill milk stables a year after his exposé, wrote that despite swill milk's greater threat to public health, "the poor owners of the piggeries are thus punished, while the wealthy owners of the swill stables escape with impunity."[61] Perhaps if they had enjoyed more wealth and political influence, like the distillery owners, the piggeries would have remained longer. New York's politics during this period—whether Democrat, Whig, Reform, or Republican—ran on money, bribes included.

Waste recycling highlighted the difficulties and dangers of urban food production, while also raising fears among the middle and upper classes about the immigrant outsiders who were affecting the city's health. Ethnic stereotyping played an enormous role in the ways these industries were treated. Politicians and the media drew on stereotypes about the German and Irish offal-boiling piggery owners, just as they did in the case of the Irish laborers working in the milk industry. Artists drew coarse versions of their features, writers dwelled on their accents and broken English, and immigrants were subsequently cast as backward outsiders threatening the city and consumers alike. The explicit ties between the immigrants and foul urban food both reflected and reinforced ethnic divisions in the city.

As New York grew beyond recognition, the amount of waste it produced far outpaced the ability of public services to handle its removal. Add to this a growing need for local and inexpensive dairy and meat, and you get the haphazard solutions devised by the distillery and piggery owners. These entrepreneurs recycled the city's waste and turned it into something marketable and edible. After the introduction of better infrastructure, more efficient services, and technological innovations such as refrigeration, these industries would be supplanted, but for the time being they played a specific economic and environmental role in the city.

New York's progress toward public health reform and increased control over its environment was far from steady or even. As the city government's power over the urban environment grew, the opportunities for corruption increased. City officials sought out opportunities to profit personally from initiatives and programs, and in doing so stopped responding to the needs of their constituents. Politicians also acted unjustly, giving preference to noxious industries when they themselves would benefit financially or politically, all the while attacking easier targets instead. The results? Offal boilers and piggery owners were pushed off the island, but swill milk continued to be sold on street corners for decades. Calling an industry a nuisance was not a failsafe way to have it condemned. While reformers and wealthy critics considered most practices of immigrants and lower-class New Yorkers to be nuisances, ringing that alarm did not always produce desired results in city government, due to deep-seated corruption. Unhappy with the city government's intervention, reformers increasingly turned to the state legislature for support, as was the case with the development of the Metropolitan Board of Police, which aided the city in taking control of its spaces.

Despite the corruption and the extent of inefficiency, the reform evident in the Piggery War showed that the city government had the ability, when it desired, to crack down on unwanted land uses and use the police to control public and private spaces. In effect, the city government pushed industries and land uses that seemed incompatible with residential neighborhoods—industries such as the piggeries—farther and farther from the center of town. The so-called "rural wards" that were home to the piggeries were transforming. With the development of Central Park and the promise of new, upscale neighborhoods on its borders, the squatters and renters of the once-marginal lands would have to be pushed out, the smells eradicated, and the pigs evicted. New York was starting a new chapter for this area that would involve redefining the neighborhood and specifying appropriate land uses within the metropolis. Through the selective targeting of certain nuisances, though, the inequalities in the drive to regulate the uses of city land become clear. Bourgeois reformers, frustrated with the city's corruption and its uneven attempts to take control of the urban environment, were also attempting to transform urban space during this era. Their efforts to take control of the streets and police parks would prove perhaps even more effective than those of the city government.

5

Clearing the Lungs of the City

When a tourist from rural Virginia visited New York City in the summer of 1848, he was struck by the contrasts between the city he was visiting and the community in which he lived. Compared with "his quiet home and the fresh atmosphere of the country," Manhattan was a "dusty, smoky, noisy, busy, great and animating emporium." Class differences were also conspicuous. He observed on the one hand "the princely dwelling, the costly equipage and the splendid appearances; and on the other hand the squalid hut of poverty, of filth, of extreme misery and degradation." The midcentury city was marked by extremes. The tourist seemed dizzied by the "eddying throngs gathering and whirling, scattering and hurrying hither and thither." Most notable in the commotion were the crowds of "Frenchmen, Spaniards, Italians, Austrians, Swiss, Germans, Russians, Chinese, Jews, Turks, Africans, Portuguese, English, Southrons [Southerners] and Yankees; all commingling in the same hour, in the same street, in the same scene and all of whom, perhaps are numbered in the census of this great metropolis." Immigration was rising to astonishing levels, stretching the urban housing stock to its limits. By 1850, 40 percent of New Yorkers were foreign-born. The city's population had grown fivefold in just two decades. The "blessed babel" on the city's streets brought with it increasingly visible poverty and destitution, as immigrants struggled to find their footing. Responding to the crowdedness of the city's tenements and sidewalks in the late 1840s and 1850s, reformers began calling not only for more aid to the poor but also for breathing room, for a park that could serve as "the lungs of the City."[1]

Two men who hurried along in the throngs of people were childhood friends from Hartford, Connecticut: Charles Loring Brace and Frederick Law Olmsted. Like many of their contemporaries, these reformers were troubled by what they saw on the streets. Using different methods, both men sought to transform the city by raising the poor out of degradation. For Brace and Olmsted, the differences between the countryside and the city loomed large, and both, to different degrees, came to believe that rural virtues were the solution for urban ills. Brace addressed the plight of the urban poor through the Children's Aid Society, a philanthropic organization he established with a dozen influential New Yorkers in 1853, while Olmsted considered the social implications of park development when designing and administering Central Park. Their concerns, though seemingly at opposite ends of the social spectrum, were actually intimately related, not only intellectually but also socially and environmentally. The ideas that inspired Brace and Olmsted were firmly grounded in the landscapes of the city.[2]

Though the government in the 1850s exerted far more control than it had during the hog riots of the 1810s or even the cholera epidemics of the 1830s, the Manhattan that Brace and Olmsted encountered was still filled with the types of unregulated and uncontrolled uses of the urban environment that worried reformers. Poor New Yorkers were settling into shantytowns on the edge of town, growing vegetables and raising livestock in ways that seemed inimical to the increasingly tamed city. In addition, an informal economy based on repurposing urban waste was thriving, with many men, women, and children scavenging for rags, bones, and other salable items in New York's perpetually filthy streets. The ever-present ragpickers were a visible reminder of the city's poverty and uncontrolled environment. While New Yorkers like Brace and Olmsted saw the ways shantytown settlers and ragpickers used the resources of the urban environment as problems worthy of reform, such practices were also a safety net for those who were barely scraping by.

Budding Reformers

Though Brace came from a humbler background than Olmsted, the two shared many experiences that helped to shape their understanding of the problems facing New York. Though they had known each other as children, they grew closer as young adults during Olmsted's frequent trips to New Haven to visit his brother John Hull Olmsted, who roomed with Brace at Yale. The two regularly exchanged witty letters in which they debated politics and discussed their futures. By 1848 both men had moved to New York, where Brace studied theology at the Union Theological Seminary and Olmsted established himself as a farmer on Staten Island.[3]

Two years later, in 1850, they traveled to England, Ireland, and Germany with Olmsted's brother John. As soon as they arrived in England that May, they were captivated by the rural landscape. In *Walks and Talks of an American Farmer,* a travel journal Olmsted published upon returning to New York, he wrote of falling in love with the English countryside. "There we were right in the midst of it! The country—and such a country!—green, dripping, glistening, gorgeous! We stood dumb-stricken by its loveliness." Brace wrote of the "luxuriant appearance of the landscape," filled with "endless shades of green and glitter of water and an occasional peep at a brown cottage wall." Yet despite this romantic enthusiasm for pastoral landscapes, neither man was naïve

FIGURE 27. Frederick Law Olmsted gazes at his childhood friend Charles Loring Brace in this daguerreotype from 1846. The image includes other friends studying at Yale: Charles Trask, Frederick Kingsbury, and John Hull Olmsted. (Courtesy of the National Park Service, Frederick Law Olmsted National Historic Site.)

about the conditions of farm workers. Olmsted wrote very candidly about their harsh existence, their mode of "life so low, so like that of *domestic animals*," but that did not take away from his appreciation of the transformative effect that the rural landscape could have on people. It certainly transformed Olmsted. In a letter to the famed landscape architect Andrew Jackson Downing, his mentor and friend, Olmsted wrote: "I feel as if I had not merely seen the rural character, but lived in it, and made it a *part* of me."[4]

Parks were of special interest to Brace and Olmsted. One of their excursions was to a new park in Birkenhead (near Liverpool) that was specifically designed for the people—a novelty in England, where most parks were on royal or private property. Olmsted considered it remarkable "that in democratic America there was nothing to be thought of as comparable with this People's Garden." He "was glad to observe that the privileges of the garden were enjoyed about equally by all classes. There were some who were attended by servants, . . . but a large proportion were of the common ranks, and a few women with children . . . were evidently the wives of very humble labourers." The idea of a park that all classes were encouraged to visit was novel for residents of New York, where for decades parks had been fiercely protected by members of the city's elite, who considered them their spaces.[5]

In addition to the countryside and parks, the men also toured common schools (public schools), ragged schools (charitable institutions for destitute children), and model lodgings for the poor. In famine-ravaged Ireland, Brace was surprised to find "nothing of the Irish beggary we had expected," given his experience with the Irish in Manhattan. Brace seemed to realize that the desperation of Irish immigrants in New York stemmed partly from the squalid conditions and limited opportunities available to them in the city. While Olmsted would later regret that he had not "seen more of the better, more polished classes," Brace and Olmsted's exposure to society outside elite circles certainly had an influence on the work these men would do later in life, albeit to different degrees.[6]

Brace and Olmsted, despite their affinities, did not embrace identical political or social ideals. Right before they returned to New York, Congress passed the Fugitive Slave Act, which required citizens to return runaway slaves to their owners, as part of the Compromise of 1850. While Brace was a staunch abolitionist who argued that the act placed the evils of slavery on "our free Northern shoulders," Olmsted hesitated to take such a strong position. Olmsted believed that slavery was justified, as long as it was a civilizing institution. The men argued fiercely about these issues. Perhaps hoping that firsthand experience would change Olmsted's mind, Brace used a connection with the *New-York Daily Times* (predecessor of the *New York Times*) to obtain an assignment for his friend: Olmsted would tour the South and report back to the paper about his findings. During his travels, he stayed with a slaveholder and former Yale classmate of Brace's, Samuel Perkins Allison, in Tennessee. Olmsted arrived at Allison's home convinced of the North's social superiority, but left with a clearer view of the inequalities that existed even in the free-labor North. In a heated discussion with Allison, Olmsted reluctantly acknowledged "the rowdyism, ruffianism, want of high honorable sentiment & chivalry of the common farming & laboring people of the North," which made him "very melancholy." As he recounted this to Brace, he concluded that in order for America to attain its democratic ideals, "We need institutions that shall more directly *assist* the poor and degraded to elevate themselves. The poor and wicked need more than to be let alone. . . . The poor need an education to refinement and taste and the mental & moral capital of gentlemen." Both men believed that for the sake of democracy and the stability of their city, the impoverished conditions they saw around them had to be eliminated.[7]

In working to transform the city, Brace and Olmsted chose paths that circumvented the city government. New York's municipal government in the 1850s was plagued with corruption, exemplified by the offal and swill milk scandals. In an effort to curb corruption, the state revised the city's charter—but did this in such a way that it fragmented municipal power, making city-led reform even more difficult. Reformers began bypassing the municipal government to petition the state government directly for laws regarding temperance, health reform, and municipal corruption. Brace's work with philanthropic organizations and Olmsted's work with the state-controlled Central Park Board of Commissioners illustrate two different ways in which reformers worked to reshape the city without involving the municipal government. Olmsted and Brace were just two of many reformers negotiating the city's political thickets to find ways to take control of public space.[8]

After returning from Europe and settling back into their lives in New York, Brace and Olmsted had new reference points from which to assess American society. Having met and studied Irish and German laborers on their home turf, Brace likely felt that he had a better understanding of the immigrants who flocked to the city seeking a better life. He had lost interest in theological orthodoxy. Now he set out to make a difference in the lives of New York's poor, first through preaching at institutions on Blackwell's Island and at the Five Point Mission, and later through his work with the Children's Aid Society. Olmsted, with images of the undulating landscapes of England's parks and countryside in his mind, was well equipped when presented with the opportunity to co-design and manage a public park for New York. As they began their careers, Olmsted told Brace to throw his "light on the path in Politics and Social Improvement and encourage me to put my foot down and *forwards*. There's a great *work* wants doing in this our generation, Charley, let us off jacket and go about it." Both saw themselves as suited to transform New York for the better.[9]

The "Dust-Eaters of New York" and Their "Straggling Suburbs"

In 1850, after a few years of living in New York, Brace was agonizing over the social problems that faced the city: "What an immense vat of misery and crime and filth much of this great city is! I realize it more and more. Think of *ten thousand children* growing up almost sure to be prostitutes and rogues!" In the mid-nineteenth century, a massive wave of immigration hit the shores of Manhattan Island. Fueled by economic and political unrest mainly in western Europe, a large proportion of the new immigrants ended up struggling on the streets of New York, adding to what Brace saw as a "vat of misery." The New York that Brace and Olmsted hoped to reform was a city that knew both extreme wealth and extreme poverty. Given the economic conditions and the housing supply, this poverty was most evident in the immigrant neighborhoods and shantytowns, and in the number of men, women, and children picking through the city's waste and selling their wares on the streets. This was the urban landscape that inspired both men as they embarked on their projects.[10]

The deluge of immigrants during these decades was largely made up of men, women, and children ill-equipped to thrive immediately upon arrival. Uprooted as a result of economic, environmental, and political troubles, immigrants were typically poor and often weakened by their travels. Though New York received newcomers from every part of the world, at midcentury the majority came from Ireland and Germany. The recent Irish immigrants were at a particular disadvantage, coming from an already impoverished agrarian economy that had been further devastated by potato blight and the subsequent famine. Since these farmers had few trade skills to aid them in finding urban employment, they filled the lowest-paid positions as domestics and day-laborers, competing directly with the city's African American population. Even then, not everyone found work. Without adequate welfare systems to match the constant flow of immigrants, New York's institutions—its almshouse, orphanages, hospitals, and prisons—were filled to capacity. New York lacked a wide-enough safety net to catch these struggling newcomers.[11]

As early as the 1830s, anti-immigrant Nativists were gaining a foothold in municipal and state politics, showing how fearful some New Yorkers were of how these immigrants and their Catholic loyalties might change the face of the city. Native New Yorkers' fears of the urban immigrant masses extended in many directions. The influence of the European revolutions of 1848 threatened to disturb American hierarchies. Immigrants had increasingly powerful voices in city politics, and their visibility in public spaces seemed to emphasize the social disparities afflicting the city. Their visibility also threatened bourgeois sensibilities about what properly belonged inside the home and what was permissible in public spaces. With health officials blaming cholera and other urban ailments in part on the immigrants' crowded, subpar housing, it seemed that the poor were liable to spread disease as they spilled outdoors and through the streets. State politicians described tenement housing as "oozing with pollution" and "reeking with filth." There was also anxiety about maintaining racial purity, given the intermixing of African Americans, Irish, and other New Yorkers in these poor communities. The same politicians, in describing the horrors of the tenements, noted the number of "amalgamationists," mainly African American men and their Irish wives, living in these communities with their "children of various shades." While fears of "miscegenation" were not unique to New York, they further fueled the idea that the city's poor threatened to infect the urban body, politically, biologically, and morally.[12]

Immigrants were not the only impoverished people in the city. There were plenty of native-born paupers, including a sizable population of African Americans who worked in the lowest-paying jobs. While some African Americans had decently paid artisanal jobs as hairdressers, tobacconists, butchers, bakers, carpenters, and the like, the majority were employed in unskilled positions. Suffering from rampant job discrimination, African Americans had a difficult time getting licenses from the city to enter certain trades that white New Yorkers dominated. The households of African Americans were interspersed with those of immigrants and other New Yorkers, as were their troubles.[13]

While bourgeois New Yorkers worried about the immoralities of the notorious Five Points neighborhood, the extralegal shantytowns on the edge of the city stood in even sharper contrast to the increasingly controlled, gridded city. These communities were a common part of the mid-nineteenth-century urban landscape and marked the movable boundary between the city and its hinterland. They served as a partial, makeshift solution for the housing crisis that crammed countless poor New Yorkers into the downtown tenements. The *New York Times* claimed that the squatters "prefer dwelling rent-free amid filth and squalor to paying a landlord's agent monthly dues for the enjoyment of similar privileges as conferred upon the lodgers in a tenement house." If the alternative involved residing in neighborhoods like Five Points where living conditions were often worse, a shanty with access to land and the ability to maintain a semi-rural lifestyle was far preferable. While there was certainly evidence of urban squatting in the early nineteenth century, it became more widespread in the 1840s and 1850s as immigration swelled. Several of Manhattan's shantytowns began as temporary housing for workers laying railroad ties, building the Croton Aqueduct, or working in quarries, but they ended up surviving for thirty or forty years, with shanties regularly changing hands. The Catholic Church recognized how established these communities were and built churches nearby, in hopes of attracting more parishioners.[14]

These shantytowns are the forgotten and neglected early suburbs of New York. While picturesque enclaves like Brooklyn Heights certainly gained more fame, New York's suburbs consisted of more than bourgeois residential retreats from urban problems. The term "suburb" in the mid-nineteenth century referred to any kind of exurban community, planned or unplanned. While those celebrating Brooklyn Heights used the term, so too did those decrying the existence of the shantytowns, though they qualified it with adjectives like "straggling" and "unlovely." The erasure of such communities from many contemporary descriptions of the city and their characterization as not quite belonging to the city indicate how wealthier neighbors viewed them and their use of the land. Yet these unplanned immigrant and African American communities, built largely from scraps of wood, were part of the expanding metropolitan periphery. Clustered around the edges and along the infrastructural supports that would make it possible for the city's population to move farther north, they were an urban borderland—part city, part country. They were not, however, the idealized rural landscapes that elite New Yorkers like Brace and Olmsted dreamt about. In 1846, the editor of the *New York Herald* commented on the dramatic boundary between the city and its shanty suburbs: "There are the palaces of the Fifth avenue and Union place, and there are the hovels of the squatters on the 'meadows,' where pigs, chickens and children, grow in dirty profusion."[15]

While shantytown residents sometimes had leases or informal arrangements with the landowners, journalists assumed they were squatters, basing this view on the haphazard nature of the shanties and their own stereotypes about the poor and often foreign people who lived in the wooden structures. The *New York Times* called squatters "a terror and a scourge," believing them lawless: "They pay no rent,—they will submit to none." In the eyes of the journalists who chronicled their lives for general readers, squatters were outsiders, likely dangerous, and certainly ungovernable.[16]

Typically located on marginal land amid the piggeries and offal-boiling establishments, the shantytowns hardly resembled the city to their south. These communities existed on all types of land, with many on rocky outcroppings, where landowners delayed the expensive work of leveling their property to street grade until real estate values rose high enough to make it worthwhile. Poor New Yorkers took advantage of this and constructed their homes atop the schist and along other undeveloped lands. In comparison to the regularity of the grid and the permanent brick and stone structures that met each other at right angles throughout the better part of the island, the shantytowns developed in a seemingly random fashion. After visiting one squatter community, Brace suggested that a visitor to New York's shantytowns would "hardly suspect he was in an American city." He provided detailed descriptions of the squatters' lifestyles and living situations to the readers of the *Times*, as if the communities were located in a foreign country. To many New Yorkers, they might as well have been.[17]

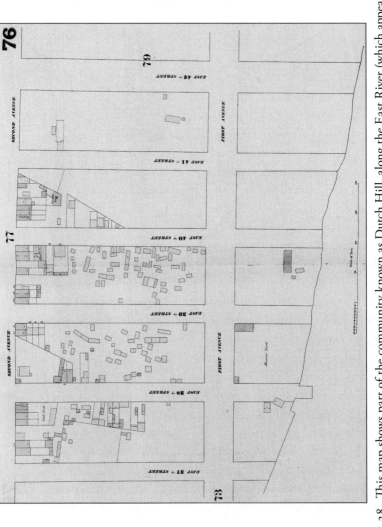

FIGURE 28. This map shows part of the community known as Dutch Hill, along the East River (which appears at the bottom). The shanties are indicated by the haphazardly placed wooden structures within the blocks. The construction of brick row houses on nearby property by speculators was an attempt to transform the neighborhood, though the Dutch Hill shanties would remain until the late nineteenth century. William Perris, Plate 76, *Atlases of New York City*, 1857. (Col-

Visitors were struck by the rustic conditions and rough architecture that differentiated the shantytowns from the rest of the city. Brace referred to one such community as a "collection of wigwams" made of wood boards and mud. He found single-story buildings of all shapes and sizes, some with flat roofs, others with arches, and occasionally one with a "sharp Gothic gable." Some residents even converted old railroad cars into dwellings. Squatters usually built their homes on Sundays, when family and friends could help. They typically covered their wooden roofs with scraps of metal and used a simple opening or stovepipe for a chimney. Some shanties had extensions, gardens, and pigpens. If the residents were inclined and the land would permit, they grew potatoes, cabbage, Indian corn, and other produce to feed their families and sell on the streets. The *New York Times* described the way shanty dwellers typically organized the property outside their homes: "When the shanty is completed a small space of ground in the rear is generally enclosed within a dilapidated fence and a few poles are driven in the ground at either extremity. Clothes-lines are stretched from upright to upright, some wretched specimens of wearing apparel are thrown over the ropes to dangle about at the caprice of the winds." To outsiders, very little about these homes seemed orderly or admirable. The disorganization of the buildings was almost symbolic of their existence outside the established, comparatively orderly city and beyond the rule of the government.[18]

The fact that squatters raised livestock further separated them visually and culturally from their wealthier neighbors. Squatters lived in close proximity with their livestock, sometimes even under the same roof. Shanty dwellers set their geese, hens, goats, cows, and pigs free to forage in the neighborhood during the day, locking them up at night in an outbuilding or the family's residence. The *New York Times* claimed that "wherever a group of melancholy animals is to be seen clustering about a heap of garbage in a street of orthodox appearance, the suspicion that a squatter settlement is not far distant is likely to prove correct." Visitors to the shanties described stumbling over "flocks of fowls,

FIGURE 29. *Squatter Settlement, between 1st and 2nd Aves. near 38th St., 1858.* In Dutch Hill, pigs and goats circulated among the cluster of shanties. The community was located on the East River. Lithograph by A. Weingärtner for D. T. Valentine, *Manual of the Corporation of the City of New York,* 1859. (Collection of the New-York Historical Society.)

hogs, goats, cats and dogs" as they entered dark rooms caked in dirt and filled with pails of foul-smelling swill intended for the animals. While Brace worked hard to convey the humanity of the inhabitants of these dwellings, he described their lives in ways that made them seem worlds apart from those of the bourgeois men and women downtown. With animals roaming inside and outside the buildings, the communities hardly seemed urban at all.[19]

Shantytowns were not the only locations where the poor made use of the city's natural resources to scrape by. New York's perpetually filthy streets provided a wealth of materials for scavengers, beyond even the offal and kitchen scraps collected for the piggeries. Salvaging materials out of garbage heaps kept many people afloat when wages for unskilled workers could barely cover the basic needs of a family. Ragpicking, though grueling and far from lucrative, was a safety net that allowed adults as well as children to scavenge as a temporary solution for unemployment or underemployment. It was a business in which any individual, practically regardless of age or sex, could work to make a living. While jobs might come and go, New Yorkers could count on their streets being filthy. The same fetid heaps that helped to feed the hogs, dogs, and other loose animals and to fertilize the countryside also provided income for the poor and raw materials for the urban manufacturing system.[20]

Ragpickers became increasingly visible on the streets in the 1840s, from a combination of rising poverty levels and demand for raw materials from various local industries. In 1843, the *New-York Evening Post* announced to its readers that in the previous few years a visible class of "degraded hunters" known as ragpickers or chiffonniers had developed. They would set out early in the morning "furnished with their apparatus of labour, consisting of a long-handled iron hook, with which they rake the [gutters], and overturn the heaps of rubbish and filth, in search of rags, bones, bits of paper, &c., and a basket on one arm, or a large bag slung across the shoulder, which receives their gatherings, reeking with mud and filth." Some pickers brought along drays (low carts) and dogs to protect their bounty, but many just carried bags filled with their collections. The author called ragpickers a "new sore upon the face of this city," suggesting that the only antidote was to clean the streets and thus remove their source of work. The heaps of garbage filled with rags, woodchips, scrap metal, crockery, and bones were fodder for these urban recyclers, who saw value in the items that they could sell to junk dealers, offal boilers, and collectors on the street or use to feed their families and heat their homes. Though called "ragpickers," the classification usually included all scavengers who were after any kind of lost treasure.[21]

Those who found their livelihoods in the city's trash were barely subsisting. In 1853, Brace visited a community of German pickers and described the difficult financial straits and workdays of these families. Kleindeutschland, the German enclave between Third Avenue and the

East River, was buzzing by 5:00 A.M., which in January was long before daybreak. By Brace's calculations, there were approximately 2,000 people in the Eleventh Ward alone who "make it their sole business to glean bones, rags, and garbage from the streets." In one apartment he visited where the mother was ill, the father and children worked hard to pay the rent. They picked through the city's trash and earned approximately $3 each week, which they "could hardly get along on." Facing the cold weather, the family needed to pay not only for their usual provisions, but also for fuel to heat their apartment. The family, like many other pickers, washed their rags at home and hung them to dry on any surface they could find, not only in their apartments but also in courtyards, alleys, or any railing or banister. New York State assemblymen visiting these neighborhoods described ragpickers' housing as "canopied by myriads of rags fluttering from lines crossing their filthy yards, where bones of dead animals and noisome collections of every kind were reeking with pestiferous smells." With so much time and work necessary for collecting and then cleaning the treasures, it was no wonder that parents and children alike had to contribute to the family's wages in order to keep the household afloat.[22]

There was a large system of entrepreneurs who acted as middlemen, purchasing goods from pickers and selling them to manufacturers. Brace met a thirteen-year-old girl on the street who could typically make 10 cents a day by selling bones to men with carts as they passed through the neighborhood and 2 cents for each pound of rags she sold to a local shop. The Board of Aldermen licensed various businesses such as junk shops, pawnshops, and secondhand stores where New Yorkers could buy and sell items. Junk shops, specifically, were a major stopping point for those who picked scrap metal and bits of rope. These businesses were a crucial link in the urban recycling network that made picked-over treasures available to manufacturers who needed rags to make paper, metal for machinery, and bones for comb handles, fertilizer, or sugar refining.[23]

Critics often conflated the legal and illegal aspects of this informal economy of reselling garbage. Police, for instance, arrested children who scavenged in the garbage as thieves and vagrants. While adults played a large part in the informal economy, reformers and critics paid special attention to the increasing number of children sifting through the trash and selling their wares on street corners. To New Yorkers anxious about the moral solvency of the city, it seemed that juvenile vagrants would soon graduate from the relatively benign practices of picking rags to become career thieves and prostitutes. The visible presence of these poor children was a symbol of the urban disorder that bourgeois New Yorkers worried about, especially during a period when the city was experiencing vast changes due to immigration. Their visibility is also what convinced reformers like Brace and Olmsted that real social and environmental change was necessary in New York.[24]

Regardless of the threats that ragpickers, hawkers, and hucksters may have posed, such people made a relatively honest living on the urban commons. Brace tried to elevate their position in the eyes of bourgeois readers of the *New-York Daily Times* by describing their lives and the virtues of their work. He called on readers to be kind to the people hunting through the garbage and selling their wares.

> To all this petty and dirty work done by children and foreigners in our city, none has the right to utter a word of objection. It is immeasurably better than begging. The little muddy, dripping girl, with her rough hair and torn dress, who is sweeping the walk, and flying about with her broom in the storm, like an ugly little sprite, may be just keeping herself and an old mother from the alms-house, by these hard-earned pennies. Possibly she has not any very clear ideas of purity and virtue—but possibly society never gave her much chance to gain them. However that may be, she, and the little match-seller, and the ragpicker, and "the boner," and the apple peddler, are *in honest work,* and even if it be not very clean or very extensive, it is at least *work*—and worth generally all it is paid.

The urban environment, filled as it was with recyclable garbage and possible wares, provided options for the poor as they gained their footing on American shores, as they augmented their family income when a parent fell sick, and as they struggled to save enough money to move out of the city. While their lives and characters were rarely romanticized by writers, the few like Brace who ventured into their communities saw virtue in their work. A writer for the *New York Times* maintained that although they were "the least respected and least regarded denizens of the City," they actually lived respectable lives. In 1857, as the economy collapsed and fears of riots and class warfare haunted the minds of bourgeois New Yorkers, a writer for the *New York Daily Tribune* remarked that the informal economy so many of the elite despised could actually save the city from crisis: "Yet with all this risk of the 'swinish multitude,' we conjure some of the 'unemployed' to set up the pop-corn business, and grow wise and wealthy." The informal economy was the safety net that rescued many poor New Yorkers, and, in doing so, perhaps saved bourgeois residents from the types of revolutions and riots they feared. Without the minor income so many of New York's poorest gleaned from the urban environment, both they and the city would have certainly been in an even more desperate situation.[25]

Bringing Order to the Streets

Despite the safety net that peddling and picking provided, crime in New York appeared to be on the rise. Urban violence and unrest were endemic in the middle of the nineteenth century, with over 200 major gang wars between 1834 and 1844, as well as large-scale riots such as the 1837 flour riot, the 1849 Astor Place Riot, and the Dead Rabbits Riot of 1857 (the Dead Rabbits were a notorious gang). Since few New Yorkers ventured into troubled neighborhoods like Five Points or the uptown squatter villages, their understanding of the city's lower-class immigrants and African Americans came from the peddlers and ragpickers they encountered on the streets and the sensational accounts of the haunts and livelihoods of the "swinish multitude." Authors ranging from Charles Dickens to George G. Foster visited the city's "ulcer of wretchedness," Five Points, and composed graphic descriptions of the impoverished, rum-soaked people they found there. Like many later writers, Dickens guided readers into the rickety wooden tenements: "Ascend these pitch-dark stairs, heedful of a false footing on the trembling boards, and grope your way with me into this wolfish den, where neither ray of light nor breath of air, appears to come." Five Points and other poor neighborhoods seemed to be a nexus of physical filth and moral darkness. Literature such as this helped to confirm middle-class fears about the unruly lower class that lived in these neighborhoods, threatening the peace of the entire city.[26]

The poor seemed like a completely different species, closer to animals than to their bourgeois neighbors. Time and again, writers made reference to the animalistic qualities of poor immigrants and African Americans. Noting that many of the city's pigs came from the Five Points neighborhood, Dickens mused, "Do [the pigs] ever wonder why their masters walk upright instead of on all-fours? And why they talk instead of grunting?" Foster went further, continually referring to Five Points residents as "human swine." These animal references may have comforted some bourgeois readers into believing that poor people were intrinsically different from themselves and that they could never reach such debased and uncivilized lows. Unfortunately, descriptions of this type also made it difficult for elite and middle-class New Yorkers to relate to those who were struggling in their midst. Similar animal comparisons were used in the South during this period to make slavery seem natural and justifiable. By referring to New York's underclass as animals, writers emphasized the uncontrolled, uncivilized, and untamed aspect of the city's indigent residents.[27]

Through his writings, Charles Loring Brace worked hard to humanize the poor, especially their children, by repeatedly bringing stories of their lives to the armchairs of elite New Yorkers. He did not shy away from sensational writing, but there was an undercurrent of sympathy and hope in his descriptions. Like Foster and Dickens, he made references to the animalistic qualities of the poor; but unlike them, he placed the blame for those qualities elsewhere. In Five Points, he wrote, "Human beings were herded like animals in every possible nook and cranny of it." Similarly, he routinely described children as looking much older than their years, having "low animal features," and "growing up like brutes." He attributed their condition not to the children themselves but rather to their parents' depravity and to the landlords who valued profits more than livable apartments. Their environment had essentially turned them into animals. This philosophy opened up the hope that if removed from these conditions or taught new habits, the children could rise from the ranks and culture of the poor.[28]

Despite his sympathy for poor New Yorkers, Brace saw them as a threat to the politics, property, and peace of the city. In one of the early annual reports for the Children's Aid Society (CAS), he laid out the importance of the organization's work. He must have struck fear in the hearts of potential funders when he wrote: "The greatest danger that can threaten a country like ours, is from the existence of an ignorant, debased, permanently poor class, in the great cities. It is still more threatening if this class be of foreign birth, and of different habits from those of our own people. The members of it come at length to form a separate population." If left unguided by the supposedly wiser upper classes, these immigrants were "liable to be played upon by demagogues," easily becoming a force that could sway elections. Brace, a steadfast abolitionist, saw a threat in the growing Irish support for the Democratic Party in New York. Democrats had taken hold of municipal politics in the late 1840s, leaving Whigs and their Republicans successors struggling to maintain their footing. Steering the poor toward acceptable bourgeois habits and lifestyles and giving them opportunities to work would be one way to avert this social crisis and perhaps also regain political power. In Brace's eyes, the benefits of assimilation were manifold: from cleaner streets and a more orderly environment to fewer riots and the ascendancy of the Republican Party.[29]

As the director of the CAS, Brace adopted a fresh take on how to handle the poverty plaguing New York. Having ministered to the poor for several years, he was familiar with the city's asylums and had become increasingly disappointed with their inefficacy in reforming vagrant children. The previous generation of reformers and government officials had embraced asylums as a way to enforce discipline in the lives of children and adults alike, and with the support of elite New Yorkers, institutions such as the House of Refuge and workhouses had sprung up throughout the city. Instead of working within the existing city institutions, Brace and the other gentlemen who founded the CAS chose to work apart from the bureaucracy, avoiding the mess of city and state politics that might inhibit their efforts. Theirs was a private solution to an urban problem. Brace, one of the most vocal reformers in New York at midcentury, argued that families and industrial schools, not asylums, could best serve the youth of the city. Children, after all, were malleable and ready for reform. Though convinced that it was much more difficult to reform adults, Brace hoped that he could eventually reach the parents through their children.[30]

Within the city, Brace opened several industrial schools for children of both sexes and a lodging house for homeless and runaway newsboys. The lodging houses and industrial schools of Germany, England, and Scotland had inspired Brace during his trip with Olmsted in 1850. Brace staffed the New York schools with middle- and upper-class women and men who he hoped would impart bourgeois values as they instructed the children. The teachers were to "show the fruits of high civilization" to the "little barbarians." Brace put a lot of confidence in the idea that bringing the classes together could benefit everyone in society. Not only would the poor children benefit, but so, too, would their teachers. "No lady can long attend these classes, hear the little story of the rag picker or the beggar, become familiar with their petty joys and troubles, and afterwards pass one of them in rags and dust in the street, as indifferently as before. They are no longer parts of the street scenery like the animals; they become human beings, with warm hearts, and souls formed for an immortal destiny." By teaching children useful skills, the CAS could guide them in finding employment off the streets, away from the "petty and dirty work" of the informal economy.[31]

Removing the children from the city completely was another option. By sending children out west and separating them from the shanties that they had grown up in, Brace believed the organization could help children rise above their family's station and problems. While the CAS placed children of both sexes in rural households, boys made up the majority. Girls tended to stay closer to home, enrolling in the industrial schools. Brace took pride in the fact that children who had grown up in shanties on Dutch Hill "more often became ashamed of their paternal piggeries and nasty dens," after getting a taste of country life outside the city. The children essentially learned where rural land uses belonged. Through the influences of the industrial schools and the placing-out system, the CAS was in the business of imparting bourgeois values and ideals to lower-class urban children. Brace was confident that bourgeois values, in the form of domestic, industrial, or farm skills, would be the saving grace for immigrant children. These tools would separate the children from the informal economy on which their families relied. It gave them the ability to be employed indoors, away from public spaces.[32]

For Brace, the country was an antidote to the problems of the city. He did not, however, see the country in a romantic light; his writings were not filled with lyrical prose about the benefits of rural lifestyles. Instead, he saw it as a place in need of labor when the city had a glut of unemployed and underemployed people. In his memoir about his work with the CAS, Brace boasted that the "United States have an enormous advantage over all other countries, in the treatment of difficult questions of pauperism and reform, that they possess a practically unlimited area of arable land." He recognized the energy and ingenuity of street urchins and thought these qualities could be better directed on farms, under the guidance of families, rather than in asylums or on the streets. By sending children west, Brace believed that the CAS could have a profound influence in changing their lives and freeing them from the constraints of the environment—both physical and social—that they were growing up in. In his second annual report for the society, Brace explained: "It is a simple plan, but it is capable of forming almost another world for the young city vagrant; the boy or girl who[m] sad fortune brings to birth amid the miasmata of vice and filth, which a city engenders. It gives him pure country air, instead of the gases of sewers, and the exhalations of filthy lodging houses; trees and fields and harvests, in place of the narrow alleys, the drink-cellars, and the thieves' haunts of a poor quarter. It gives him a life, where those around him will further him to virtue and industry, instead of dragging him down." Brace was confident that farmers would have a positive influence on New York's poor. When he placed children from the shanties onto farms, he was doing his part to bring an end to rural land uses within city limits. In doing so, he was working to define a more stable boundary between city and country. Part of New York's problem, in the opinion of Brace and many other bourgeois New Yorkers, was the urban agriculture and informal economy they saw as tied to the lower classes. Their uses of space transgressed the boundaries of what was acceptable in the public space of a refined city.[33]

Brace was not the first reformer to think of training urban children in rural settings. For more than twenty-five years before the Children's Aid Society was founded, reformers in New York sent children into the country. The House of Refuge, for instance, typically placed reformed juvenile delinquents in apprenticeships in the country. The aldermen also established the Long Island Farms in 1832 in what is now Astoria, Queens, where they housed abandoned and orphaned children with the idea that they would do better in a rural setting, separated from the adult poor in the almshouse. Brace continued this tradition, but took it a step further by sending children into semi-permanent arrangements outside the city, with the general goal of dispersing part of the poor population into the West. This was part of a larger cultural movement that saw the West as a safety valve for the social unrest in eastern cities.

While most advocates of western migration could only suggest it as an option for the poor, Brace was actively making it happen through his placing-out system.[34]

Brace's goals for the city were attractive to bourgeois New Yorkers. Through the refining of poor boys and girls in his industrial schools and the dispersal of children into the countryside, the city streets would ideally become a more orderly place, with fewer people picking through the trash, fewer hawkers, street sweepers, and beggars on the street corners pestering passersby, and fewer shanties on the outskirts of the city. Crime and the threat of revolution and riot would diminish, and if the children returned to the city, they would have the training and social skills necessary to rise above their parents' station. At stake was who had control over public space. Taking control of the streets was a means to define boundaries between public and private, urban and rural, rich and poor. There was a strong element of paternalistic elitism behind Brace's earnest conviction that the CAS was improving the lives of poor children. In his eyes, bourgeois values and habits could save these children and the city from ruin. By properly training these children to join the middle class or by sending them out of the city entirely, public spaces would be brought under control and urban order restored.[35]

The city, Brace argued, did not just need order; it also needed a park for the working class that would help to inspire them. In an article for the *New-York Tribune* in 1855, he implored elite New Yorkers to open their hearts to the plight of the working man, who did not have the luxury to escape to the country each weekend or the leisure time to enjoy concerts at night. The poor who crowded the city's slums were not another species, as many seemed to assume: "In each worn, overworked body, is the same heart as in you and me. Music is as sweet to their ears—the rustle of summer leaves, the splash of fountains, the glimmer of sunlight as pleasant to them as to us." Yet they needed a space in the city that was accessible and that could accommodate their growing numbers. A large public park, Brace wrote, would not only allow these citizens to breathe fresh air, but would also improve their cultural tastes. "One of the elevating influences most needed in our City, is a Park for the working classes; grounds where statuary, and flowers, and objects of beauty, should call away some, at least, of the crowd from rum-shops, and gambling-halls, and prize-fights." Brace believed that *"the taste for a higher pleasure is the best means for eradicating the taste for a lower."* Just as coming into contact with the upper classes of New York might help to elevate the impoverished, so too might an appreciation for a beautiful, rural landscape.[36]

The Lungs of the City

Charles Loring Brace was not the first to call for a new park for the city. In fact, when he wrote that article in 1855, a campaign had been underway for a decade and the city government had already chosen the site that would become Central Park. As early as the 1840s, cultural figures, gentlemen, and politicians had been advocating for a park that would fulfill New York's "manifest destiny" and provide the city not only with a monument to its magnificence, but also with "lungs" to preserve the public health from the increasing density of the social and built environment. The small parks downtown were measly compared to what the city's burgeoning population required.[37]

Park advocates wrote extensively about the city's need for breathing space. Suffocated by the crowdedness of the city, and having felt the blows of two waves of cholera, many were desperate to secure the health of the city. "More than a million lungs are hard at work day and night," wrote the *New-York Daily Times*, "respiring the city's air, many of them in lanes crowded to excess, and buildings bursting with repletion. We have no competent breathing-place." If the city was a living organism, it was sick. The solution?

Let us infuse a little more Country into our City. Let our eyes be rejoiced by resting upon something else than interminable rows of brick and freestone. Let us have a place richly equipped with natural

beauty and verdant, in the midst of this present aridity—embosomed
in foliage and filled with fragrant air to tempt us from our too en-
grossing pursuits—well kept and guarded; and within its shaded
precincts, the loveliest artistic creations—where genius may bring
its offerings, and Nature and Art blend together to work out images
of serene and placid beauty—open equally to rich and poor—
contributing alike to the pleasure and improvement of the sick and
the well, the man of leisure and the man of work.

Rural landscapes, the editors argued, would save the city from its unhealthy downfall. The *New York Herald* published a similar plea. The
"unnatural mortality" of the city, the editor insisted, was a sign that
change was needed. While the commissioners who laid out the grid in
1811 had seen the rivers as a distinct benefit for the city's health to the
point that they avoided reserving park space, the rivers were now a liability: "The masses of people are shut off from the country by an intervening river on either hand." With neighboring cities growing ever more
populous, the country was disappearing. Suffocating from urbanization, the editor pleaded: "Give us oxygen. Give us that great central
park." A park would save the city's public health and culture, while
benefiting *all* New Yorkers, "rich and poor."[38]

The conviction that the park would benefit the working class was a
typical refrain. Andrew Jackson Downing—landscape architect, editor
of the *Horticulturist,* and friend of Frederick Law Olmsted—was one of
the early proponents of the park. Along with other advocates, including
William Cullen Bryant and Horace Greeley, Downing believed that
the park would help to civilize the lower classes, thus benefiting not
only their neighbors but also democracy in general. A landscaped park,
he argued, would help to raise the "social civilization and social culture" of Americans. "The higher social and artistic elements of every
man's nature lie dormant within him," he continued, "and every laborer
is a possible gentleman, not by the possession of money or fine clothes—
but through the refining influence of intellectual and moral culture."

As politicians continued to fight over the prospects of an uptown park, their pleas were made much more compelling when they included the needs of the lower classes. At one point, when Mayor Ambrose Kingsland was fighting for the park's survival amid political clamor, he declared to the Common Council that the city's investment in a large park would bring rich returns in the form of "health, happiness, and comfort of those whose interest are specially intrusted to our keeping— the poorer classes." Whether strategically crafted political rhetoric or earnestly espoused belief, the notion that a park could benefit the city's poor had gained traction by the middle of the nineteenth century.[39]

The idea that parks could help to raise the lower classes out of their filthy homes and jobs picking through the trash and bring them closer to the culture of elite New Yorkers was a philosophy that had developed in the two decades since the park boom of the 1830s. By the 1850s the city's poverty was significantly more visible, in the form of the omnipresent ragpickers, the growing belt of shantytowns, and the increased focus of journalists and other writers on neighborhoods like Five Points. While 1830s New Yorkers were certainly concerned about poverty, it had not seemed as threatening to them as it did to New Yorkers in the 1850s. Of course, as with the earlier parks, many of the benefits a park would bring to elite New Yorkers drove the campaign for Central Park. For instance, speculators and landowners of the surrounding property stood to profit handsomely from the rise in property values, even though they would have to pay significant assessments. Wealthy New Yorkers hoped to use Central Park as a refined space, where it would be safe for women to move freely and for the "Upper Ten" to promenade and display their wealth. The idea that this would be a space for the working class, however, was new, and to many critics these uses were completely incompatible. The designers and proponents of the park wrestled with balancing these competing interests in an attempt to make their goals a reality.[40]

Ironically, though many supporters touted the benefits for the working class, few members of the working class were outspoken supporters of the park. Horace Greeley, in his *New-York Daily Tribune,* lamented that those who had taken an interest in the park were a "mere handful of liberal, foreseeing men—of philanthropists and artists." They worked to procure park space "without any aid from the masses for whom they have thus labored." Frustrated, Greeley called on members of the working class to throw their support behind the park. While he may have overestimated the power that the masses had in affecting the outcome of the park, Greeley was correct in noting that the park had become the project of elite politicians, landholders, newspaper editors, and other outspoken reformers such as Brace, Olmsted, and Downing.[41]

The site for Central Park was not the first choice of these elite politicians and advocates. Initially, the mayor and aldermen focused on Jones Woods on the East River between 66th and 75th streets. Comprising 150 acres, Jones Woods included the two country estates of the Jones and Schermerhorn families, who were unwilling to sell. Through a technicality in court, they were able to block the acquisition of their property when the city and the state attempted to assert eminent domain. As a result, in 1852 the Special Committee on Parks recommended a more central location between 59th and 106th streets, Fifth and Eighth avenues. A portion of this land was already owned by the city, including the Croton receiving reservoir and the proposed site of another reservoir. In addition, the price for the remaining acreage would be kept low, advocates promised, because of the rugged topography. Its large rocky outcroppings were matched by low swampy marshes. Central Park was, essentially, marginal land. The Board of Aldermen reported that "Central Park will include grounds almost entirely useless for building purposes, owing to the very uneven and rocky surface, and also to its lying so far below the proper grade of the streets as to render the grading very costly." Political advocates used the marginal qualities of the land to sell the park to opponents—not only would the land be less expensive, but it would also have been very difficult to develop. Not much, in other words, would be lost by setting aside this land. Although park administrators would later grumble over the difficulty of planting the acreage with lush verdure, the effort required made the transformation all the more dramatic and inspiring.[42]

As was true in other parts of the island, marginal land was attractive to poor New Yorkers looking to find an unused spot in the city to call home. The southern reaches of the park were dotted with piggeries, shanties, and bone-boiling establishments, primarily owned by Irish and German immigrants. A well-established, mainly African American community known as Seneca Village, with churches, cemeteries, and a school, lay north of that, between 82nd and 87th streets, near Eighth Avenue. Other homes and businesses were scattered throughout the rest of the park property. Despite the existence of these neighborhoods, several early government documents describing the park completely ignore them. In an 1852 report for the Board of Aldermen, the Special Committee on Parks informed them that there were "very few improvements, such as private dwelling-houses." Similarly, Mayor Fernando Wood, in defending the size of the park, declared that it was an "almost uninhabited part of the island." By downplaying the presence of homes, politicians glossed over the number of victims who would be affected, making it easier to pass the legislation necessary to build the park.[43]

When the park's engineer-in-chief, Egbert Viele, set out to survey the land, the reports he presented to the Central Park Board of Commissioners made no mention of the park's residents. Mapping the site was perhaps the first step toward making the land legible and consequently conquerable. Viele divided the park into four divisions and had the surveyors write up specific reports on the state of each section. Not one of these reports mentioned the communities located on the uneven marshy land in the south or on the higher, more evenly graded land of Seneca Village. The reports were written as if the surveyors were examining the site from a map rather than on the ground. The residents were an afterthought. Yet Viele was very aware of the people in the park. The buildings were missing from early surveyor maps, but by the time Viele

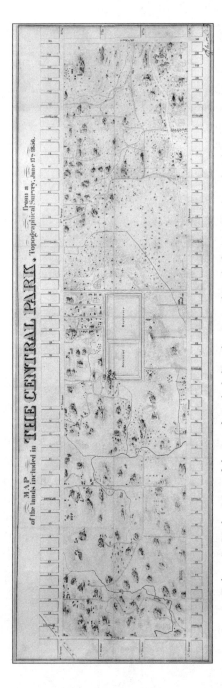

FIGURE 30. Egbert L. Viele, *Map of the Lands Included in the Central Park, from a Topographical Survey, June 17, 1856.* The map shows the many homes and businesses of park residents, including Seneca Village just west of the reservoir. (Collection of the New-York Historical Society.)

submitted his survey in the summer of 1856, he had included the structures along with the trees and topographic features.[44]

Viele was not fond of the park residents. Later in life, he recounted that "the entire ground was the refuge of about five thousand squatters, dwelling in rude huts of their own construction, and living off the refuse of the city, which they daily conveyed in small carts, chiefly drawn by dogs, from the lower part of the city." Viele was offended by their lack of "knowledge of the English language," and their disrespect for the law. "Like the ancient Gauls, they wanted land to live on, and they took it; and, like the Gauls, they prepared to defend their occupancy at the very suggestion of its invasion, no matter by whom. Such was the danger of the situation, that the designer of the park was compelled to go armed while making his studies, and, in addition to this, to carry an ample supply of deodorizers." Though Viele likely exaggerated the threat in the same way that he exaggerated the number of squatters in order to play up his heroism, there was reason for the park residents to resist the intrusion of surveyors onto the property around their homes. Those who did not own the land where they resided stood to lose everything without any compensation. The city was responsible only for remunerating the landowners, and while many of the Seneca Village residents owned their property, the Irish communities to the south were made up of lessees and squatters. The surveyors acted as the face of the government that was evicting the residents from their homes. In addition to whatever compelled Viele to tour the park armed, residents performed nonviolent acts of resistance by pulling up the surveyors' stakes and making it more difficult for the city to take complete control of the park.[45]

Residents were wise to be suspicious of visitors' motives. When writers from the *New York Herald* took a tour of the park in 1856, they did so with the specific aim of not only describing the park but also interviewing its inhabitants. "Our appearance among this farming population, as we drove up hills, and down valleys and through places where wheeled vehicles had never dared venture, produced quite a sensation.

FIGURE 31. Photograph of land slated to be flooded for Central Park, ca. 1857. The clusters of houses and farms threatened by plans for the park are visible on the horizon. (Collection of the New-York Historical Society.)

They seemed to be thoroughly pested up in regard to the great Central park and the designs of the city upon their little plantations, and evidently regarded our presence among them as the beginning of the invasion which was to end in their total expulsion." The writers approached a German gardener, whom they described as a "burly looking agriculturist," and complimented his garden. Skeptical about their intentions, the man angrily retorted: "Vat you say 'bout mine garden?" He continued to ready himself for the defense of his property and ended the conversation by telling them not to take away his land. As was common in many of the papers during this period, the *Herald* playfully and condescendingly transcribed the conversation in broken, heavily accented English, underscoring the difference between its readers and the foreigners its reporters were interviewing. This likely helped to temper whatever sympathy a reader might have felt for the soon-to-be-evicted farmer. The trope of a farmer being forcibly evicted had the potential to be particularly compelling, especially due to the expected deep connection between a farmer and his land, but the *Herald* was able to transform this reaction by emphasizing the foreignness and irrational aggression of the man being interviewed. While papers might make arguments against the park because of tax increases or the fact that land was being taken off the market, they were not about to use the plight of the residents as a reason to hold back the project.[46]

The government and newspaper reports that mentioned the park residents made their lifestyles seem so foreign and lowly that they might as well have been intruders standing in the way of civilization. They were, it seemed, pests needing eradication. The Board of Commissioners described the parkland at the time of its purchase as "part of [the city's] straggling suburbs, and a suburb more filthy, squalid and disgusting can hardly be imagined." The author of an 1864 guidebook to the park referred to the region as one of the city's "most unlovely suburbs," filled with "tribes of squalid city barbarians." Though some of the residents cultivated market gardens, reports typically focused more on the nuisances and public health threats posed by the communities, such as the proliferation of domestic animals and foul-smelling offal-boiling plants. "If some of the hogs, goats, and other inmates of the shanties in this vicinity do not die of the yellow fever this Summer," the editor of the *New York Times* wrote, "it will only be because Death himself hesitates to enter such dirty hovels." Writers also emphasized that the residents were squatters, even though 20 percent actually owned their land and others had formal and informal arrangements with the landowners. By calling them squatters, newspapers and government officials could gain more support for their removal.[47]

Less attention was paid to Seneca Village, probably because destroying their more established working- and middle-class neighborhood would not have fit so neatly into the clearance literature as did the hodgepodge, illegal wooden shanties filled with animals and barefooted Irishmen. One of the few articles that mentioned the African American community described it admirably. The "neat *little settlement,* known

FIGURE 32 AND 33. *Harper's Weekly* published these illustrations of the shantytown residents in which their "otherness" is signaled by their bare-footedness, languor, and closeness with animals. From "The Central Park," *Harper's Weekly*, November 28, 1857. (Beinecke Rare Book and Manuscript Library, Yale University.)

as 'Nigger Village' " contrasted nicely with the Irish shanties filled with hogs and goats, according to the *New York Times*. Yet the writer for the *Times* did not hide his condescension: "The policemen find it difficult to persuade them out of the idea which has possessed their simple minds, that the sole object of the authorities in making the Park is to procure their expulsion from the homes which they occupy. It is hoped that their removal will be effected with as much gentleness as possible." Faced with racism throughout the city, African Americans had established Seneca Village far from the city's center in 1825, two years before slavery ended in New York State. It included the largest collection of African American landowners in the city. Over the decades, the community had expanded to include several Irish and German families. Seneca Village's three churches—the Episcopalian All Angels' Church, the AME Zion Church, and the African Union—served many of the nearly 250 local residents. All Angels' Church, which had begun as a mission project of St. Michael's Church in 1833, had transformed into a regular place of worship by 1849. Its minister reported that "white and black and all intermediate shades worshipped harmoniously together" in his church. Residents had already faced eviction when the city purchased the land for the Croton Reservoir, just to their east. In 1853 the city was in the process of acquiring land to their north for a new reservoir, which involved the eviction of still more nearby park residents. To the residents of Seneca Village, this was the third in a series of incursions into their neighborhood by the government.[48]

Once the state authorized the acquisition of park lands and buildings through eminent domain in 1853, everything began to change. Though residents were able to stay in their homes for four more years, their ability to use the land as they once had began to diminish. In the spring of 1856, the newly organized Central Park police force took up residence in a "neat little Station-house" on 86th Street, in the middle of the park. With the authority of an ordinance approved by Mayor Fernando Wood, Captain Bennett and his corps of twenty men helped to lead the survey of residents so that the city could collect rent from those who chose to stay. The police also began arresting people who used the park's resources. While residents had previously harvested fuel from nearby trees, such an act was now considered "plundering." The police posted signs on fences throughout the park, alerting residents and trespassers to the law. Since the park was desperately in need of trees, administrators now saw a formerly common practice as intolerable: the "rapacious occupants of the cabins" were aggressively attacking the nascent park. By the summer, the force had expanded to thirty-one men, with a night patrol to monitor the "nocturnal depredations that have been so frequent on the grounds." Even with the expanded force, however, the Board of Commissioners had a difficult time maintaining control over how the park's resources were used.[49]

A year later, as the summer of 1857 approached, many residents began asking if they could renew their leases. Those who had cultivated market gardens had "spent considerable sums of money for manures" and had expended a great deal of labor in preparing the ground. If evicted, they would not recoup their investment at harvest time. Though their plight inspired sympathy, the Board of Commissioners' Committee on Buildings in the Park found many of the other residents troublesome. The residents who kept pigs, goats, dogs, and cows, for instance, allowed them to run at large in the park, "destroying the trees and otherwise injuring the public property in our charge." Other lessees included those who ran foundries, ropewalks (long, covered walks or buildings where ropes were made), and bone-boiling establishments— all industries that were inappropriate downtown because of their size or their threat to public safety and health. The committee added that keeping these industries would not produce enough profit to counter their annoyance, especially given the "class of person who are employed in them." Some residents had begun to enclose lands for grazing illegally, while milkmen and others from elsewhere in the city pastured "their cattle within the bounds, using it as a common, and doing great injury." Downtown horse owners, whose animals were about to die, also set them out to pasture in the parklands. The committee warned that more staff was needed to take charge of the park and sell the extant buildings. Chief engineer Egbert Viele reiterated this point in a report to the commissioners a few months later. While there had been a proposal to house policemen and their families in the vacated shanties, he dismissed this as a bad idea. "Until the ground ceases to be occupied as residences," he wrote, "it will not be a public Park." He urged the commissioners to evict the residents, clear the buildings, enclose the park, and establish a public pound so that they could "keep it free from trespassers."[50]

That September, the residents' eviction was settled. The *New York Times* triumphantly reported that "the kingdom of shantydom, which has long been dominant in that region, is to be swept away." The city uprooted park residents just as the Panic of 1857 was setting in. The Board of Commissioners sold any shanty that was not dismantled by its owners and, with just a few exceptions, workers cleared the park of what was left of its more than 300 buildings, preparing it for the massive transformation about to take place. Problems with free-roaming livestock persisted, but the new public pound helped to ease the situation.[51]

Just two weeks after the final eviction of the park residents, the Board of Commissioners announced a design competition for the park. Frederick Law Olmsted, who had served under Viele as the park's superintendent for a few months, applied in partnership with Calvert Vaux, an English landscape architect, who had worked with the recently deceased park advocate Andrew Jackson Downing. The "Greensward Plan" that they designed followed in the tradition of English landscape design, something that Olmsted had admired during his European trip. The aesthetic, championed by Downing in *The Horticulturist,* involved creating a landscape that appeared as if it had been crafted by Mother Nature rather than by man. Art was not just an imitation of nature, but *"an expressive, harmonious, and refined imitation."* By the

1850s, cutting-edge landscape design was moving away from formal gardens based on symmetry and sculpture and toward this more natural design, with undulating hills, irregularly shaped lakes, and natural tree formations. The park encompassed the ideals of a rural landscape without the pitfalls of its reality. There would be no impoverished farmers or unruly domestic animals, just paths through picturesque fields and wooded areas with a scattering of mainly decorative buildings. Central Park was to be a truly rural retreat from urban life. By incorporating a significant dose of open, green space, the city could continue to expand at its current pace without fear that it would lack breathing room.[52]

Central Park was a completely rewritten landscape. In the "Greensward Plan" that Olmsted and Vaux submitted for the competition, they included several sepia-toned photographs of the park's current condition, taken by famed photographer Matthew Brady, along with lush artistic renderings of the landscape they envisioned on that site. One of the photographs showed evidence of residents' agriculture, with a stone wall separating tilled land divided into neatly arranged rows. This was not the rural landscape, however, that Olmsted and Vaux were after; Vaux's painting of the "effect preferred" shows a verdant tree-lined lake in place of the farms. Olmsted and Vaux promised a return to an idealized landscape—reforested, beautified, and cleared of all evidence of its previous occupants.[53]

Political struggles between the city and state played a significant role in Olmsted's initial appointment as superintendent, and it likely also played a partial role in the selection of Olmsted and Vaux's "Greensward Plan." In his uncompleted autobiography "Passages in the Life of an Unpractical Man," Olmsted recounted how one of the Central Park commissioners, Charles Elliott, had encouraged him to apply for the superintendent position, as he was a Republican but not a practicing politician—something that would have made him palatable to the Democrats on the commission. At the time, the city government, which had been dominated by Democrats, was emerging from a series

EFFECT PROPOSED.

FIGURE 34 AND 35. Images from the Central Park competition entry by Frederick Law Olmsted and Calvert Vaux. The photograph shows evidence of park residents' farms in the tilled fields and stonewalls. The painting, by Vaux, which depicts the proposed landscape, illustrates a completely different type of rural ideal, one that is at odds with the rural reality it replaced. (Courtesy of the NYC Municipal Archives.)

of corruption scandals, and its powers were deeply fragmented by the state-designed city charters of 1849 and 1853. The Republican state legislature used its power to take over some city functions, including the governance of the new Central Park, in a supposedly nonpartisan way. The legislators appointed eleven commissioners, six of whom were Republicans, four were Democrats, and one was a Know Nothing. By pursuing Olmsted, the Republican commissioners hoped to gain more control of the park, given that in a show of nonpartisanship they had appointed Democrats as their president, treasurer, and engineer-in-chief (Viele). When they were judging the thirty-three entries for the design competition, artistic merit and practicality certainly took precedence, but politics continued to play an important role. This was evident from the political affiliations of those who voted for Olmsted and Vaux's plan: all six Republicans and just one Democrat. Along with the adoption of the Greensward Plan in the spring of 1858, the board ousted Viele and appointed Olmsted architect-in-chief. For a man who had worked as a sailor, merchant, farmer, and writer, this was a career-changing moment for Olmsted, who would gain fame for his work in landscape design. With his new powers as architect-in-chief, Olmsted leaped at the opportunity to transform New York's society through his work in the park.[54]

Olmsted embraced the philosophy espoused by Downing, the newspaper editors, and his friend Charles Loring Brace that parks could have a positive influence on lower-class New Yorkers while also serving as a space for their wealthier neighbors. "The Park," wrote Olmsted, "is intended to furnish healthful recreation for the poor and the rich, the young and the old, the vicious and the virtuous." Just as Brace hoped to bring the classes together in the industrial schools of the Children's Aid Society, Olmsted envisioned doing the same in Central Park. A space where classes could meet would not only elevate members of the lower class by cultivating their love of beauty and rural landscapes, but would also help to bridge the deepening chasm between the classes. Olmsted seemed to harbor a sincere hope that the park would be a tool to create a better republic. He believed that the upper class had a responsibility to raise those beneath them to higher standards, primarily through education. This paternalistic role was central not only in slaveholding states, but also in the North. Central Park was his way of serving society and civilizing the "uncivilized" lower class. The Board of Commissioners year after year continued to boast that Central Park could influence all New Yorkers regardless of class and "convey very positive ideas in regard to natural scenery, even to a person who might never see anything more country-like than will ultimately be contained within its limits." Central Park was just the dose of country that the city needed.[55]

Not everyone was confident that this melding of classes would work, however. While workers were still in the process of clearing the park for development, James Gordon Bennett published an editorial in the *New York Herald* in which he fueled the fear that Central Park would be controlled by the "lower denizens of the city." He claimed that public parks worked well in European cities because the social hierarchy there was clearly defined and "no annoyance is caused to the peasant if he be excluded from the places haunted by his recognized 'superiors.'" The European nobility could keep the "vulgar" out of their parks by "simply stationing watchmen at the gates, with directions not to admit the 'lower orders.'" In America, however, Bennett claimed that the social order had been upended, and "Sam the Five Pointer is as good a man as William B. Astor or Edward Everett." If the city opened a public park, therefore, "Sam will air himself in it. He will take his friends, whether from Church street [Five Points] or else where. He will enjoy himself there, whether by having a muss, or a drink at the corner groggery opposite the great gate. He will run races with his new horse in the carriage way. He will knock any better dressed man down who remonstrates with him. He will talk and sing, and fill his share of the bench, and flirt with the nursery girls in his own coarse way." What hope did gentlemen like William B. Astor and Edward Everett have of enjoying such a place? Bennett fanned the flames of this class anxiety by announcing that German lager dealers and Irish groggery owners were in the process of purchasing the property surrounding the park. Central Park, he argued, was devolving into "nothing but a huge beer garden"—"the greatest of all blunders of our city improvements." *Harper's Weekly* accepted Bennett's prediction, and called on the "power of the leading capitalists of the city" to purchase the property around the park. "If the lager beer dealers are allowed their own way, it will soon be undistinguishable from the slums, and the benefit of the Central Park will be lost to the rich, the peaceable, and the well disposed."[56]

Olmsted was offended by these critiques, calling them the "fallacy of cowardly conservatism." He steadfastly believed that the park could be a public space peacefully used by all classes, particularly if it was well regulated. Olmsted actively tried to recruit journalists to tour the park, in order to disprove the theory that the rich and poor could not successfully share a space. Henry W. Bellows published an article in 1861 in the *Atlantic Monthly* that was sympathetic to Olmsted's mission. Bellows assured readers that "so thoroughly established is the good conduct of people on the park, that many ladies walk daily in the Ramble without attendance." Alongside Mr. Astor, the park induced "many a poor family, and many a poor seamstress and journeyman," to maintain their relationship with "purer Nature" while also improving their "strength, good humor, and safe citizenship." Bellows tried to dispel the anxiety that the classes could not share Central Park, embracing Olmsted's vision instead. The bourgeois could be assured that the lower class was surprisingly quiet, well-behaved, and civil on park grounds.[57]

In order to keep the space from slipping out of the positive influence of New York's elite, careful policing was necessary. As early as 1853, when the park was still merely an idea, the state senators who were considering the practicalities of a large public space assumed that the space would need to be heavily policed in order to remain safe for "unprotected ladies—for children and young persons—for the sick and infirm, and the aged." While European cities had police forces "sufficiently strong to keep these great and desirable accessories to city life and comfort in good order—to guard them from annoying vagrants," New York lacked comparable protection. Olmsted fully embraced the need to police the park, not only for its routine maintenance and the protection of its plantings, but also to control the way visitors used the space. His enthusiasm for this control was so immense that his partner Calvert Vaux bitterly referred to him as "Frederick the Great, Prince of the Park Police." Olmsted's governance over park visitors' behavior began with his control of the police officers and sergeants themselves. He wrote a set of rules and conditions meant to govern when they could speak, what they would wear, and how they should walk. Olmsted also required that they never drink, even when off duty, and subjected them to military drills and discipline. The park police received authority from the city's Metropolitan Police Commissioners, but were paid by the park fund and recruited from the maintenance and construction workers employed on the park. Olmsted's dream of influencing the city's lower classes through the park was extended through his control of the men serving on the park police. Not only would they represent the park to visitors, but they too would be refined through the discipline and proper behavior he required of them.[58]

Olmsted governed Central Park as if it were a city within the city. The park had a set of ordinances separate from the city's that governed the behavior of visitors and kept things respectable. Published in the newspapers, posted throughout the park, and kept in the pockets of the police force, the park's ordinances were intended to "protect the plants and other property, guard against accidents, and otherwise aid the superintendence" of the public space. While some of the ordinances governed traffic and the proper use of the carriage roads and pedestrian paths, other rules seemed specifically aimed at controlling lower-class visitors. The ordinances sent the message that the park was not a commons. No one was permitted to turn cattle, goats, horses, or swine out into the park to graze. Similarly, hunting was declared illegal by the ordinance restricting visitors from carrying firearms. Olmsted kept visitors from harvesting fuel and building materials by making it illegal to "cut, break, or in any way injure or deface the trees, shrubs, plants, turf, or any of the buildings, fences, bridges, or other constructions upon the Park." The resources could not be *used* by the public; they could only be appreciated. These formerly acceptable uses of the land were now completely incompatible with the mission and function of the park. Olmsted and the commissioners added new ordinances as necessary, such as a law against picking flowers, fruit and nuts, a law against annoying birds, and laws preventing people from bathing and fishing in the park's lakes and ponds. Olmsted remained actively in control of the police force during his tenure with Central Park.[59]

Olmsted saw the police force as essential to the success of the park's mission. While the apparent need for these laws is proof that the space remained contested, Central Park was a highly controlled space. By closely regulating how people used the park, Olmsted preserved elite New Yorkers' control of the space. As Olmsted and the Board of Commissioners wrote in 1861, "The preservation of order on the Park, and its exemption from the presence of influences that would render it a disagreeable or unsafe resort for all classes of society, is of the very first importance, and requires constant vigilance, as, if it is not well understood that disorder or obscenity on the Park are promptly punished, the virtuous and orderly will be banished from it." A public space intended to welcome rich and poor alike had to be carefully regulated in order to keep all visitors comfortable—or at least in the eyes of Olmsted and the commissioners, to keep the *bourgeois* visitors comfortable. By preventing unrefined uses of parkland, whether this meant the harvesting of food and fuel or the use of water, Olmsted and the commissioners hoped to instill elite values and sensibilities in lower-class visitors. New York's elite certainly should have felt comfortable in the park. Crime was very low, and the elite uses of park space had triumphed. The promenade was one of the first features that the workers completed. Visitors commented on the "gay equipages occupied by the beauty and fashion of the upper-ten portion of the community." Even if the poor were welcomed into the space, Central Park catered to the fashions and needs of the city's wealthy denizens, those who had the loudest voices in government and the fullest representation on the park's Board of Commissioners. The poor were welcome in the park, but only if they respected the rules. Olmsted believed that policing tamed the park and its visitors.[60]

Ironically, though politicians, advocates, and its designers celebrated Central Park as a democratic space, the park police had to dispossess hundreds of people from their homes in order to make that space possible. This magnificent public works project that has remained the pride of the city for over 150 years was not a generically benevolent public good. It had its share of victims, from the residents of Hogtown, Seneca Village, and the other shanties scattered throughout the park, to the lower-class residents living just outside the park who were forced to sell their homes or abandon their leases because of the high assessments levied against their property in order to finance the public space. For the most part, the park police were able to eliminate the foraging, hunting, grazing, and wood harvesting that had been so common on the park lands before its conversion. Using military precision, the police, the commissioners, and Olmsted hoped to turn the park into an elegant, bourgeois space meant to assimilate poor and foreign New Yorkers.

Central Park was a space where Olmsted hoped to introduce the peace of a rural landscape into New York's urban chaos. Yet these carefully orchestrated elements of rural life—the undulating hills, the lakes, and the breathing room—eliminated the urban agriculture that had been thriving in the form of market gardens, piggeries, and grazing spaces. The rural antidote for urban ills came at the expense of what was truly rural about the city. What survived was an elite ideal of rural life, something more akin to country estates than working farms. The artificial rural landscape no longer contained chickens, swine, cows, or goats but rather was home to increasing numbers of exotic animals, such as coypu, cockatoos, and ant bears, donated by wealthy New Yorkers and foreigners. New Yorkers also donated animals that would

enhance the impression that this was a landscape suitable for the elite—
animals such as deer, swans, and foxes. Some of the animals that survived found a home in the new zoo, while others were set free in the
park. These animals were part of the image the commissioners and elite
New Yorkers were hoping to cultivate, and the domestic animals that
the poor had relied on had no part in this imagery. By 1864 the commissioners would introduce a flock of sheep onto the Sheep Meadow,
but again, this was mainly to cultivate a pastoral ideal.[61]

Central Park was as much a social experiment as it was a rural antidote to New York's urbanity. Whether Olmsted and the commissioners succeeded in fostering democracy through the meeting of rich and
poor among the rolling hills and lush landscapes is less important than
the fact that they, like Brace and other like-minded reformers of this
period, felt that they could influence the city's social conditions through
the control of its environment. They believed that control was within
their reach. By writing ordinances and hiring police, and by introduc-
ing specific ingredients to the park that were meant to perfect the rural
image, Olmsted intended to educate and train the masses while also
giving them a space in which they could recreate and breathe.

Brace and Olmsted were earnest in their determination to lift up the
city's poor through their projects. They saw social relations in the city
as increasingly tense and unsustainable. For Brace, the country served
as a safety valve to release some of the pressure by dispersing the poor.
For Olmsted, the country could be infused into the city in the form of
a park that would give visitors a psychological and cultural respite from
the unceasing activity on the city's streets. The park would be a place
for those who could not afford to escape to the country to catch their
breath, especially during the unhealthy summer months. There were
countless immigrants who rioted, flooded the ballot boxes, and seemed
content to lay claim to and build shanties on others' property in the
city's increasingly unattractive suburbs, while sifting through garbage

for a living. Brace and Olmsted believed that these problems could be solved in part if the city's poor would just embrace bourgeois values and cultures. Certainly there was arrogance in this view, but they also had sympathy for the plight of the poor, as was especially true of Brace.

Both the Children's Aid Society and Central Park were projects that bypassed the troubled municipal government. Brace, Olmsted, and those they worked with found it more effective to control public space and those within it by finding power elsewhere. The municipal government was struggling not only with an antagonistic state legislature, but also with its own corruption and the massive urbanization transforming the city. With the local government leaning heavily toward the Democrats, who were supported in large part by immigrants, those who had elite visions for the city's public space found power through privately funded philanthropic organizations like the CAS or through state-controlled public works projects like Central Park. At a time when it seemed to elite New Yorkers that their power was threatened by the urban masses and their unregulated use of the environment, they found alternative ways to transform the city in their own image. The danger of these solutions that circumvented the municipal government was that they removed lower-class representation from decisions on how the urban environment would be shaped, at least in political forums. This might have been exactly what was attractive to the reformers.

Brace and Olmsted sought to make New York's public spaces safer and more refined in a way that dismissed alternative uses of the land by the urban poor. By implementing these changes, the two believed that they were making the city more democratic. Despite the problems facing the city government, Brace and Olmsted were interested in the expansion of government's role in Americans' lives. In 1853, just as Brace was beginning his work with the Children's Aid Society, Olmsted wrote him a letter telling him to "go ahead with the Children's Aid and get up parks, gardens, music, dancing schools, reunions which will be so attractive as to force into contact the good & bad, the gentlemanly and the rowdy. And the state ought to assist these sort of things as it does

Schools and Agricultural Societies." Olmsted argued that a democratic government's job was not only to preserve a democratic distribution of power, but also to foster democracy socially. Accordingly, the government should take proactive steps to foster social cohesion by supporting the arts in a way that would bring all New Yorkers together. Neither man was personally interested in subverting the local government or eliminating its power. Brace probably saw more room for growth and outreach in the world of public pleas and private philanthropic donations, without the political maneuverings of mayors and aldermen. As the state legislature was negotiating its control over the Central Park Board of Commissioners, Olmsted had little power in the situation. Yet however frustrated he may have been with the political pressure on the park's hiring practices, he would have had an incredibly difficult time exerting the kind of control he sought if the park's administration had been tied directly to local constituents.[62]

Central Park was a physical manifestation of the government's growing power. Despite the awkward power struggle between the city and the state, the two, in concert, were in the process of taking enormous steps to provide public goods for the city, in the form of a professional police force, public schools, clean water, and an impressive public park. Alongside this progress, however, were the losses faced by those New Yorkers who had built wooden shanties on forgotten land and harvested resources from the urban environment. These losses were felt most deeply by those who used the city's resources as their economic safety net.

Brace and Olmsted were both looking to reform the city by taking control of its public spaces. Faced with disorderly shantytowns, immigrants picking through piles of trash, unsightly urban agriculture, rising crime rates, riots, and the threat of class warfare, they chose to educate the poorest New Yorkers so as to instill bourgeois habits and values. Their ideal city would be tamed, with streets clear of visible poverty and refined parks filled with orderly visitors of all classes. Children would be off the streets, slums would be less crowded, the city's suburbs would be more attractive, filthy livestock would be far from the city, and fewer citizens would frequent groggeries and engage in crimes. Some would move west onto farms; others would embrace bourgeois domestic rituals, train for trades or professional jobs, abandon the informal economy, and learn to appreciate the beautiful rural landscape of Central Park.

Epilogue

After barricading the windows and doors with bales of water-soaked newsprint to prevent rioters from setting the building on fire, Horace Greeley and his staff at the *New-York Tribune* offices managed to publish accounts of the Draft Riots erupting at their doorstep and throughout the city. To those who lived through the riots in July 1863, Manhattan was anything but tame. Although the riots had begun as a protest against the federal Conscription Act, which unfairly affected those too poor to pay their way out of it, the rioters quickly expanded their targets to include not just draft offices, but figures of authority, African Americans, and wealthy Republicans. The uprising evolved from a protest into a race riot and class war. The *Tribune* reported that the "vast crowd swayed to and fro, racing first in this direction, then in that, attacking indiscriminately every well-dressed man. The general cry was, 'Down with the rich men.' Three gentlemen talking together on Lex-

FIGURE 36. *Charge of the Police on the Rioters at the "Tribune" Office.* In this image, which is reminiscent of the Piggery War four years earlier, police officers struggle to control rioters protesting the federal Conscription Act in front of the New York Tribune building. From *Harper's Weekly,* August 1, 1863. (Collection of the New-York Historical Society.)

ington avenue were set upon and knocked down, narrowly escaping with their lives." The Draft Riots shook New Yorkers. Though the city was familiar with various forms of rioting and gang violence, the Draft Riots had a different tenor. The number of participants, the level of destruction to public and private property, and the diverse set of victims left a significant impression on those who witnessed the events.[1]

The grievances that brought the rioters out were extensive. The most immediate, of course, was the new draft. Two years into the Civil War, the Lincoln administration faced a dwindling number of volunteers and increasing incidents of desertion from the Union Army. In March 1863 Congress passed the Conscription Act, which immediately enlisted all men between the ages of twenty and forty-five. Their names were called in a lottery, and very few were granted exemptions. They could get out of the draft, though, by finding a substitute or paying a $300 commutation fee. Young, lower-class families who were dependent on the father's income were particularly hard hit. With the urban commons shrinking after decades of laws and reforms, and wartime inflation making necessities even more expensive, many of these families faced serious problems. Though the government used the $300 price tag as a way to cap the fees paid to substitutes, this was prohibitively expensive for working-class people, who perceived the conflict to be a rich man's war but a poor man's fight.[2]

The city's poor and working-class residents were primarily Democrats, and while New York Democrats had mixed feelings about the war, they were less than enthusiastic about the Republican consolidation of power embodied in the Conscription Act. New York's Republicans were most often represented by the city's elite. These included the merchants, the philanthropists, the industrialists—in short, the bosses whom the working class dealt with on a daily basis and the reformers who visited their homes, suggested they send their children out west to live on farms, attempted to shut their groggeries, and instructed them on better housekeeping and personal habits. These abolitionists, Nativists, and Lincoln supporters were often the same New Yorkers who were able to pay their way out of the draft, something their poorer, mainly immigrant, and Democratic neighbors could not do.

In addition, racial tensions were high. The Conscription Act, though it did not mention race directly, affected only "citizens" or, rather, white Americans. Following the Emancipation Proclamation, issued earlier that winter, Democratic orators warned the city's workers that they would be displaced and devalued by an influx of free blacks to New York. Adding to this fear, a shipping company had recently used African Americans to break a strike of Irish longshoremen that spring. In the eyes of these white laborers, wealthy Republicans were forcing them to fight a war to free African Americans who would inevitably make it harder for them to find jobs that were already difficult to come by.[3]

The conditions seemed set for an explosion. Few people expected that the draft would be implemented smoothly. A clerk began pulling names on Saturday, July 11, at the Ninth District headquarters at Third Avenue and 46th Street, directly abutting the Irish and German shanty-towns. By 4:00 P.M. the clerk had called 1,236 names. Conscripted men began assembling in bars and on the streets, to discuss the inequities of the system and how they might protest. Hours before the draft office was set to reopen the following Monday, it was clear that workers for the railroads, factories, foundries, construction sites, and shipyards would fail to show up at their jobs. Half of those building the new reservoir in Central Park missed work to assemble at a meeting in the park with other rioters, who formed into two columns and headed downtown. Volunteer firemen, angered that they had not been exempted from the draft as was customary, sacked and burned the Ninth District headquarters with the draft officers barely escaping. Rioters fanned out across the city, forcing factories to close and pressuring workers to join them. By Monday night, rioters had pulled down telegraph poles, torn up train tracks, disrupted streetcar service, and burned down the Colored Orphan Asylum, sending 237 children rushing out the back door to a police station for protection. That week, rioters beat and lynched African Americans, ransacked their homes, and sent them fleeing into Central Park and station houses. Rioters burned down the homes of the city's wealthy, especially those assumed to be Republicans, stealing their possessions and breaking what they could not take with them. Businesses shut down and criminals took advantage of the chaos to loot. Before federal troops arrived on Thursday, havoc reigned. Vigilante committees formed to protect private property and the lives of citizens, but their power was limited.[4]

While the rioters were mainly Irish immigrants, they also included native-born Americans, Germans, French, and other lower-class New Yorkers. Though not at risk of being drafted themselves, the rioters also included women, as well as men who were too young or too old to have been drafted. Drawn to the battle out of support for the drafted, out of anger at injustices they faced as families and communities, or purely out of excitement for the melee and for having the city's hierarchy turned on its head, thousands joined together in this show of violence and revolt.

The Draft Riots were, in part, a culmination of all the discord and conflicts over public space and the urban environment that had marked the previous half-century. The rioters seem to have included many of the city's piggery owners, swill milk producers, and squatters. Five Points, notorious among contemporaries as a hotbed of disease and unrest, surprisingly did not supply the majority of rioters, perhaps because residents were pro-war Tammany Democrats or perhaps because their community was racially integrated. Most of the rioters instead lived uptown, in the shantytowns and other neighborhoods on the outskirts of the city. Several had faced previous arrests or media attention for violating sanitary regulations. The uptown squatters and piggery owners had been struggling to save their homes and livelihoods in the years leading up to the war, with the development of Central Park and the various attacks on uptown "nuisance" industries, and these resentments perhaps made them even more likely to lash out. Reliant on the urban commons in their efforts to make ends meet, they saw the government and reformers making concerted efforts to push their livelihoods farther and farther from the city. As the urban commons shrank and their tenuous grip on economic stability was further threatened by the draft, rioters expressed their anger against wealthy residents, Republicans, and the government, in addition to African Americans.[5]

The Draft Riots embodied everything that reformers like Charles Loring Brace feared. The chaos and violence made it clear to Brace that more work was needed to assure control of the city. Convinced that an "ignorant, debased, permanently poor class" was the greatest threat to the property and safety of cities, Brace had argued for reform programs that would raise the city's children to middle-class values and culture. The riots added weight to his and other reformers' programs. More than ever, as a result of the Draft Riots, Brace saw communism as a true threat to American society: "All these great masses of destitute, miserable, and criminal persons believe that for ages the rich have had all the good things of life, while to them have been left the evil things. Capital to them is the tyrant." If the wealthy lost control over such people, "we should see an explosion from this class which might leave this city in ashes and blood"—a situation not unlike what he and his contemporaries were witnessing in the Draft Riots. He viewed the rioters as wild animals. During that week, Brace was struck by the "marvelous rapidity with which the better streets were filled with a ruffianly and desperate multitude . . . creatures who seemed to have crept from their burrows and dens to join in the plunder of the city—how quickly houses were marked out for sacking and ruin. . . . It was evident to all careful observers then, that had another day of license been given the crowd, the attack would have been directed at the apparent wealth of the city—the banks, jewelers' shops, and rich private houses." While the rioters had many different aims, as was evident from the "wild and brutal crimes . . . committed on the unoffending negroes," it was the class war that truly shook Brace. In the days, months, and years following the riots, illustrators depicted rioters not only lynching African Americans and shooting over barricades at the army, but also looting and destroying the city's wealthier neighborhoods. In the eyes of Brace and many other elite reformers, serious changes needed to be made if New York had any chance of avoiding further threats to the social order.[6]

Just five months after the riots, a bipartisan group of New York's most "influential citizens" joined together, despite the exceedingly partisan war taking place, to form the Citizens' Association of New York. It included a variety of prominent New Yorkers, from Democrats like August Belmont and Peter Cooper to Republicans like John Jacob Astor and Hamilton Fish—a group of the city's wealthiest men. Calling for widespread municipal reform in terms of public health safeguards, charter revisions, tax policies, and anticorruption measures, the Citizens' Association was driven by the city government's inability to tame the city by preventing social unrest and protecting lives and private property.[7]

The association's Council of Hygiene and Public Health produced a landmark report that catalogued the city's environment in remarkable

FIGURE 37. *The Riot in Lexington Avenue.* Sacking the homes of New York's wealthy, rioters looted possessions, destroyed furniture, and set fires, cementing in the minds of the city's elite the belief that this was as much a class as it was an anti-draft protest and a race war. From J. T. Headley, *The Great Riots of New York, 1712 to 1873* (New York: E. B. Treat, 1873), 169. (Collection of the New-York Historical Society.)

detail and gave hope to reformers that control of the city's conditions would have significant social benefits. The council formed a team of twenty-nine physicians who volunteered to serve temporarily as sanitary inspectors for the entire city. Collecting an immense amount of data on New York's inhabitants and environment, the inspectors compiled a report that laid out the city's major problems and proposed solutions. Despite all the progress that had been made in the previous half-century, the inspectors still faced what they saw as an uncontrolled urban environment. The physicians concluded that the city's filth not only created dangerous public health threats, such as epidemics and high mortality rates, but had serious social repercussions as well. While reformers such as Brace had already been working to change the environmental conditions that they believed fostered poverty, the Draft Riots spurred New York's elite to consider the consequences of failing to improve the lives and conditions of their poor neighbors. "The elements of popular discord," "social evils," and "unholy passions," the Council of Hygiene argued, were embedded in the wretched filth and ramshackle housing of the city's impoverished neighborhoods. Ensuring peace, prosperity, and the safety of people's property meant addressing these issues head on. Ezra R. Pulling, a surgeon who volunteered to inspect the Fourth Ward, argued in his report that his subjects were the victims of their environment: "The terrible elements of society we saw brought to the surface during a great popular outbreak, are equally in existence at the present moment; nay, more, they are increasing year by year. The tocsin which next summons them from their dark and noisome haunts may be the prelude to a scene of universal pillage, slaughter, and destruction. We must reap that which we sow. Pestilence and crime are fungi of hideous growth, which spring up side by side from such pollution as we allow to rankle in our midst." From the perspective of the Citizens' Association, the city government was not intervening in any significant way to control this physical and social pollution, so private citizens would have to do the legwork necessary to make this control possible.[8]

In order to gain the information they needed to fully catalogue the city's condition, the inspectors had to enter the homes and spaces of the city's residents. In a sense, missionaries and reformers had already been opening these doors throughout the previous decades, when they met with New York's poor in their kitchens and reported about their living conditions. Yet the inspectors' visits were even more intrusive. An immense amount of information was collected about people's bodies, health, intelligence, private property, personal habits, and even the amount of air space contained in their apartments. The inspectors analyzed the topography of the neighborhood, the drainage capacity of the streets, and the proximity and cleanliness of urban animals. They clearly believed that poverty and epidemics resulted directly from environmental conditions. They did not absolve the residents of all blame, however, and in each district report, inspectors routinely included evidence that the residents had despicable habits that likewise needed reform. The inspectors served as a private, invasive Board of Health. With this vast amount of information about the lives and environmental conditions of the city's residents, the Council of Hygiene hoped to inspire the city agencies to take control of the urban environment and remedy the city's physical and social ills. In their introduction to the report, members of the council expressed great optimism: "The rapid progress of knowledge, the marvelous increase of human power over the elements of nature, by means of the applied sciences, the requirements of humanity, and an advanced civilization, together with the lessons and the light of past experience in great cities, combine to make plain the duty and practicability of Sanitary works and regulations which shall redeem the city of New York." With evidence of success after half a century of battles over the urban environment, these reformers were confident that control was possible and that it would improve both nature and human nature.[9]

Following the Draft Riots, New Yorkers interested in taming the city could have learned two very different lessons. One was that even more control was necessary if reformers were to govern the unruly environment and the even more unruly people. The other lesson was that prior efforts to tame the city had backfired. By chipping away at the urban commons, reformers and politicians had, perhaps inadvertently, eliminated an economic safety net that had kept the city's poor afloat. While the Citizens' Association as a whole embraced the call for further control, one of the inspectors, L. A. Rodenstein, hesitated. He was wary of the project of urbanization. Finding the least healthy New Yorkers in the areas where there had been the most environmental interventions—areas where the city had intercepted the natural flow of the waters by building avenues, grading land, and altering the drainage—he concluded: "The natural conformation of the surface has been disturbed by the art of man which makes the city, and makes it badly; . . . an incipient city defaces Nature, and deprives it of its own provisions for restoring the equilibrium of its disturbed elements, and art has not yet provided any substitute for the natural outlets of accumulated moisture." Perhaps it was hubris or just optimism that led New Yorkers to believe that they could fully control their environment.[10]

Yet this group of wealthy New Yorkers and their team of medical experts, who gave authority to the Citizens' Association report, believed that additional control was the solution. They wanted the city and state governments to tame the urban environment, no matter how intrusive the interventions. They praised the efforts of the city government in New Orleans, where the "strong arm of a sanitary police, enforced by military authority," had transformed the disease-ridden city into "one of the most salubrious ports on the continent." The Citizens' Association called for extensive educational programs to teach the poor better habits, for continued investigations into their living conditions, and for a strengthened role of the Metropolitan Police in enforcing "strict obedience to sanitary regulations," especially in poor neighborhoods. Such interventions would have been unimaginable in the 1810s, when certain New Yorkers had hoped the government would control the city's loose hog and dog populations. Fifty years later, they were not nearly so farfetched. With the police more actively involved in campaigns such as the Piggery War of 1859, and with the extensive control over public spaces like Central Park, the recommendations of the Citizens' Association likely seemed reasonable. The initiatives of these elite New Yorkers were a critical step in the city's efforts to control the urban environment.[11]

While it would take decades and the work of generations of reformers and bureaucrats to bring about some of the systemic changes the Citizens' Association called for, the *Report of the Council of Hygiene and Public Health* immediately helped to build support for the state's Metropolitan Health Act of 1866. This act created the Metropolitan Board of Health, the country's first modern municipal public health authority. The board oversaw both Manhattan and Brooklyn and included a health officer, four police commissioners, and four additional commissioners appointed by the governor. The council's report likewise spurred the state legislature to approve an 1866 law standardizing construction practices, as well as the Tenement House Act of 1867, the first of many attempts to improve lower-class housing. These three state laws were part of a concerted effort by the government to take charge of the urban environment, both built and natural. Aided by these laws, state and local authorities could attack the city's environmental problems with a stronger bureaucracy, equipped with the strength to eliminate nuisances. This expression of government power and its allegiance with the interests of the city's elite did not emerge out of nowhere. The momentum had been building for half a century.[12]

The Metropolitan Board of Health and the Tenement Law did not solve all of New York's problems in one fell swoop. Filthy streets and waste management issues would continue to plague the city through the end of the century. The urban commons remained a contested space, as was evident in Jacob Riis's famous late nineteenth-century photographs of ragpickers, in the persistent presence of shantytowns and squatters throughout the city, and in the continued battles over how visitors used the city's parks. Yet the formation of the Citizens' Association and the comprehensive work that group did to study and catalog the city's people and environment show the culmination of a movement among the city's elite to take control of the urban environment and its seemingly uncontrollable residents.[13]

Restraining loose animals, eliminating or minimizing urban agriculture, building elite neighborhoods around parks, regulating how people used the parks, and sanitizing the city were all efforts aimed at making the city more livable, pleasant, and sustainable. To bourgeois reformers, a tightly controlled environment meant civilized politics and social interactions, certainly not riots that could upend the social hierarchy and call into question the stability of their positions and of the city itself. Controlling the urban environment held the promise of controlling what seemed most uncontrollable about the city: the overwhelming flow of immigrants, the deepening pits of poverty, and the upheavals of constant change. The optimism embedded in this philosophy would propel reform movements in the decades to come. Yet the increasingly tamed city privileged one group's vision for the city and its environment, while amplifying environmental and economic disparity. It led to new boundaries between the city and the country, but did little to alleviate social tensions. Perhaps the city was never truly tamed at all.

Notes

Introduction

1. For more on the ecological history of Manhattan Island, see Eric W. Sanderson, *Mannahatta: A Natural History of New York City* (New York: Abrams, 2009). The first published recounting of this farmer's tale seems to have been in the 1896 edition of Martha J. Lamb and Mrs. Burton Harrison's *History of the City of New York*. Edwin Burrows and Mike Wallace retold the tale in their 1998 historical survey of New York City, *Gotham*. Regardless of whether the landowner threw vegetables, Randel did face several arrests due to "numerous suits instated against me as agent of the Commissioners, for trespass and damage committed by my workmen, in passing over grounds, cutting off branches of trees, &c., to make surveys under the instructions from the Commissioners." *Manual of the Corporation of New-York* (New York: D. T. Valentine, 1864), 848; Martha J. Lamb and Mrs. Burton Harrison, *History of the City of New York: Its Origins, Rise, and Progress* (New York: A. S. Barnes, 1877, 1880, 1896), 3: 571–572; Edwin Burrows and Mike Wallace,

Gotham: A History of New York to 1898 (New York: Oxford University Press, 1998), 420.

2. Joseph J. Salvo and Arun Peter Lobo, "Population," *Encyclopedia of New York City,* ed. Kenneth T. Jackson, 2nd ed. (New Haven: Yale University Press, 2010), 1018–1020.

3. For examples of this nostalgia, see Gene Schermerhorn, *Letters to Phil: Memories of a New York Boyhood, 1848–1856* (New York: New York Bound Books, 1982); Charles Haynes Haswell, *Reminiscences of an Octogenarian of the City of New York* (New York: Harper and Brothers, 1896).

4. The informal economy has received varied treatment by scholars, from historians focusing on the embattled "moral economy" following the growth of a more formal market system, to sociologists and journalists who have studied the present-day underground economy across the world. "Moral economy," as E. P. Thompson initially coined it, comprises a set of principles governing market activities that were accepted as a way to protect lower-class consumers from exploitation and unfair pricing. With the transition to a more market-based or capitalist economy, many of these tenets began to be abandoned by merchants and farmers, and governments issued fewer paternalistic controls. Thompson uses this model to explain the logic and reasoning behind seemingly irrational or spasmodic riots. The danger of the "moral economy" model is that it romanticizes these people as a "people of the past" working under different philosophies and economic models, rather than seeing them as people adapting to the changes occurring in their societies. It is easy to romanticize their "premarket" ways. Thomas Clay Arnold, "Rethinking Moral Economy," *American Political Science Review* 95.1 (2001): 85–95; Ruth Bogin, "Petitioning and the New Moral Economy of Post-Revolutionary America," *William and Mary Quarterly,* 3rd ser., 45.3 (1998): 391–425; John Bohstedt, "The Moral Economy and the Discipline of Historical Context," *Journal of Social History* 26.2 (1992): 265–284; Karl Jacoby, *Crimes against Nature: Squatters, Poachers, Thieves, and the Hidden History of American Conservation* (Berkeley: University of California Press, 2001); Barbara Clark Smith, "Food Rioters and the American Revolution," *William and Mary Quarterly,* 3rd ser., 51.1 (1994): 3–38; E. P. Thompson, "The Moral Economy of the English Crowd in the Eighteenth Century," *Past and Present* 50 (Feb. 1971): 76–136; Philip Mattera, *Off the Books: The Rise of the Underground Economy* (London: Pluto Press, 1985); Sudhir Alladi Venkatesh, *Off the Books: The Underground Economy of the Urban Poor* (Cambridge, MA: Harvard University Press, 2006).

5. Historians who have focused on the intersection of social and environmental issues, often contrasting spaces of leisure and those of labor, include: Louis S. Warren, *The Hunter's Game: Poachers and Conservationists in Twentieth-Century America* (New Haven: Yale University Press, 1997); Jacoby, *Crimes against Nature;* Jake Kosek, *Understories: The Political Life of Forests in Northern New Mexico* (Durham, NC: Duke University Press, 2006); Gunther Peck, "The Nature of Labor: Fault Lines and Common Ground in Environmental and Labor History," *Environmental History* 11.2 (2006): 212–238; Matthew Klingle, *Emerald City: An Environmental History of Seattle* (New Haven: Yale University Press, 2007); Lawrence M. Lipin, *Workers and the Wild: Conservation, Consumerism, and Labor in Oregon, 1910–1930* (Urbana: University of Illinois Press, 2007); Scott E. Giltner, *Hunting and Fishing in the New South: Black Labor and White Leisure after the Civil War* (Baltimore: Johns Hopkins University Press, 2008); Connie Chiang, *Shaping the Shoreline: Fisheries and Tourism on the Monterey Coast* (Seattle: University of Washington Press, 2008); Thomas G. Andrews, *Killing for Coal: America's Deadliest Labor War* (Cambridge, MA: Harvard University Press, 2008). For more on the history of environmental inequalities, see Ellen Stroud, "Troubled Waters in Ecotopia: Environmental Racism in Portland, Oregon," *Radical History Review* 74 (1999): 65–95; Matthew Gandy, *Concrete and Clay: Reworking Nature in New York City* (Cambridge, MA: MIT Press, 2002); Harold L. Platt, *Shock Cities: The Environmental Transformation and Reform of Manchester and Chicago* (Chicago: University of Chicago Press, 2005); Ari Kelman, *A River and Its City: The Nature of Landscape in New Orleans* (Berkeley: University of California Press, 2006); Klingle, *Emerald City;* Coll Thrush, *Native Seattle: Histories from the Crossing-Over Place* (Seattle: University of Washington Press, 2007); Julie Sze, *Noxious New York: The Racial Politics of Urban Health and Environmental Justice* (Cambridge, MA: MIT Press, 2007).

6. Michael Rawson, *Eden on the Charles: The Making of Boston* (Cambridge, MA: Harvard University Press, 2010), 22–74; Ted Steinberg, *Down to Earth: Nature's Role in American History* (New York: Oxford University Press, 2002), 157; Andrew Hurley, "Busby's Stink Boat and the Regulation of Nuisance Trades, 1865–1918," in *Common Fields: An Environmental History of St. Louis,* ed. Andrew Hurley (St. Louis: Missouri Historical Society Press, 1997), 145–162; Mary Ryan, *Civic Wars: Democracy and Public Life in the American City during the Nineteenth Century* (Berkeley: University of California Press, 1998); Andrew Robichaud, "Living on the Edge: Humans and Animals in San Francisco Shantytowns, 1880–1900," paper presented at the American Society

for Environmental History Conference, San Francisco, March 2014; Robichaud, "Making and Remaking Animal Space in San Francisco, 1860–1900," paper presented at the American Society for Environmental History Conference, Toronto, April 2013; Kelman, *A River and Its City*, 87–118. A handful of historians, ecologists, and geographers have written about New York City's environmental and ecological history: Gandy, *Concrete and Clay;* Sze, *Noxious New York;* Betsy McCully, *City at the Water's Edge: A Natural History of New York* (New Brunswick, NJ: Rutgers University Press, 2007); Sanderson, *Mannahatta;* David Stradling, *The Nature of New York: An Environmental History of the Empire State* (Ithaca: Cornell University Press, 2010).

7. Zusha Elinson, "Urban Farming for Cash Gains a Toehold in San Francisco," *New York Times*, 13 August 2010; "Updates on Chicago Food Issues," *Chicago Tribune*, 28 September 2011; "Emmanuel Widens City's Gate to Urban Farming," *Chicago Tribune*, 27 July 2011; "Urban Farming, a Bit Closer to the Sun," *New York Times*, 17 June 2009; Christopher M. Smith and Hilda E. Kurtz, "Community Gardens and Politics of Scale in New York City," *Geographical Review* 93.2 (2003): 193–212; Lisa W. Foderaro, "Enjoy Park Greenery, City Says, But Not as Salad," *New York Times*, 29 July 2011; Manhattan Borough President Scott M. Stringer, "FoodNYC: A Blueprint for a Sustainable Food System," February 2010, www.mbpo.org/uploads/policy_reports/mbp/FoodNYC.pdf.

8. The majority of urban environmental histories, with just a few exceptions, focus on the Progressive Era and the twentieth century. Major changes and environmental transformations took place during the antebellum period, and these urban spaces deserve attention. Rebecca Edwards has argued for the "Long Progressive Era" that extends back to the end of the Civil War. Some of those seeds were planted even farther back in the antebellum period. Rebecca Edwards, *New Spirits: Americans in the Gilded Age, 1865–1905* (New York: Oxford University Press, 2006), 6–7; Robert D. Johnston, "The Possibilities of Politics: Democracy in America, 1877 to 1917," in *American History Now*, ed. Eric Foner and Lisa McGirr (Philadelphia: Temple University Press, 2011), 96–124; William J. Novak, *The People's Welfare: Law and Regulation in Nineteenth-Century America* (Chapel Hill: University of North Carolina Press, 1996).

1. Mad Dogs and Loose Hogs

1. "For the Evening Post," *New York Herald*, 15 May 1817.
2. "Corporation Intelligence," *New York Herald*, 7 May 1817.

3. Jon C. Teaford, *The Municipal Revolution in America: Origins of Modern Urban Government* (Chicago: University of Chicago Press, 1975), 47; William J. Novak, *The People's Welfare: Law and Regulation in Nineteenth-Century America* (Chapel Hill: University of North Carolina Press, 1996); Edwin G. Burrows and Mike Wallace, *Gotham: A History of New York City to 1898* (New York: Oxford University Press, 1998), 353–370.

4. Edward K. Spann, *The New Metropolis: New York City, 1840–1857* (New York: Columbia University Press, 1981), 51–56. Philadelphia, which came in second place, had a much more modest 4,023 per councilman. Leonard P. Curry, *The Corporate City: The American City as a Political Entity, 1800–1850* (Westport, CT: Greenwood Press, 1997), 16.

5. Spann, *The New Metropolis,* 47.

6. For more on the role of animals in history, see Dorothee Brantz, ed., *Beastly Natures: Animals, Humans, and the Study of History* (Charlottesville: University of Virginia Press, 2010); Harriet Ritvo, "Animal Planet," *Environmental History* 9 (April 2004): 204–220.

7. New York also had its fair share of pet and working cats, but they caused considerably less trouble. They did not face the sort of targeted campaigns that dogs did. For more on urban cats, see Katherine C. Grier, *Pets in America: A History* (Chapel Hill: University of North Carolina Press, 2006), 215–216.

8. On pest control: Grier, *Pets in America,* 60, 62–63, 76.

9. A few examples of countless cures: "Mad Dogs," *New York Herald,* 25 May 1811; "Cure for Hydrophobia," *New York Herald,* 7 February 1816. The phrase "epidemic terror" comes from an essay critiquing the fear of mad dogs by English poet Oliver Goldsmith that was reprinted in the *Public Advertiser* almost forty years after his death. "Essay," *Public Advertiser,* 24 May 1811.

10. Harriet Ritvo, *The Animal Estate: The English and Other Creatures in the Victorian Age* (Cambridge, MA: Harvard University Press, 1987), 174. Jeffrey C. Sanders finds similar issues with loose dogs and public order in late-twentieth-century Seattle, where loose animals were often seen as symbols of urban blight and the impotence of city government. Jeffrey C. Sanders, "Animal Trouble and Urban Anxiety: Human-Animal Interaction in Post–Earth Day Seattle," *Environmental History* 16 (April 2011): 226–261.

11. *Minutes of the Common Council of the City of New York* (New York: Published for the City of New York, 1918), 16 October 1785, 1:183; 22 July 1802, 3:93; 28 February 1803, 3:214; 11 January 1808, 4:705; 11 July 1808, 5:191; 18 July 1808, 5:210; 27 May 1811, 6:600, 603; "Communication," *New-York Gazette,* 1

April 1811; "Communication," *New-York Evening Post,* 25 April 1811; "Mad Dogs," *Public Advertiser,* 26 April 1811; "Mad Dogs," *New-York Evening Post,* 29 April 1811.

12. "Law Concerning Dogs," *The Columbian,* 29 May 1811; *Minutes of the Common Council,* 27 May 1811, 6:603.

13. John Duffy, *A History of Public Health in New York City, 1625–1866* (New York: Russell Sage Foundation, 1968), 297–329.

14. "Dog Law," *New-York Evening Post,* 1 June 1811; "Communication," *The Columbian,* 3 June 1811. Harriet Ritvo describes London in the later part of the nineteenth century as being much more divided in terms of classes of dogs: clear distinctions were drawn between the animals belonging to upper-class owners and those of the lower class. New York in the early nineteenth century seems to have drawn fewer lines among classes of dogs. Reports referred to the animals generally as "dogs," rather than specifying their breed (or lack of breed) or even their physical attributes. Defining which class of dog was particularly susceptible to disease was also relatively rare during this period in New York. Ritvo, *The Animal Estate,* 167–202. Similarly, Neil Pemberton and Michael Worboys describe the fierce social judgments that were passed on the roaming dogs of England: "Roaming, mischievous, biting, dogs were a metaphor of the rootless, uncouth, brutal criminal classes, whose behavior seemed to threaten to infect the whole working class." Neil Pemberton and Michael Worboys, *Mad Dogs and Englishmen: Rabies in Britain, 1830–2000* (New York: Palgrave Macmillan, 2007), 37. Direct metaphors such as these were not being drawn in the New York newspapers or government reports.

15. Asa Greene, *A Glance at New York* (New York: A. Greene, 1837), 90–92; *Minutes of the Common Council,* 24 August 1818, 9:766; 22 July 1822, 12:473; "Dogs! Dogs!" *The Columbian,* 19 June 1815.

16. Yi-Fu Tuan discusses the complicated dynamics between this affection and the power relations inherent in the dependency of pets in *Dominance and Affection: The Making of Pets* (New Haven: Yale University Press, 1984). See also Richard Bushman, *The Refinement of America: Persons, Houses, Cities* (New York: Vintage, 1993); Grier, *Pets in America,* 154–166.

17. *Minutes of the Common Council,* 30 September 1811, 6:720; "Notice," *Mercantile Advertiser,* 30 May 1811; "Dog Law," *New-York Evening Post,* 1 June 1811; "Communication," *The Columbian,* 3 June 1811; "In Common Council," *Mercantile Advertiser,* 12 June 1811; *Minutes of the Common Council,* 10 June 1811, 6:625.

18. Adrian Lubbersen, "To the Editors of the Atheneum Magazine," *New York Review and Atheneum Magazine,* November 1825, 461. Horses would start to lose their status in cities only in the early twentieth century, when automobiles began replacing them. Not only were regal horses a status symbol for wealthier New Yorkers, they were considered "living machines," as Clay McShane and Joel Tarr have termed them, and were useful for rich and poor alike. On the role of horses in the urban landscape: Clay McShane and Joel A. Tarr, *The Horse in the City: Living Machines in the Nineteenth Century* (Baltimore: Johns Hopkins University Press, 2007); Ann Norton Greene, *Horses at Work: Harnessing Power in Industrial America* (Cambridge, MA: Harvard University Press, 2008); Clay McShane, "Gelded Age Boston," *New England Quarterly* 74 (Aug. 2001): 274–302.

19. "Dog Law," *New-York Evening Post,* 1 June 1811; "For the Public Advertiser," *Public Advertiser,* 24 May 1811; "Essay," *Public Advertiser,* 24 May 1811.

20. Unfortunately the archivists at the New York Municipal Archives were unable to locate the original files for these cases, so I was only able to reference the dockets with summaries. *People v. Francis Passman et al.,* June 11, 1811, NYCGS; *People v. John Gillespie et al.,* June 11, 1811, NYCGS; Paul Gilje, *The Road to Mobocracy: Popular Disorder in New York City, 1783–1834* (Chapel Hill: University of North Carolina Press, 1987), 226–227, 230; *Longworth's American Almanac, New York Register, and City Directory* (New York: Longworth, 1815), 223, 335; *Minutes of the Common Council,* 30 September 1811, 6:720.

21. "Dog Law," *New-York Spectator,* 26 June 1811.

22. "Notice," *The Columbian,* 3 June 1812; "Last Notice," *The Columbian,* 15 July 1812; "Notice," *New-York Evening Post,* 3 July 1813; "Dogs! Dogs!" *The Columbian,* 19 June 1815; "Another Mad Dog . . . ," *New York Herald,* 1 July 1815; *Minutes of the Common Council,* 25 September 1815, 8:299–300; 3 January 1816, 8:380–381; 8 April 1816, 8:468; 15 January 1818, 9:703; "Dogs! Dogs!" *The Columbian,* 19 June 1815; "Mad Dogs," *The Columbian,* 17 June 1815; "Hydrophobia Again," *The Columbian,* 21 June 1815; "Mad Dog," *New-York Evening Post,* 16 June 1815; "The Common Council . . ." *New York Herald,* 5 July 1815; "A Law Concerning Dogs," *New York Herald,* 8 July 1815; "Notice," *New-York Courier,* 24 July 1815; "Beware of Mad Dogs," *The National Advocate,* 19 September 1815; "Last Evening," *New York Herald,* 13 April 1816.

23. "A Law Concerning Dogs," *The National Advocate,* 26 June 1818; "Mayor's Office," *Commercial Advertiser,* 21 August 1818; *Minutes of the Common Council,*

24 August 1818, 9:765–766; *Wm. Bowder vs. Ebenezer Janson,* New York City Police Office Watch Returns, New York Municipal Archives, Roll 13, 2 September 1818; *Benjamin Watson vs. George Lynch,* New York City Police Office Watch Returns, New York Municipal Archives, Roll 13, 2 September 1818; *Benjamin Watson v. George Lynch & Boy,* New York City Police Office Minutes Before Special Justices for Preserving the Peace, New York Municipal Archives, Roll 4, 2 September 1818; *Benjamin Watson v. Peter Crawbuck,* New York City Police Office Minutes before Special Justices for Preserving the Peace, New York Municipal Archives Roll 4, 2 September 1818; *People vs. Charles Williams,* New York City Court of General Sessions Records, New York Municipal Archives, Roll 8, 16 September 1818. Paul Gilje also looks at these riots in *Road to Mobocracy,* 227. Arrests were also made in 1819: *Benjamin Watson v. Michael Sherlock & Francis Bownie,* New York City Police Office Minutes Before Special Justices for Preserving the Peace, New York Municipal Archives, Roll 4, 29 June 1819; *Benjamin Watson vs. Nathan Johnston,* New York City Police Office Watch Returns, New York Municipal Archives, Roll 13, 20 July 1819.

24. *Minutes of the Common Council,* 14 June 1819, 10:434; 13 November 1820, 11:382; 25 June 1821, 11:704; 8 July 1822, 12:468; "Law Concerning Dogs," *New-York Evening Post, for the Country,* 28 June 1822; "A Mad Dog . . . ," *New-York Evening Post, for the Country,* 9 July 1822; "At the Last Meeting . . . ," *New-York Evening Post, for the Country,* 13 June 1823; "Proceedings of the Common Council," *New-York Spectator,* 15 April 1825.

25. "Dog Days," *New-York Spectator,* 27 July 1830; "Mad Dogs," *New-York Spectator,* 17 August 1830; "Death by Hydrophobia," *New-York Spectator,* 21 June 1831; *Proceedings of the Board of Aldermen* (New York: Printed by Order of the Common Council, 1835), 15 June 1831, 1:102; *Proceedings of the Boards of Aldermen and Assistant Aldermen, and Approved by the Mayor, From May 16, 1831, to May 14, 1833* (New York: Printed by Order of the Common Council, 1835), 1:11–12; "Common Council," *New-York Spectator,* 28 June 1831. The section of the 1831 law that created the generous bounty was repealed in October of that same year, only to be reinstated in 1836. This section that legalized the killing of all loose dogs was highly contentious, as visible in the frequent revisions of the law in the years following. *Proceedings of the Board of Aldermen* (New York: Printed by Order of the Common Council, 1835), 17 October 1831, 1:377; "Document No. 13," "Document No. 4," and "Document No. 14," *Documents of the Board of Aldermen of the City of New York* (New York: Printed by

Order of the Common Council, 1839) 5:175–178; *By-Laws and Ordinances of the Mayor, Aldermen, and Commonalty of the City of New York, Revised* A.D. 1838–1839 (New York: Printed by William B. Townsend, 1839), 349–350.

26. These were not the first calls of animal cruelty. Particularly wrenching scenes, such as a groomer's public beating to death of a horse in 1823, caused public outcry for anticruelty legislation. The number of calls, however, increased significantly with the city-wide dog wars. "Cruelty to Horses," *New-York Evening Post,* 23 September 1823. "Dogs," *New-York Spectator,* 2 September 1831; "Document No. 4," *Documents of the Board of Aldermen of the City of New York* (New York: Printed by Order of the Common Council, 1837), 3:25–29, "Harvest of Dogs," *New-York Spectator,* 30 July 1836; "The Dog War," *New-York Spectator,* 3 October 1836; "Die the Death of a Dog," *New-York Spectator,* 6 October 1836; "Document No. 13," *Documents of the Board of Aldermen of the City of New York* (New York: Printed by Order of the Common Council, 1838), 86; L. Maria Child, *Letters from New-York* (New York: Charles S. Francis, 1943), 11.

27. For more on what Katherine Grier has termed the "domestic ethic of kindness" see: Grier, *Pets in America,* 127–181; Karen Halttunen, "Humanitarianism and the Pornography of Pain in Anglo-American Culture," *American Historical Review* 100.2 (1995): 303–334. On the seventeenth- and eighteenth-century development of theories about the treatment of animals in England, see Keith Thomas, *Man and the Natural World: A History of Modern Sensibility* (New York: Pantheon Books, 1983). James Turner chronicles the evolution of ideas regarding pain, and how that affected human relations with animals and conceptions of animal cruelty in James Turner, *Reckoning with the Beast: Animals, Pain, and Humanity in the Victorian Mind* (Baltimore: Johns Hopkins University Press, 1980). L. H. Sigourney, *Letters to Mothers* (Hartford: Hudson and Skinner, 1838), 39–40. Attesting to the popularity of this book, it was reprinted at least five times between 1838 and 1854.

28. Grier, *Pets in America,* 127–181; Bushman, *The Refinement of America;* Child, *Letters from New-York,* 11; "Dogs," *New-York Mirror: A Repository of Polite Literature and the Arts,* 2 July 1851; Greene, *A Glance at New York,* 87–90; "Document No. 13," 86.

29. Richard Stott, *Jolly Fellows: Male Milieus in Nineteenth-Century America* (Baltimore: Johns Hopkins University Press, 2009).

30. Quote from "Hydrophobia," *New-York Spectator,* 18 July 1836.

31. Greene, *A Glance at New York,* 90.

32. In *The Road to Mobocracy,* Paul Gilje analyzes the antebellum dog and hog riots, and sees them as evidence that the middle class was interested in attacking the rights of the urban poor for the sake of creating a more commercially friendly city. Focusing exclusively on riots, he sees hogs and dogs as the interests solely of the lower class, whereas I argue that dogs, at least, had supporters across the socioeconomic categories. The wealthy just expressed their displeasure with the dog law in print and political pressure, rather than through riots. Gilje, *Road to Mobocracy,* 224–232.

33. On the Dutch, see I. N. Phelps Stokes, *The Iconography of Manhattan Island, 1498–1909* (New York: R. H. Dodd, 1915–1928), 15 March 1640, 4:92; 27 June 1650, 4:121; 15 November 1651, 4:124–125; 28 July 1653, 4:140; 15 November 1651, 4:124–125; Duffy, *A History of Public Health in New York City,* 11–12. On the English, see *Minutes of the Common Council of the City of New York, 1675–1776* (New York: Dodd Mead, 1905), 23 March 1703, 2:258; 20 July 1708, 2:358; 14 October 1758, 6:152; 22 November 1770, 7:244. Virginia Anderson looks at the havoc hogs and other livestock wreaked in the British colonies of New England, though she does not dwell too much on urban animal issues. Virginia DeJohn Anderson, *Creatures of Empire: How Domestic Animals Transformed Early America* (New York: Oxford University Press, 2004).

34. Jane Allen, "Population," in *The Encyclopedia of New York City,* ed. Kenneth T. Jackson (New Haven: Yale University Press, 1995), 920–924; "The People vs. Isaac Baptiste," *New-York Daily Advertiser,* 16 August 1820; Charles H. Haswell, *Reminiscences of an Octogenarian, 1816–1860* (New York: Harper and Brothers, 1896), 86.

35. It is difficult to determine on the basis of available records how New Yorkers were able to identify their own hogs. In contrast to cities or towns where hogs were legal, New York did not seem to have any earmark registers associating owners with specific symbols imprinted on their animals' ear. Howard B. Rock, "A Delicate Balance: The Mechanics and the City in the Age of Jefferson," *New York Historical Society Quarterly* 63 (1979): 93–114; Sean Wilentz, *Chants Democratic: New York City and the Rise of the American Working Class, 1788–1850* (New York: Oxford University Press, 1984). Seth Rockman looks at a similar transition in early republican Baltimore; see Rockman, *Scraping By: Wage Labor, Slavery, and Survival in Early Baltimore* (Baltimore: Johns Hopkins University Press, 2009).

36. For more on the ways hogs have been used symbolically in politics and writing, see Carl Fisher, "Politics and Porcine Representation: Multitudinous

Swine in the British Eighteenth Century," *LIT: Literature Interpretation Theory* 10 (2000): 303–326; Peter Stallybrass and Allon White, *The Politics and Poetics of Transgression* (Ithaca: Cornell University Press, 1986), 45–59, 147–148; Brett Mizelle, "I Have Brought My Pig to a Fine Market," in *Cultural Change and the Market Revolution in America, 1789–1860,* ed. Scott C. Martin (New York: Rowman and Littlefield, 2005), 184; Robert Malcolmson and Stephanos Mastoris, *The English Pig: A History* (London: Hambledon Press, 1998), 1–28.

37. Charles Henry Wilson, *The Wanderer in America; or, Truth at Home* (Thirsk, U.K.: Henry Masterman, 1824), 18–19; Ole Munch Raeder, "Correspondent from the Homeland," in *This Was America,* ed. Oscar Handlin (Cambridge, MA: Harvard University Press, 1949), 217; Lady Emmeline Stuart Wortley, *Travels in the United States, etc. during 1849 and 1850* (New York: Harper and Brothers, 1851), 16 May 1849, 13; New York City Common Council Papers, 1670–1831, City Inspector Petitions, Municipal Archives Collections, Roll 65, 1818.

38. Raeder, "Correspondent from the Homeland," 217; Malcolmson and Mastoris, *The English Pig,* 40–44. Examples of authors complaining about the disgrace brought on by hogs include: "Hogs in the Streets," *New-York Evening Post,* 27 April 1819; "Swine," *New-York Evening Post,* 3 November 1819. For more on the quest for refinement among middle-class and wealthy Americans, see Bushman, *The Refinement of America.* For more on Pittsburgh's animal troubles, see John Duffy, "Hogs, Dogs, and Dirt: Public Health in Early Pittsburgh," *Pennsylvania Magazine of History and Biography* 87.3 (1963): 294–305.

39. Elizabeth Blackmar, *Manhattan for Rent, 1785–1850* (Ithaca: Cornell University Press, 1989), 44–71; Wilentz, *Chants Democratic;* Raymond A. Mohl, *Poverty in New York, 1783–1825* (New York: Oxford University Press, 1971), 3–13; Peter R. Gluck and Richard J. Meister, *Cities in Transition: Social Changes and Institutional Responses in Urban Development* (New York: New Viewpoints, 1979), 3–9, 36–43; Rockman, *Scraping By.* Until 1821, the Common Council controlled the cost and weight of bread sold within the city limits with a bread assize. For more on this long-lasting, politically charged debate, see New York (N.Y.) Common Council, *Laws and Ordinances Ordained and Established by the Mayor, Aldermen, and Commonalty of the City of New-York, in Common Council Convened* (New York: T. and J. Swords, 1817), 51–56; "Assize of Bread," *New York Herald,* 15 March 1815; "The Poor . . . ,"

New York Herald, 18 March 1815; "Bread," *New-York Evening Post, for the Country,* 5 March 1822; "Rise of Milk," *New York Herald,* 30 November 1816; "Milk," *New York Herald,* 7 December 1816; "Soup House in Frankfort-Street, near the Arsenal," *New York Herald,* 19 February 1817; Society for the Prevention of Pauperism in the City of New York, *Plain Directions on Domestic Economy* (New York: Printed by Samuel Wood and Sons, 1821).

40. On the difficulties of determining hog ownership, see note 35 above. "Remonstrances against Law to Prohibit Swine from Running at Large," New York City Common Council Papers, Municipal Archives, Box 60V, Folder No. 497 Flat, 19 May 1817.

41. "Remonstrances against Law to Prohibit Swine from Running at Large"; "The Petition of the Subscribers Inhabitants of the City of New York," New York City Common Council Papers, 1670–1831, 2 February 1818, Roll 67.

42. "To the Mayor and Corporation of the City of New-York," *Republican Watch-Tower,* 13 June 1809; "For the Public Advertiser, Dirty Streets, No. 1," *Public Advertiser,* 11 April 1810, 2. For an overview of urban American sanitation, see Martin V. Melosi, *Garbage in the Cities: Refuse, Reform, and the Environment, 1880–1980* (College Station: Texas A&M University Press, 1981), 13–20.

43. *Minutes of the Common Council,* 18 May 1812, 7:146–147; 14 November 1814, 8:84; 1 June 1818, 9:668; "Communication," *New-York Evening Post,* 29 June 1819.

44. "New York, May 15, 1799," *Daily Advertiser,* 15 May 1799; correspondence between Peter Burtsell and John Pintard, Inspector of Health, 20 January 1806, New York City Common Council Papers, 1670–1831, Roll 29; *Minutes of the Common Council,* 28 May 1810, 6:209; "Public Health," *New-York Evening Post,* 12 August 1825; "Cholera Statistics," *New-York Mercury,* 15 August 1832; "City Intelligence," *New York Herald,* 18 May 1849; Isaac Candler, *A Summary View of America: Comprising a Description of the Face of the Country, and of Several of the Principal Cities* (London: T. Cadell, 1824), 22–24.

45. Raeder, "Correspondent from the Homeland," 217; "Health of the City," *New-York Daily Advertiser,* 29 October 1819. "The Swinish Multitude," *New-York Evening Post,* 10 October 1816.

46. For examples of boys riding hogs and getting into trouble, see *The People v. Christian Harriet,* in *The New-York Judicial Repository,* ed. D. Bacon, Esq. (New York: Gould and Banks, 1818), 262–263; "Swine," *New-York Evening Post,* 17 March 1818; "More Serious Accidents from Hogs," *New-York*

Evening Post, 29 October 1818. For descriptions of victimized women and girls, see "A Congratulation," *New-York Evening Post,* 31 December 1817; *The People v. Christian Harriet,* in *The New-York Judicial Repository,* 262; "Communication," *New-York Evening Post,* 26 June 1819; "New-York, May 28, 1810," *New-York Evening Post,* 29 May 1810; "To the Editor of the Evening Post," *New-York Evening Post,* 28 June 1819; "Yesterday Afternoon," *New-York Columbian,* 1 July 1820; "Mr. Stone," *Northern Whig,* 1 August 1815.

47. For more on women and household economy, see Jeanne Boydston, *Home and Work: Housework, Wages, and the Ideology of Labor in the Early Republic* (New York: Oxford University Press, 1990); Rockman, *Scraping By,* 158–193; Christine Stansell, *City of Women: Sex and Class in New York, 1789–1860* (1982; Urbana: University of Illinois Press, 1987).

48. Allen, "Population"; Charles Lockwood, *Manhattan Moves Uptown: An Illustrated History* (Boston: Houghton Mifflin, 1976), 50–71. In his famous article, "Pigs and Positivism," Hendrik Hartog also notes that 1816 marked a turning point at which complaints about pigs grew louder. While I contend that this change has more to do with the growing population of hogs and the increased density of the city, he attributes it to a cultural change that made New Yorkers more concerned with their property and the legality of keeping pigs. Hendrik Hartog, "Pigs and Positivism," *University of Wisconsin Law Review 4* (1985): 903–904.

49. *Minutes of the Common Council,* 5 November 1816, 8:670; 17 May 1817, 9:130; Burrows and Wallace, *Gotham,* 353–356. The archivist at the Municipal Archives of New York was unable to locate the original petition. Howard Rock makes reference to the fact that the petition was signed by about 200 names. See Rock, "A Delicate Balance." "The Swinish Multitude," *New-York Evening Post,* 26 May 1817. "Remonstrances against Law to Prohibit Swine from Running at Large"; "The Swinish Multitude," *New-York Evening Post,* 26 May 1817.

50. "Common Council," *New-York Evening Post,* 21 May 1817; Alice Eicholz and James M. Rose, eds., *Free Black Heads of Households in the New York State Federal Census, 1790–1830* (Detroit: Gale Research, 1981); Howard Rock and Paul Gilje, "'Sweep O! Sweep O!': African American Chimney Sweeps and Citizenship in the New Nation," *William and Mary Quarterly,* 3rd ser., 51 (July, 1994), 507–538; Shane White, *Somewhat More Independent: The End of Slavery in New York City, 1770–1810* (Athens: University of Georgia Press, 1991); Leslie M. Harris, *In the Shadow of Slavery: African Americans in*

New York City, 1626–1863 (Chicago: University of Chicago Press, 2003), 116–118; Leonard P. Curry, *The Free Black in Urban America, 1800–1850: The Shadow of a Dream* (Chicago: University of Chicago Press, 1981), 88, 217–218.

51. "The Hogs and the Corporation," *New-York Evening Post,* 27 May 1817; "The Hogs and the Corporation," *New York Herald,* 28 May 1817; *Minutes of the Common Council,* 23 June 1817, 9:215–216; Gilje, *The Road to Mobocracy,* 225; "Quadroped Toleration, Intolerable," *New-York Columbian,* 23 July 1817; "The Yankee in New-York," *Exile,* 26 July 1817; "Dogs and Hogs," *Albany Argus,* 22 August 1817; "Communication," *New-York Evening Post,* 13 September 1817; "For the New-York Evening Post," *New-York Evening Post,* 3 September 1817; *Minutes of the Common Council,* 7 October 1817, 9:310; "Swine," *New York Herald,* 11 October 1817; "A Congratulation," *New-York Evening Post,* 31 December 1817; "A Law Respecting Swine," *New-York Columbian,* 15 January 1818, 9:3.

52. *Minutes of the Common Council,* 15 December 1817, 9:393; 2 February 1818, 9:462; "Repeal of the Law Prohibiting Swine Running at Large," *New-York Evening Post,* 29 December 1817; "The Petition of the Subscribers Inhabitants of the City of New York." The race of the signers was determined by checking them against New York State census records: Eicholz and Rose, *Free Black Heads of Households.*

53. "Hogs," *New-York Evening Post,* 16 February 1818. Anger at the repeal can also be seen here: "Repeal of the Swine Law," *New-York Columbian,* 10 February 1818; "Swine Once More," *New-York Evening Post,* 21 February 1818.

54. "Swine Once More," *New-York Evening Post,* 21 February 1818. Information about the party affiliation of the aldermen was found in D. T. Valentine, *Manual of the Corporation of the City of New York for 1854* (New York: McSpedon and Baker, Printers, 1854).

55. Mayors during this period served as judge of the Court of General Sessions, as part of their position. "Correspondent," *New-York Evening Post,* 7 December 1818; *The People v. Christian Harriet, The New-York Judicial Repository,* 258–259. See also Hartog, "Pigs and Positivism," 904–905. Hartog has written an article on the difference between laws and reality that traces the custom of keeping pigs in New York City in the 1810s and 1820s. Specifically focusing on *The People v. Christian Harriet,* Hartog's legal history shows that the court case did not, in the end, have the authoritative teeth to make a difference in the ways hog owners used public space or even in the ways the Common Council handled legislation.

56. Novak, *The People's Welfare*, 60–71, 191–233. In addition, nuisance law and its use in the judicial system is discussed in Martin V. Melosi, *The Sanitary City: Urban Infrastructure in America from Colonial Times to the Present* (Baltimore: Johns Hopkins University Press, 2000), 21–22; *The People v. Christian Harriet,* in *The New-York Judicial Repository,* 264, 269. For a more detailed analysis of this case from a legal historian's perspective, see Hartog, "Pigs and Positivism"; Hendrik Hartog, *Public Property and Private Power: The Corporation of the City of New York in American Law, 1730–1870* (Chapel Hill: University of North Carolina Press, 1993), 139–142.

57. A similar case to *The People vs. Christian Harriet* was the indictment of Isaac Baptiste, following the complaint of a grocer who had a run-in with Baptiste's hogs. An article discussing this case makes reference to the fact that at least twenty such cases had been heard previously, all ruling hogs to be a nuisance. "The People vs. Isaac Baptiste," *New-York Daily Advertiser,* 16 August 1820. "Hogs Running at Large in the City," *New-York Evening Post,* 1 July 1819; "Hogs," *New-York Daily Advertiser,* 7 April 1819; "Hogs Avaunt!" *New-York Columbian,* 7 January 1819; "Hogs in the Streets," *New-York Evening Post,* 27 April 1819; "The People vs. Isaac Baptiste," *New-York Daily Advertiser,* 16 August 1820; "Salutary Conviction," *New-York Evening Post,* 9 June 1820.

58. *Minutes of the Common Council,* 30 April 1821, 11:600; "Proceedings of the Common Council," *New-York Evening Post,* 1 May 1821; Permission from the State Legislature to seize privately-owned pigs for the Alms-House was requested on January 8, 1821: *Minutes of the Common Council,* 8 January 1821, 11:444. The law was passed on April 30, 1821, and reported in the newspapers immediately following: *Minutes of the Common Council,* 30 April 1821, 11:600; "Proceedings of the Common Council," *New-York Evening Post,* 1 May 1821.

59. "The Law Respecting the Running of Swine," *New-York Spectator,* 1 June 1821; "Hogs in the Streets," *New-York Evening Post,* 12 June 1821. *Minutes of the Common Council,* 25 June 1821, 11:704.

60. *Minutes of the Common Council,* 21 July 1821, 11:722; "Hogs Running at Large in the Streets," *New-York Evening Post,* 4 August 1821; "Police," *New-York Spectator,* 7 August 1821; "From the Daily Advertiser," *New-York Evening Post,* 4 August 1821.

61. Harris, *In the Shadow of Slavery,* 117–119, 133. Harris argues that it was at this point that a division grew between middle-class and working-class blacks over acceptable means for political activism. Paul Gilje contextualizes these hog riots as being part of a larger set of public demonstrations in

nineteenth-century New York. He attributes the growing violence of riots in the 1820s and 1830s to the increasing economic disparity and evolving ideas of what constituted a public good. Perhaps restriction of suffrage rights also impacted the changing tenor of these events. Gilje, *Road to Mobocracy.*

62. *New-York Spectator,* 7 August 1821; "In Proceedings of the Corporation . . . ," *New-York Evening Post, for the Country,* 5 April 1822; "Cleanliness," *New-York Evening Post, for the Country,* 15 July 1823.

63. "Hog Law," *New-York Spectator,* 8 April 1825; *Minutes of the Common Council,* 14 March 1825, 14:365; 28 March 1825, 14:410–411; "Hog Law," *New-York Spectator,* 8 April 1825. Regarding Henry Bourden's role in the riot: "Court of Sessions," *Weekly Commercial Advertiser,* 19 April 1825; *People vs. Henry Bourden,* New York City Court of General Sessions Records, New York Municipal Archives, 9 April 1825, Roll 11. Henry Bourden is likely the "Henry Borden" listed in the 1830 and 1840 U.S. censuses, living in the Eighth Ward. 1830 United States Federal Census, New York Ward 8, New York County, New York, Roll 97, 273; 1840 United States Federal Census, New York Ward 8, New York County, New York, Roll 302, 334; Haswell, *Reminiscences of an Octogenarian,* 130; *People vs. Allaire & Allaire,* NYCCGSR, 9 April 1825, Roll 11; *People vs. Thompson and Phalen,* NYCCGSR, 11 April 1825, Roll 11.

64. Thomas F. De Voe, *The Market Book: Containing a Historical Account of the Public Markets in the Cities of New York, Boston, Philadelphia, and Brooklyn* (1862; New York: Burt Franklin, 1969), 1:482–483; "If the Laws . . . ," *New-York Evening Post,* 8 September 1826; "Hog Law," *New-York Evening Post,* 8 September 1826; "Where Is the Hog Cart?" *New-York Evening Post,* 27 February 1827; De Voe, *The Market Book,* 1:482–483; *New-York Evening Post,* 2 July 1830, quoted in Stokes, *Iconography of Manhattan Island,* 5:1693; Gilje, *Road to Mobocracy,* 231; "Hog Thieves," *New-York Evening Post,* 20 February 1829. The law continued to be reconfigured following the riots, but enforcement was scant. *Proceedings of the Board of Aldermen* (New York: Printed by Order of the Common Council, 1834), 27 May 1833, 5:41–42; 30 September 1833, 5:262; 5 February 1834, 6:153.

65. "We Are Daily Required . . . ," *New-York Tribune,* 12 June 1841.

66. Jon C. Teaford writes that historians should consider inertia "a force in the decision-making process," and this was certainly the case when it came to governing New York's streets in the early nineteenth century. Jon C. Teaford, "New Life for an Old Subject: Investigating the Structure of Urban Rule," *American Quarterly* 37.3 (1985): 353.

67. McShane and Tarr, *The Horse in the City,* 47–53.

68. "Dogs," *New-York Mirror,* 2 July 1851; "Address of the Swine," *New-York Evening Post,* 21 February 1818.

2. Unequally Green

1. "Grand Canal Celebration by the City of New-York," *New-York Spectator,* 25 October 1825; "THE WORK IS DONE!" *New-York Spectator,* 28 October 1825; "Celebration of the Fourth of November," *New-York Spectator,* 8 November 1825; William L. Stone, *Narrative of the Festivities Observed in Honor of the Completion of the Grand Erie Canal Uniting the Waters of the Great Western Lakes with the Atlantic Ocean* (New York: City of New York, 1825). For more on the canal's impact on the state, see Carol Sheriff, *The Artificial River: The Erie Canal and the Paradox of Progress, 1817–1825* (New York: Hill and Wang, 1996). For the impact of the real estate boom on Chicago and elsewhere during the 1830s, see William Cronon, *Nature's Metropolis: Chicago and the Great West* (New York: W. W. Norton, 1991), 32.

2. "Corporation Property," *New-York Evening Post, for the Country,* 18 March 1823; *The Picture of New-York, and Stranger's Guide to the Commercial Metropolis of the United States* (New York: A. T. Goodrich, 1828), 435–440; James Hardie, *The Description of the City of New York* (New York: Samuel Marks, 1827), 158.

3. Public health crises were catalysts in bringing significant changes to public spaces. For more on cholera outbreaks and their impact on New York City's landscape, see Chapter 3.

4. The literature on New York City's parks typically starts with the world-famous Central Park, glossing over the park craze of the 1830s, if mentioning it at all. In *The New Urban Landscape,* David Schuyler describes a growing intellectual movement in the 1830s and 1840s that embraced the idea that the countryside could be a positive influence if introduced to the city. He aims to show the intellectual traditions that eventually culminated in the work of Frederick Law Olmsted and his contemporaries. By focusing his work on Central Park and the country's other midcentury parks, Schuyler loses sight of the motivations that drove 1830s park advocates. He argues that public health, national pride, and the goal of elevating the lower classes drove park development. This is certainly true for Central Park; but in the 1830s economic motivations proved more central, and in the 1840s politicians did not try to hide these

motivations. Other authors who begin histories of New York's parks with Central Park criticize Frederick Law Olmsted and his contemporaries for focusing on the benefits the park would bring to real estate interests. This had a much longer tradition, however, extending back to the 1830s. See Galen Cranz, *The Politics of Park Design: The History of Urban Parks in America* (Cambridge, MA: MIT Press, 1982), 157–181; David Schuyler, *The New Landscape: The Redefinition of City Form in Nineteenth-Century America* (Baltimore: Johns Hopkins University Press, 1986); Roy Rosenzweig and Elizabeth Blackmar, *The Park and the People: A History of Central Park* (Ithaca: Cornell University Press, 1992); Mona Domash, *Invented Cities: The Creation of Landscape in Nineteenth-Century New York and Boston* (New Haven: Yale University Press, 1996); David M. Scobey, *The Making and Meaning of the New York City Landscape* (Philadelphia: Temple University Press, 2002). For more on Arcadian ideals in cemetery and park design, see Aaron Sachs, *Arcadian America: The Death and Life of an Environmental Tradition* (New Haven: Yale University Press); Peter J. Schmitt, *Back to Nature: The Arcadian Myth in Urban America* (New York: Oxford University Press, 1969).

5. "An ACT Relative to Improvements, Touching the Laying Out of Streets and Roads in the City of New-York, and for Other Purposes, Passed April 3, 1807," *Laws of the State of New-York, Passed at the Thirtieth Session of the Legislature, Begun and Held at the City of Albany, January 27th, 1807* (Albany: Webster and Skinner, 1807), ch. 115, 125.

6. "Document No. 8," *Documents of the Board of Assistant Aldermen* (New York: Printed by Order of the Common Council, 1835), 1:51–52.

7. William Bridges, *Map of the City of New York and Island of Manhattan* (New York: T. and J. Swords, 1811); David T. Valentine, *Manual of the Corporation of New-York* (New York: D. T. Valentine, 1864), 848. While a range of critics from John Reps to Lewis Mumford have expressed their dislike of the grid in strong terms, Elizabeth Blackmar, Mary Ryan, and Hendrik Hartog place the commissioners' philosophy about city planning within the context of neoclassical design aesthetics and republican political thought. In 2011–2012, the Museum of the City of New York hosted an exhibit entitled "The Greatest Grid: The Master Plan of Manhattan," curated by Hilary Ballon, which put the grid's influence in an overall positive light, emphasizing how the grid "speaks to the city's optimism about its future and its courage to do big things." Comparing grids in Kazakhstan and Montana, Kate Brown finds that leaders used grids because they ultimately sought to destroy the "revolu-

tionary and spontaneous quality of urban space." Regardless of the commissioners' reasoning for deciding on the grid, the grid had a significant impact on Manhattan Island's environment, as it involved significant leveling of the topography and removal of natural waterways and other characteristics. I. N. Phelps Stokes, *Iconography of Manhattan Island, 1498–1909* (New York: Robert H. Dodd, 1915), 1:407–408; Hilary Ballon, *The Greatest Grid: The Master Plan of Manhattan, 1811–2011* (New York: Columbia University Press, 2012), published in conjunction with the exhibition "The Greatest Grid: The Master Plan of Manhattan, 1811–2011," shown at the Museum of the City of New York; Elizabeth Blackmar, *Manhattan for Rent, 1785–1850* (Ithaca: Cornell University Press, 1989), 94–99; Hendrik Hartog, *Public Property and Private Power: The Corporation of the City of New York in American Law, 1730–1870* (Ithaca: Cornell University Press, 1983), 158–175; Mary Ryan, *Civic Wars: Democracy and Public Life in the American City during the Nineteenth Century* (Berkeley: University of California Press, 1997), 26–38; Lewis Mumford, *The City in History: Its Origins, Its Transformations, and Its Prospects* (New York: Harcourt, 1961), 421–426; John Reps, *The Making of Urban America: A History of City Planning in the United States* (Princeton: Princeton University Press, 1965), 298–299; Robert T. Augustyn and Paul E. Cohen, *Manhattan in Maps, 1527–1995* (New York: Rizzoli, 1997), 100–105; Kate Brown, "Gridded Lives: Why Kazakhstan and Montana Are Nearly the Same Place," *American Historical Review* 106.1 (2001): 17–48.

8. Bridges, *Map of the City of New York*, 25–28, 37–38; *Manual of the Corporation of New-York* (1864): 838–840, 847–856.

9. *Minutes of the Common Council of the City of New York* (New York: Published for the City of New York, 1918), 17 January 1812, 7:2–3; 17 February 1812, 7:40–43; 2 March 1812, 7:56–57; 9 March 1812, 7:61–62; 16 March 1812, 7:69.

10. *Minutes of the Common Council*, 17 February 1812, 7:42–43; 28 February 1814, 7:704–705; 1 March 1813, 7:391–392; 12 April 1813, 7:430; 24 January 1814, 7:669; "An ACT relative to opening, laying out and forming, and extending, enlarging, and otherwise improving streets, avenues, squares, and public places in the city of New-York," *Laws of the State of New York, Passed at the Thirty-fifth Session of the Legislature Begun and Held at the City of Albany, the Twenty-Eighth Day of January, 1812* (Albany: S. Southwick, 1812), ch. 174, 332–354; "AN ACT to Amend an Act, Entitled 'An Act Relative to Improvements Touching the Laying Out of Streets and Roads in the City of New

York, and for Other Purposes,' Passed April 15, 1814," in Henry E. Davies, ed., *A Compilation of the Laws of the State of New York, Relating Particularly to the City of New York* (New York: Printed by Order of Common Council, 1857), 576–578.

11. *Minutes of the Common Council,* 20 October 1817, 9:315; 22 December 1817, 9:408; 18 January 1818, 10:201–207; 8 February 1819, 10:233–238; 27 March 1826, 15:302. Schieffelin's conflict of interest came out years later in Council minutes when he more virtuously excused himself from the discussion of the Parade's future. Yet he had had no problem contributing to the discussion of the land's future in the decade prior. Mr. Schieffelin continued to get involved with the discussion inappropriately, calling for amendments to resolutions that would benefit him personally, such as by arranging for the compensation for buildings built on the Parade after the map was submitted.

12. *Minutes of the Common Council,* 27 February 1826, 15:229; 19 March 1827, 16:165; 25 February 1828, 16:762; 31 March 1828, 16:82–85. James W. Anderson published many advertisements for his real estate business. *New-York Literary Gazette and American Athenaeum* (New York: Dixon and Sickels, 1827), 3:84, 94, 96, 108, 116, 120, 132, 140, 144, 156, 180.

13. "City Improvements," *New-York Evening Post, for the Country,* 6 June 1828.

14. "City Improvements." For more on the issue of purity and categorizing spaces, see Richard White, "The Problem with Purity," Tanner Lecture on Human Values, delivered at the University of California at Davis, May 10, 1999. Available at http://tannerlectures.utah.edu/_documents/a-to-z/w/white00.pdf.

15. *Laws of the State of New-York, Passed at the Fifty-First Session, Second Meeting, 1828; and Fifty-Second Session, 1829* (Albany: E. Croswell, 1829), ch. 269, 400. The *New-York Evening Post* was not the only publication to chastise the aldermen about their decision to erase the park. The *New-York Mirror* published a scathing article before the state act was passed in 1829, describing the aldermen's decision as marked by "the grossest folly, not to say stupidity." *New-York Mirror,* 21 March 1829, 295.

16. Tourists regularly remarked on New York's elegant promenading. A few examples include Frederick Fitzgerald De Roos, *Personal Narrative of Travels in the United States and Canada in 1826* (London: William Harrison Ainsworth, 1827), 45–55; Frances Trollope, *Domestic Manners of the Americans* (London: Printed for Whittaker, Treacher, 1832), 268–271; George Foster, *New*

York in Slices, by an Experienced Carver: Being the Original Slices Published in the N.Y. Tribune (New York: W. F. Burgess, 1849), 3–5, 7–13. The most detailed work on antebellum promenades can be found in David Scobey, "Anatomy of the Promenade: The Politics of Bourgeois Sociability in Nineteenth-Century New York," *Social History* 17.2 (1992): 203–227. See also John F. Kasson, *Rudeness and Civility: Manners in Nineteenth-Century America* (New York: Hill and Wang, 1990). Examples of rules or requests for rules being published in newspapers include "How to Walk the Public Streets," *New-York Evening Post, for the Country,* 19 September 1823.

17. Foster, *New York in Slices,* 7–12; Karen Halttunen, *Confidence Men and Painted Women: A Study of Middle-Class Culture in America, 1830–1870* (New Haven: Yale University Press, 1982).

18. Scobey, "Anatomy of the Promenade."

19. Asa Greene, *A Glance at New York* (New York: A. Greene, 1837), 216–217.

20. "The Battery," *New-York Spectator,* 22 June 1830; *Proceedings of the Board of Aldermen,* 15 June 1831, 1:97–98; 20 July 1831, 1:107; "The Battery Assaults," *New-York Spectator,* 20 June 1833.

21. "For the New York Enquirer," *New-York Evening Post, for the Country,* 26 September 1826; Trollope, *Domestic Manners of the Americans,* 279; Carla L. Peterson, *Black Gotham: A Family History of African Americans in Nineteenth-Century New York City* (New Haven: Yale University Press, 2011), 147–187; Christine Stansell, *City of Women: Sex and Class in New York, 1789–1860* (Urbana: University of Illinois Press, 1987), 92, 190.

22. The sale of horse manure constituted another major income source for the municipal government. This is discussed at length in Chapter 3.

23. Board of Assistant Aldermen, "Document No. 3, December 5, 1831" (New York, 1831), Appendix. For more on the building boom, see Blackmar, *Manhattan for Rent,* 164–166; Charles Lockwood, *Manhattan Moves Uptown: An Illustrated History* (Boston: Houghton Mifflin, 1976), 73–78.

24. D. G. Brinton Thompson, *Ruggles of New York* (New York: Columbia University Press, 1946), 56, 60; Stephen Garmey, *Gramercy Park: An Illustrated History of a New York Neighborhood* (New York: Balsam Press, 1984), 27.

25. Charles King, *Progress of the City of New-York, during the Last Fifty Years* (New York: D. Appleton, 1852), 60–61; Garmey, *Gramercy Park,* 31–39; "Document No. 47," *Documents of the Board of Assistants, from May 21, 1832 to May 12, 1834* (New York: Printed by Order of the Common Council, 1838), 2/3:289–291.

26. Mark Girouard, *The English Town: A History of Urban Life* (New Haven: Yale University Press, 1990), 157−170. For an example of the sort of travelers' account typical in newspapers of this period, see "Letters from Europe," *New-York Spectator,* 15 September 1836.

27. Charles Lockwood, *Bricks and Brownstones: The New York Row House, 1783−1929, an Architectural and Social History* (New York: McGraw Hill, 1972), 40−42; Stokes, *Iconography of Manhattan Island,* 3:604.

28. *New-York Evening Post,* 17 August 1847; E. Porter Belden, *New-York: Past, Present, and Future; Comprising a History of the City of New-York, A Description of Its Present Condition and an Estimate of Its Future Increase,* 2nd ed. (New York: G. P. Putnam, 1849), 31−34; Lockwood, *Bricks and Brownstones,* 36−37; Garmey, *Gramercy Park,* 28.

29. *Proceedings of the Board of Aldermen,* 28 December 1831, 2:43; 19 January 1832, 2:64; 6 February 1832, 2:121; 18 February 1833, 4:222; 26 November 1833, 5:409; 26 May 1834, 7:20; 21 July 1834, 7:136−137; 4 August 1834, 7:156; 4 August 1834, 7:162; 23 June 1834, 7:76; 13 October 1834, 7:278; 27 October 1834, 7:329.

30. "Document No. 47," *Documents of the Board of Assistants, from May 21, 1832, to May 12, 1834* (New York: Printed by Order of the Common Council, 1838), 2 and 3, 289−291; *Proceedings of the Board of Aldermen and Assistant Aldermen, and Approved by the Mayor* (New York: Printed by Order of the Common Council, 1835), 1:380.

31. *Proceedings of the Board of Aldermen,* 2 September 1835, 9:224.

32. Thompson, *Ruggles of New York,* 60−61. Thompson sings Ruggles's praises throughout the biography, yet lays out proof of this questionable arrangement without really delving into what it meant for Ruggles or the assessment system. Eugene P. Moehring, *Public Works and the Patterns of Urban Real Estate Growth in Manhattan, 1835−1894* (New York: Arno Press, 1981), 76−77.

33. The praise for Ruggles that began among his contemporaries has continued among modern historians. Allan Nevins, for instance, lauded him as being one of the founders of the "small-parks movement" that was later championed by reformers such as Jacob Riis. Allan Nevins, "Introduction," in Thompson, *Ruggles of New York,* 11−14. Original Deed of Gramercy Park (1831), reproduced in Garmey, *Gramercy Park,* Appendix. For more on the tradition where noblesse oblige is tied to property ownership, see Carol Rose, *Property and Persuasion: Essays on the History, Theory, and Rhetoric of Ownership* (Boulder: Westview Press, 1994), 49−70.

34. Original Deed of Gramercy Park (1831). Other local landowners such as Peter G. Stuyvesant and Cornelius Williams followed suit, adding restrictive convenants to their deeds when they sold their property, in order to ensure its status. New York City Landmarks Preservation Commission, *East 17th Street–Irving Place Historic District Designation Report* (New York: City of New York, 1998), 12.

35. "Document No. 47," *Documents of the Board of Assistants, From May 21, 1832, to May 12, 1834* (New York: Printed by Order of the Common Council, 1838), 2/3:289–291; Board of Assistant Aldermen, "Document No. 3, December 5, 1831" (New York, 1831), 7–8.

36. *Proceedings of the Board of Aldermen*, 28 December 1831, 2:32, 43, 48–49; the petition by Charles Wilkes and the residents of Hudson Square was logged in the minutes of the Aldermen on 28 December 1831: *Proceedings of the Board of Aldermen*, 28 December 1831, 2:32. "Document No. 3," 1, 2, 8.

37. *Proceedings of the Board of Aldermen*, 6 February 1832, 2:121, 131–133.

38. Greene, *A Glance at New York*, 217.

39. *Minutes of the Common Council*, 18 October 1831, 19:291; 29 November 1830, 19:369–370.

40. Davies, ed., *A Compilation of the Laws of the State of New York*, 814; Valentine, *Manual of the Corporation of New-York*, 1864, 850. Another contemporary park built on marginal land was the "Public Square at Harlem," a site that the aldermen deemed too difficult to grade and therefore unsuitable for building. "Document No. 10," *Documents of the Board of Aldermen* (New York: Printed by Order of the Common Council, 1836), 2:39–41. On national parks, see Alfred Runte, *National Parks: The American Experience* (Lincoln: University of Nebraska Press, 1979), 48–64.

41. Documents of the Board of Assistants, 1:153–161, quoted in Stokes, *Iconography of Manhattan Island*, 5:1705. D. T. Valentine lifts this description, almost word for word in D. T. Valentine, *Manual of the Corporation of the City of New York for 1857* (New York: D. T. Valentine, 1857), 480–481; *Minutes of the Common Council*, 29 November 1830, 19:369–370.

42. *Proceedings of the Board of Aldermen*, 2 January 1833, 4:107–108; 21 January 1833, 4:130; 4 February 1833, 4:189; 14 February 1833, 4:208–209.

43. *Minutes of the Common Council*, 7 March 1831, 19:540–541; 25 April 1831, 19:676; *Laws of the State of New York, Passed at the Fifty-Fourth Session of the Legislature* (Albany: Wm. and A. Gould, 1831), ch. 252; Stokes, *Iconography of Manhattan Island*, 7 November 1831, 5:1705; 5 April 1832, 5:1710; 20

April 1833, 5:1719; 14 January 1834, 5:1725; *Proceedings of the Boards of Aldermen and Assistant Aldermen, and Approved by the Mayor* (New York: Printed by Order of the Common Council, 1835), 1:127–128, 170; *Proceedings of the Board of Aldermen,* 15 April 1833, 4:378; 13 May 1833, 4: 476; 23 July 1833, 5:167–168; 26 November 1833, 5:388; "Document No. 8," *Documents of the Board of Assistant Aldermen* (New York: Printed by Order of the Common Council, 1835), 1:51.

44. *Proceedings of the Board of Aldermen,* 24 October 1834, 7:317–320; "Document No. 8," 69–74.

45. "Document No. 8," 71–72; *Proceedings of the Board of Aldermen,* 24 October 1834, 7:317–320.

46. For more on the fountain's place in the celebration of the Croton Aqueduct, see Chapter 3. "New York and Its Prospects," *New-York Mirror,* 9 March 1839.

47. *Proceedings of the Board of Aldermen,* 30 September 1833, 5:246; 11 November 1833, 5:367; 23 December 1833, 6:40; 6 January 1834, 6:97–100.

48. *Proceedings of the Board of Aldermen,* 26 November 1833, 5:390; 6 January 1834, 6:97–100; 6 January 1834, 6:94–95, 97–100; Blackmar, *Manhattan for Rent,* 9–10.

49. *Proceedings of the Board of Aldermen,* 6 January 1834, 6:97–100.

50. Stephen Diamond, "The Death and Transfiguration of Benefit Taxation: Special Assessments in Nineteenth-Century America," *Journal of Legal Studies* 12.2 (1983): 202, 204, 205; Robin L. Einhorn, *Property Rules: Political Economy in Chicago, 1833–1872* (Chicago: University of Chicago Press, 1991), 87, 101. Mary Ryan discusses how special assessments and local debates over improvements fostered a particular antebellum form of urban democracy among "local publics." Ryan, *Civic Wars,* 94–108.

51. Einhorn, *Property Rules,* 14; Diamond, "The Death and Transfiguration of Benefit Taxation," 201, 239; Rose, *Property and Persuasion,* 49–70.

52. Diamond, "The Death and Transfiguration of Benefit Taxation," 210; *New York Municipal Gazette,* 11 March 1841.

53. Differentiating between assessments and taxes, of course, was a matter of semantics. Assessments were essentially another form of taxation but the government prided itself on not using the citywide property taxes to pay for local improvements. *Proceedings of the Board of Aldermen,* 7 March 1834, 6:267–269.

54. For more on the ways class divisions played a role in the distribution of New York's public works, see Blackmar, *Manhattan for Rent,* 158–169.

55. For more on the 1830s slum clearance efforts in Five Points, see Black-mar, *Manhattan for Rent*, 175–177. *Documents of the Board of Assistant Alder-men*, 19 December 1831, 1:163–168, quoted in Stokes, *Iconography of Manhattan Island*, 5:1707; *Proceedings of the Board of Aldermen*, 28 December 1831, 2:23–24; 10 June 1833, 5:66; 24 June 1833, 5:86; *Proceedings of the Board of Aldermen and Assistant Aldermen, and Approved by the Mayor*, 25 July 1832, 1:254; "Board of Aldermen," *New-York Spectator*, 3 June 1833; "The Five Points," *New-York Spectator*, 2 August 1831; G. G. Foster, *New York by Gas-Light: With Here and There a Streak of Sunshine* (New York: Dewitt and Davenport, Tribune Build-ings, 1850), 56.

56. "Document No. 36," *Documents of the Board of Aldermen of the City of New York* (New York: Printed for the Common Council, 1836): 2:153–162; "Document No. 85," 2:439–446; "Document No. 98," 2:513–519; "Board of Al-dermen," *New York American*, 16 February 1836; "Board of Assistants," *New-York Spectator*, 9 May 1836; *Proceedings of the Board of Aldermen*, 27 Feb 1837, 12:359; 20 March 1837, 12:434–435; 19 November 1849, 37.2:341–345; "Chap. 177: An Act to alter the map or plan of the city of New-York, by establishing a public square or place in the sixteenth ward of said city," *Laws of the State of New-York, Passed at the Sixteenth Session of the Legislature* (Albany: E. Cro-swell, 1837), 102.

57. Greene, *A Glance at New York*, 212.

58. Frances Trollope complained in 1832 that there were not enough trees to provide the shade she would have liked to find in New York's hot summers. Trollope, *Domestic Manners of the Americans*, 280–282.

59. *Minutes of the Common Council*, 20 May 1791, 1:643; 30 May 1791, 1:648; 22 April 1793, 2:4; 14 April 1794, 2:72; 10 April 1799, 2:535; 19 August 1802, 3:109; *Daily Advertiser*, 28 May 1791.

60. *Minutes of the Common Council*, 1 April 1822, 12:294; 15 April 1822, 12:325; 29 April 1822, 12:354; Edwin G. Burrows and Mike Wallace, *Gotham: A History of New York City to 1898* (New York: Oxford University Press, 1998), 416; Michael and Arianne Batterberry, *On the Town in New York: The Land-mark History of Eating, Drinking, and Entertainments, from the American Revo-lution to the Food Revolution* (New York: Routledge, 1999), 42; "Shady Trees in Our Streets," *New-York Evening Post, for the Country*, 19 April 1822. Anne Whiston Spirn notes the bureaucratic and ecological threats that continued to plague urban street trees; see Spirn, *The Granite Garden: Urban Nature and Human Design* (New York: Basic, 1984), 171–206.

61. "Setting Out Shade Trees," *New-York Evening Post, for the Country,* 19 November 1822. Other examples of articles advocating street trees: "Set Out Your Trees Before It Is Too Late," *New-York Evening Post, for the Country,* 26 April 1822; "Now Is the Time to Set Out Your Trees," *New-York Evening Post, for the Country,* 15 March 1822; "Setting Out Shade Trees," *New-York Evening Post, for the Country,* 19 November 1822; "Shady Trees," *New-York Evening Post, for the Country,* 18 November 1823; "Tree-Planting," *New-York Daily Tribune,* 24 October 1845.

62. *Proceedings of the Board of Aldermen,* 13 May 1833, 4:476; 30 September 1833, 5:246; Henry W. Lawrence, *City Trees: A Historical Geography from the Renaissance through the Nineteenth Century* (Charlottesville: University of Virginia Press, 2006), 177.

63. "Shady Trees," *New-York Evening Post, for the Country,* 18 November 1823.

64. *Manual of the Corporation of the City of New York* (New York: Valentine, 1862), 689. Other sources, such as the extant plaque, date the tree's arrival as 1664. In 1862 *Harper's Monthly* declared the pear tree to be "the oldest living thing in the city of New York." "American Historical Trees," *Harper's New Monthly Magazine,* 24.144 (1862), 726. The tree was so revered that in 2003 the city planted a new pear tree on that corner in memory of the old one. *New York Evening Post,* 31 October 1837; *New York Times,* 27 February 1867.

65. *New York Evening Post,* 19 February 1831.

66. "Tree-Planting," *New-York Daily Tribune,* 24 October 1845.

67. For more on the championing of parks as democratic spaces, see Chapter 4. See also Cranz, *The Politics of Park Design,* 3–56, 183–224.

68. Belden, *New-York: Past, Present, and Future,* 31–34.

3. The Dung Heap of the Universe

1. Charles Dickens, *American Notes for General Circulation* (New York: Harper and Brothers, 1842), 34–35.

2. Dickens, *American Notes for General Circulation,* 32; "Mr. Editor," *New-York Evening Post, for the Country,* 22 July 1817. For more on San Francisco and New Orleans during this period, see Mary Ryan, *Civic Wars: Democracy and Public Life in the American City during the Nineteenth Century* (Berkeley: University of California Press, 1998).

3. "Public Health," *New-York Evening Post,* 12 August 1825; "Proceedings of the Corporation," *New-York Evening Post, for the Country,* 10 December 1824.

4. The 1829 article was reprinted eight years later in Asa Greene, *A Glance at New York* (New York: A. Greene, 1837), 171–172.

5. "Mr. Editor," *New-York Evening Post, for the Country,* 22 July 1817. New Yorkers often complained about the city's filth in newspapers, petitions, and guidebooks: Greene, *A Glance at New York,* 169–170. William Chambers, *Things as They Are in America* (1853), in *Empire City: New York through the Centuries,* ed. Kenneth T. Jackson and David S. Dunbar (New York: Columbia University Press, 2002), 226–227. *Proceedings of the Board of Aldermen,* 10 May 1850, 38:728–729; 7 September 1850, 39:676–677. Other examples of New Yorkers comparing themselves negatively to Boston: "Health of the City," *New-York Daily Advertiser,* 29 October 1819; "Cleansing the Streets," *New-York Evening Post, for the Country,* 19 April 1825; "Cleaning the Streets," *New-York Evening Post, for the Country,* 22 April 1825; "Dead Animals," *New-York Tribune,* 12 June 1857; "Boston and New York," *New-York Spectator,* 1 October 1832. "Philadelphia and New York Streets," *The American,* 13 September 1820; "From the Boston Galaxy," *Weekly Commercial Advertiser,* 27 May 1825; "Document No. 5," *Documents of the Board of Assistants* (New York: Printed by the Order of the Common Council, 1838), 4 June 1832, 2/3:12.

6. "Dirty Streets," *New-York Evening Post, for the Country,* 14 June 1822; *New-York Evening Post, for the Country,* 24 May 1823.

7. "Presentment of the Grand Jury," *New-York Herald,* 18 July 1817; "New York General Sessions," *New-York Evening Post, for the Country,* 3 August 1824.

8. "Public Health," *New-York Evening Post, for the Country,* 16 August 1822; "Our Streets," *New-York Evening Post, for the Country,* 3 May 1825; "A Law to Prevent Nuisances," *New-York Evening Post, for the Country,* 10 June 1825; "Swine," *New-York Spectator,* 7 December 1835; "The Common Council," *New-York Evening Post, for the Country,* 7 January 1823. For a survey of American urban sanitation from the perspective of civil engineers and city leaders, see Martin V. Melosi, *The Sanitary City: Urban Infrastructure in America, from Colonial Times to the Present* (Baltimore: Johns Hopkins University Press, 2000). For more on garbage and waste, see Susan Strasser, *Waste and Want: A Social History of Trash* (New York: Henry Holt, 1999).

9. John Duffy patiently details the back-and-forth of the city's decisions to choose private or public solutions in *A History of Public Health in New York City, 1625–1866* (New York: Russell Sage Foundation, 1968), chs. 8, 15. "Our Streets," *New-York Evening Post, for the Country,* 3 May 1825; "Sweeping the

Streets," *New York Evening Post, for the Country,* 29 April 1825; "Proceedings of the Common Council," *Weekly Commercial Advertiser,* 3 March 1826.

10. "The Streets! The Streets!" *New-York Evening Post, for the Country,* 3 June 1825; Anonymous, *A Clear and Concise Statement of New-York, and the Surrounding Country* (New York: Printed for the Author; and sold by John Wilson, No. 22 William-Street, Opposite the Post-Office, 1819), 7–8; Axel Leonhard Klinckowström, *Baron Klinkowström's [sic] America, 1818–1820,* trans. and ed. Franklin D. Scott from the Swedish edition (Evanston, IL: Northwestern University Press, 1952), 63–64; "Public Health," *New-York Evening Post, for the Country,* 12 August 1825; "Public Health," *New-York Evening Post, for the Country,* 16 August 1822; "Sweeping the Streets," *New-York Evening Post, for the Country,* 18 April 1823; "Cleanliness," *New-York Evening Post, for the Country,* 15 July 1823; "New York General Sessions," *New-York Evening Post, for the Country,* 3 August 1824; "The Streets! The Streets!" *New-York Evening Post, for the Country,* 3 June 1825.

11. New York State, *Census of the State of New York, for 1835* (Albany: Croswell, Van Ben Thuysen and Bourt, 1836). On the role of horses in the nineteenth-century American city: Clay McShane and Joel A. Tarr, *The Horse in the City: Living Machines in the Nineteenth Century* (Baltimore: Johns Hopkins University Press, 2007); Ann Norton Greene, *Horses at Work: Harnessing Power in Industrial America* (Cambridge, MA: Harvard University Press, 2008); Clay McShane, "Gelded Age Boston," *New England Quarterly* 74 (August 2001): 274–302.

12. A. J. Downing, ed., *The Horticulturist, and Journal of Rural Art and Rural Taste* (Albany: Luther Tucker, 1847), 1:99. For more on this early recycling ethic, see Richard A. Wines, *Fertilizer in America: From Waste Recycling to Resource Exploitation* (Philadelphia: Temple University Press, 1985), 3–21; "Dr. Lee's Report on Agriculture," *The Cultivator* (1845), 2:164. For more on the development of an "improvement ethic," see Steven Stoll, *Larding the Lean Earth: Soil and Society in Nineteenth-Century America* (New York: Hill and Wang, 2002), 19–25. Stoll contends that politics was a driving force in the decisions that farmers made to improve their lands through fertilization and other programs, rather than migrate west to establish new farms. While this was certainly part of the ethic motivating some farmers, I would argue that in the New York hinterland farmers decided to stay where they were because of the economic opportunities afforded to them. They could profit from the fact that much of the city's produce needed to be produced locally, due to its bulk or its perishability.

13. Wines, *Fertilizer in America,* 9; William Ketcham, "The Manures Used upon Long Island," *Transactions of the State of New York Agricultural Society, 1843* (Albany: Carroll and Cook, 1844), 3:463. Ketcham was a farmer in Jericho, New York, in the Town of Oyster Bay. U.S. Bureau of the Census, *1850 United States Federal Census,* Oyster Bay, Queens, New York, Roll M432_582: 191B, Image 34. In 1807, Samuel Mitchell described how Flatbush's "industrious and wealthy farmers" used New York's street manure and ashes to help raise grain and grass. Samuel Mitchell, *The Picture of New-York; or, The Traveler's Guide through the Commercial Metropolis of the United States, by a Gentleman Residing in this City* (New York: I. Riley, 1807), 160. For more about the specific ties between New York manure and Kings County, see Marc Linder and Lawrence S. Zacharias, *Of Cabbages and Kings County: Agriculture and the Formation of Modern Brooklyn* (Iowa City: University of Iowa Press, 1999), 44–51.

14. The entire cost of cleaning the streets in 1830 was $25,976.73. *Annual Report of the Comptroller* (New York: Peter van Pelt, 1831), 11, 18–19. Manure revenue was on the rise. In 1818 the government made $13,700 for its street scrapings. *The Picture of New-York, and Stranger's Guide to the Commercial Metropolis of the United States* (New York: A. T. Goodrich, 1828), 115. "Communication," *New York Herald,* 21 May 1817; "Dirty Streets," *New-York Evening Post, for the Country,* 14 June 1822; "Dirt Carts," *New-York Evening Post, for the Country,* 23 August 1822; "Communication," *New-York Evening Post, for the Country,* 29 November 1822; "Dirty Streets," *New-York Evening Post, for the Country,* 3 December 1822; "To the Public," *New-York Evening Post, for the Country,* 10 December 1824; "Sweeping the Streets," *New York Evening Post, for the Country,* 29 April 1825; "The Streets! The Streets!" *New-York Evening Post, for the Country,* 3 June 1825; "Proceedings of the Common Council," *Weekly Commercial Advertiser,* 3 March 1826; "The Streets," *New-York Mercury,* 16 May 1832; "The Streets," *New-York Spectator,* 2 August 1832; "Pine Street," *New-York Spectator,* 24 November 1836; "Cleaning the Streets by Contract," *New York Herald,* 4 August 1848; *Proceedings of the Board of Aldermen of the City of New York* (New York: McSpedon and Baker, Printers to the Common Council, 1849), 8 May 1849, 37:19–23; *Annual Report of the Comptroller* (New York: Peter van Pelt, 1831); "Common Council," *Morning Courier and New-York Enquirer, for the Country,* 28 February 1840.

15. *Minutes of the Common Council of the City of New York, 1784–1831* (New York: Published by the City, 1917), 14:456; 14:497; "Proceedings of the Common Council," *New-York Spectator,* 15 April 1825; "Communication," *New*

York Herald, 21 May 1817; I. N. Phelps Stokes, *Iconography of Manhattan Island* (New York: R. H. Dodd, 1915–1928), 5:1615–1616; "Sweeping the Streets," *New-York Evening Post, for the Country,* 18 April 1823; *Minutes of the Common Council of the City of New York, 1784–1831* (New York: Published by the City, 1917), 14:659; 15:233, 306–309; "The Streets! The Streets!" *New-York Evening Post, for the Country,* 3 June 1825. For more on the organic city, see Ted Steinberg, *Down to Earth: Nature's Role in American History* (New York: Oxford University Press, 2002), 157–172.

16. Farmers were able to purchase street dirt from the landings on Staten Island and Long Island for several decades. Selah Strong, a gentleman farmer in Brooklyn, reported in his diary that in 1820 he purchased twenty-five loads of street manure from the local docks. Selah Strong, Diary, 1817–1833, New-York Historical Society, New York; *Transactions of the New-York State Agricultural Society* (Albany: E. Mack, 1843), 2:205–206; Benjamin J. Thompson, *History of Long Island from Its Discovery and Settlement to the Present Time,* 3rd ed. (1839; New York: Robert H. Dodd, 1918), 76; "Agricultural Products of Long Island—Amount of Manures Used—Interesting Tables," *The American Agriculturist, for the Farm, Garden, and Household* (New York: Orange Judd, 1860), 19:229; *Proceedings of the Board of Aldermen,* 18 June 1849, 37.1:307–317.

17. *Transactions of the New-York State Agricultural Society,* 2:206; New York Common Council, *Laws and Ordinances Ordained and Established by the Mayor, Aldermen, and Commonalty of the City of New-York, in Common Council Convened* (New York: T. and J. Swords, 1817), 64–66.

18. *Blunt's Stranger's Guide to the City of New-York* (New-York: Edmund M. Blunt, 1817), 244–258; New York Common Council, *Laws and Ordinances* (1817), 64–66; New York City Common Council, *By-laws and Ordinances of the Mayor, Aldermen, and Commonalty of the City of New-York* (New York: John S. Voorhies, 1845), 319–320.

19. Ketcham, 3:465; *Transactions of the New-York State Agricultural Society,* 2:208.

20. "The Condition of Our Streets," *New-York Spectator,* 31 May 1831; New York City Inspector, *Annual Report of the City Inspector, of the Number of Deaths and Interments in the City of New York, during the Year 1849* (New York: McSpedon and Baker, 1850), 501–513. For more on the history of the sense of smell, see Joy Parr, "Smells Like? Sources of Uncertainty in the History of the Great Lakes Environment," *Environmental History* 11.2 (2006): 269–299; Con-

nie Chiang, "The Nose Knows: The Sense of Smell in American History," for "Roundtable: The Senses in American History," *Journal of American History* 95.2 (2008): 405–416; Connie Chiang, "Monterey-by-the-Smell: Odors and Social Conflict on the California Coastline," *Pacific Historical Review* 73.2 (2004): 183–214.

21. As citizens had to petition the Common Council to fence each vacant lot and as City Inspectors had to report on each, there are countless examples of these instances. A selection from 1830 alone includes: *Minutes of the Common Council,* 28 June 1830, 19:127; 6 September 1830, 19:218; 20 September 1830, 19:240; 18 October 1830, 19:291; 18 October 1830, 19:304. *Minutes of the Common Council,* 5 June 1815, 8:220; 8 January 1816, 8:398; 29 January 1816, 8:406. Finding an appropriate "dumping ground" was a long-standing problem and one that changed as the population of the city pushed the outer limits of its boundaries. See, for example, "We Perceive by the Proceedings . . . ," *New-York Evening Post, for the Country,* 11 July 1823. Examples of residents complaining about the location of manure docks include *Minutes of the Common Council,* 10 March 1828, 17:27; 25 April 1831, 19:665; *Proceedings of the Board of Aldermen,* 23 May 1831, 1:46.

22. *Proceedings of the Board of Aldermen,* 1 July 1831, 1:167–169; *Minutes of the Common Council,* 9 May 1831, 19:714.

23. "The North Battery," *New-York Spectator,* 12 July 1831; *Proceedings of the Board of Aldermen,* 18 July 1831, 1:203.

24. Elizabeth Blackmar, *Manhattan for Rent, 1785–1850* (Ithaca: Cornell University Press, 1989).

25. Gerard T. Koeppel, *Water for Gotham: A History* (Princeton: Princeton University Press, 2000), 70–138.

26. Cholera spread in 1831 via trade routes from Russia and Poland westward through France and England, finally reaching the Americas in the summer of 1832. "Cholera," *New-York Spectator,* 22 June 1832; "Report of the Committee on Cholera," *New-York Spectator,* 26 June 1832; "Cholera Statistics," *New-York Mercury,* 15 August 1832; Charles E. Rosenberg, *The Cholera Years: The United States in 1832, 1849 and 1866* (Chicago: University of Chicago Press, 1962), 13–14.

27. John Pintard, *Letters from John Pintard to His Daughter Eliza Noel Pintard Davidson, 1816–1833* (New York: Printed for the New-York Historical Society, 1941) 4:72; "Cholera Statistics," *New-York Mercury,* 15 August 1832; "Cholera," *New-York Spectator,* 22 June 1832; "Cholera," *New-York Spectator,*

6 July 1832; "An Intemperate Individual," *New-York Spectator,* 17 August 1832. "Cholera in New-York," *New-York Spectator,* 6 July 1832.

28. "Cholera," *New-York Spectator,* 6 July 1832. "Board of Health," *New-York Spectator,* 22 June 1832; *Proceedings of the Board of Aldermen,* 25 June 1832, 3:106; "Bathing," *New-York Spectator,* 25 July 1833; "Cholera," *New-York Spectator,* 6 July 1832; New York Board of Health, Minutes, 1798–1896 (microform). NYC Municipal Archives, Roll 2, 20 June 1832, 28 July 1832; "Relief to the Poor," *New-York Spectator,* 2 August 1832. For more on how epidemics led to a rise in social-welfare support, see Ryan, *Civic Wars,* 104.

29. "Document No. 5," *Documents of the Board of Assistants* (New York: Printed by the Order of the Common Council, 1838), 4 June 1832, 2/3:11–12; *Proceedings of the Board of Aldermen,* 14 May 1832, 3:17; 11 June 1832, 3:66–67; *Proceedings of the Boards of Aldermen and Assistant Aldermen, and Approved by the Mayor, from May 16, 1831, to May 14, 1833* (New York: Printed by Order of the Common Council, 1835), 1:223–225, 241; Greene, *A Glance at New York,* 175.

30. New York State, *Messages from the Governors,* ed. Charles Z. Lincoln (Albany: J. B. Lyon, 1909), 3:395; *Proceedings of the Board of Aldermen,* 28 July 1832, 3:155–156. For more on the spiritual response to the 1832 outbreak, see Rosenberg, *The Cholera Years,* 40–54.

31. The fact that New Yorkers were aware of the environmental causes of disease as early as 1832 counters Charles Rosenberg's interpretation that Americans did not begin to accept these ideas until the later outbreaks in 1849 and 1866. Even Governor Throop discussed sanitation in his message to the New York State legislature in 1832. New York State, *Messages from the Governors,* 3:395; Rosenberg, *The Cholera Years.* For more on the early acceptance of environmental causes of disease, see Nancy Tomes, *The Gospel of Germs: Men, Women, and the Microbe in American* Life (Cambridge, MA: Harvard University Press, 1998), 23–87, though my findings trace the support for sanitation back even further than Tomes does. *Proceedings of the Board of Aldermen,* 25 June 1832, 3:106; *Proceedings of the Boards of Aldermen and Assistant Aldermen, and Approved by the Mayor, from May 16, 1831, to May 14, 1833* (New York: Printed by Order of the Common Council, 1835), 1:237–239; "Communication," *New-York Mercury,* 1 August 1832; "The Streets," *New-York Spectator,* 2 August 1832.

32. "Relief to the Poor," *New-York Spectator,* 23 July 1832; *Proceedings of the Board of Aldermen,* 1 August 1832, 3:159; "Relief to the Poor," *New-York Spectator,* 2 August 1832; Paul Gilje, *The Road to Mobocracy: Popular Disorder in New*

York City, 1783–1834 (Chapel Hill: University of North Carolina Press, 1987), 230. The presence of hogs did not diminish significantly even during the outbreak. Observers as late as October remarked on the great numbers of them roaming the streets. "Boston and New York," *New-York Spectator,* 1 October 1832.

33. "Restoration of Health," *New-York Spectator,* 30 August 1832; "Cholera," *New-York Spectator,* 3 September 1832; "The Corporation," *New-York Spectator,* 23 May 1833; "The Streets," *Morning Courier and New-York Enquirer,* quoted in "Health of the City," *New-York Spectator,* 23 May 1833.

34. "Hint for Those Who Will Take It," *New-York Spectator,* 3 May 1834; "To the Editors of the Commercial Advertiser," *New-York Spectator,* 7 April 1834; "The Corporation," *New-York Spectator,* 8 September 1834; "The Triumph!" *New-York Spectator,* 17 April 1834; Edwin G. Burrows and Mike Wallace, *Gotham: A History of New York City to 1898* (New York: Oxford University Press, 1999), 571–575; Amy Bridges, *A City in the Republic: Antebellum New York and the Origins of Machine Politics* (New York: Cambridge University Press, 1984), 61–84.

35. Burr's Manhattan Company merged with Chase National Bank in 1955, to form Chase Manhattan Bank. Koeppel, *Water for Gotham,* 79–88; *Minutes of the Common Council of the City of New York* (New York: Published by the City of New York, 1917), 28 February 1831, 19:518; Lyceum report quoted in "Document 45," *Documents of the Board of Aldermen of the City of New York* (New York, 1835), 4 March 1835, 1:524; "Notes by the Way," *New-York Spectator,* 11 November 1831.

36. Koeppel, *Water for Gotham,* 154–156; "Document 45," 4 March 1835, 1:524; "Abridgement of the Report of the Water Commissioners," *New-York Spectator,* 26 March 1835.

37. Koeppel, *Water for Gotham,* 170–172; "The Charter Election," *New-York Spectator,* 20 April 1835; "The Whig Common Council," *New-York Spectator,* 11 May 1835; Burrows and Wallace, *Gotham,* 596–598.

38. "Local Laws," *New-York Spectator,* 13 June 1836; "A Suggestion," *New-York Spectator,* 25 December 1837; "Messrs. Editors," *Morning Courier and New-York Enquirer, for the Country,* 28 August 1838; "Board of Assistants," *Morning Courier and New-York Enquirer, for the Country,* 8 February 1839; "The Croton War," *Morning Courier and New-York Enquirer, for the Country,* 10 April 1840; "City Abuses," *New-York Daily Tribune,* 26 August 1842; Koeppel, *Water for Gotham,* 139–284; "The Croton Jubilee," *New-York Tribune,* 15 October 1842. For similar hopes and support for municipal water, see Michael Rawson, "The

Nature of Water: Reform and the Antebellum Crusade for Municipal Water in Boston," *Environmental History* 9.3 (2004): 411–435.

39. "The Croton Jubilee," E. Porter Belden, *New York, Past, Present, and Future; Comprising a History of the City of New York, a Description of Its Present Condition, and an Estimate of Its Future Increase* (New York: G. P. Putnam, 1849), 36–42.

40. New York Board of Aldermen, "Document 16," *Documents of the Board of Aldermen of the City of New York* (New York: J. F. Trow, 1845), 11:188.

41. "Document 16," 11:188. Police even fined those who dumped indiscriminately $50 for each offense. "Document 16," 11:191. The New York Poudrette Company began petitioning the city for rights to its privies in 1839. While the Aldermen were seemingly enthusiastic and felt that the program would "produce great benefits to the community" the early requests were "laid on the table" indefinitely. *Proceedings of the Board of Aldermen,* 28 January 1839, 16:133–134; 22 April 1839, 16:336; 29 April 1839, 16:390–391; 6 May 1839, 16:421; 16 December 1839, 18:71; 30 Dec 1839, 18:85; 2 March 1840, 18:328; 4 March 1840, 18:344.

42. American farmers, including many in New York State, had likely also utilized human waste, albeit informally. The poudrette companies, however, tried to make the practice extensive, common, and profitable. "Poudrette—A New Article," *The Cultivator* (1844), 1:167; Wines, *Fertilizer in America,* 26; Carl Bridenbaugh, *Cities in Revolt: Urban Life in America, 1743–1776* (New York: Alfred A. Knopf, 1955), 241; Joel A. Tarr, "From City to Farm: Urban Wastes and the American Farmer," *Agricultural History* 49 (October 1975), 599–600; "Chemical, or Prepared Manures," *The Cultivator* (1841), 8:110.

43. "Urate and Poudrette," *The Cultivator* (1840), 7:144; "Artificial Manures," *The Cultivator* (1842), 9:156; "Fertilizing Powder," *New-York Tribune,* 14 July 1841; "Price Reduced to Six Cents a Cubic Foot," *New-York Tribune,* 15 January 1842. "Curious Disclosures in Bankruptcy," *New York Herald,* 12 December 1842; New York State, *Laws of the State of New York* (Albany: E. Croswell, 1839), 350–352; "Urate and Poudrette," *The Cultivator* (1840), 7:144; "Poudrette—A New Article," *The Cultivator* (1844), 1:167. For more on how poudrette and commercially produced fertilizers were substituted for local stable manures, see Wines, *Fertilizer in America.*

44. In general, the Lodi Manufacturing Company kept its trade practices secret, never going into much detail about the process involved in converting night soil into usable manure. For instance, in a brochure distributed in 1852, the company referred to a "speedy chemical process" but provided no other

details. Lodi Manufacturing Company, *Circular* (New York: n.p., 1852), 1. The main exceptions are found in the incorporation papers published in 1840 and in an *American Agriculturalist* article from 1863. To gather information for this article, journalists apparently surprised the managers with a visit and detailed the process they observed. The incorporation papers describe some of the hopes for the structures and processes that would be developed as the company took off. The 1863 article shows how the process actually worked, over two decades later. New Jersey, *An Act to Incorporate the Lodi Manufacturing Company for Purposes of Agriculture, Passed 6th February 1840* (New York: Printed by H. Cassidy, 1840); "The 'Night Soil' of New-York City," *American Agriculturist* (June 1863), 6.197:169.

45. New Jersey, *An Act to Incorporate the Lodi Manufacturing Company,* 7; "The 'Night Soil' of New-York City," *American Agriculturist* (June 1863), 6.197:169. To a limited degree, the Lodi Manufacturing Company also produced urate, a dried form of human urine. This was separated out as much as possible from the solid waste in the night soil. The main factory building even had a separate wing for processing urate. Yet because of its low production levels and higher price (it cost 10 cents more per bushel than poudrette), urate never really caught on as a fertilizer.

46. "The 'Night Soil' of New-York City"; New Jersey, *An Act to Incorporate the Lodi Manufacturing Company,* 7.

47. New Jersey, *An Act to Incorporate the Lodi Manufacturing Company,* 6–7.

48. "Chemical, or Prepared Manures," *The Cultivator* (1841), 8:110; Lodi Manufacturing Company, *Circular* (New York: n.p., 1852), 1.

49. "Urate and Poudrette," *The Cultivator* (1840), 7:144; *Transactions of the New-York State Agricultural Society* (Albany: E. Mack, 1843), 2:205–206, 209; New Jersey, *An act to incorporate the Lodi Manufacturing Company,* 3.

50. "Poudrette," *The Cultivator* (1845), 2:151; Homer J. Wheeler, *Manures and Fertilizers* (New York: MacMillan, 1913), 18.

51. *Transactions of the New-York State Agricultural Society,* 2:209; "Poudrette," *The Cultivator* (1845), 2:306–307; "Poudrette—A New Article," *The Cultivator* (1844), 1:167; S. W. Johnson, *Essays on Peat, Muck, and Commercial Manures* (Hartford: Brown and Gross, 1859), 42–46.

52. Wines, *Fertilizer in America,* 29–30; "News of the Month," *The Cultivator* (1853), 1.7:226; Sabine Barles and Laurence Lestel, "The Nitrogen Question: Urbanization, Industrialization, and River Quality in Paris, 1830–1939," *Journal*

of Urban History 33 (2007): 806–808. For more on guano, see Wines, *Fertilizer in America,* 33–53.

53. For more on the municipal impulse toward private solutions, see Sam Bass Warner, *The Private City: Philadelphia in Three Periods of Its Growth* (Philadelphia: University of Pennsylvania Press, 1968).

54. New York Board of Health, Minutes, Roll 7, 16 May 1849, 21 May 1849; New York City Inspector, *Annual Report of the City Inspector, of the Number of Deaths and Interments,* 501–513; "City Intelligence," *New York Herald,* 18 May 1849; "The Cholera in Orange-St.," *New-York Tribune,* 18 May 1849; "The Cholera," *New-York Daily Tribune,* 21 May 1849; *Proceedings of the Board of Aldermen,* 28 May 1849, 37.2:152–154.

55. New York Board of Health, Minutes, Roll 7, 16 May 1849.

56. "The Cholera in Orange-St.," *New-York Tribune,* 18 May 1849; "The Epidemic," *New-York Tribune,* 19 May 1849; "The Cholera" *New-York Tribune,* 21 May 1849; Greene, *A Glance at New York,* 177–178; *Annual Report of the City Inspector,* 1849; "City Items," *New-York Daily Tribune,* 19 May 1849.

57. "Board of Aldermen," *New-York Daily Tribune,* 22 June 1847; New York Board of Health, Minutes, Roll 7, 17 May 1849; "City Intelligence," *New York Herald,* 18 May 1849; *Proceedings of the Board of Aldermen,* 13 June 1849, 37:256; Roy Rosenzweig and Elizabeth Blackmar, *The Park and the People: A History of Central Park* (Ithaca: Cornell University Press, 1992), 62. For more discussion of uptown swine, see Rosenberg, *The Cholera Years,* 113; "New York by Sun-Light—Thermometer 90 in the Shade," *New York Herald,* 12 July 1849; "Twelfth-Ward—Cholera Incitements," *New-York Daily Tribune,* 6 August 1849; "The Cholera Report of Last Week," *New York Herald,* 6 August 1849; "Health of the City—The Cholera Report of Last Week," *New York Herald,* 13 August 1849. For more on the piggeries, see Chapter 4.

58. *Annual Report of the City Inspector,* 1849; New York Board of Health, Minutes, Roll 7, 21 May 1849; "City Intelligence," *New York Herald,* 25 July 1849; "The Progress of the Cholera," *New York Herald,* 30 July 1849.

59. New York Board of Health, *Report of the Proceedings of the Sanatory Committee of the Board of Health in Relation to the Cholera as It Prevailed in New York in 1849* (New York: McSpedon and Baker, 1849), 53; *Proceedings of the Board of Aldermen,* 16 July 1849, 37.1:525–526; *Annual Report of the City Inspector,* 1849.

60. Alan I. Marcus has argued that fear of newcomers provoked systemic changes; see Marcus, *A Plague of Strangers: Social Groups and the Origins of*

City Services in Cincinnati (Columbus: Ohio State University Press, 1991). Criticisms of the city's progress and efficiency include: "The Cholera Report of Last Week," *New York Herald,* 6 August 1849; "Twelfth-Ward—Cholera Incitements," *New-York Tribune,* 6 August 1849; "Health of the City—The Cholera Report of Last Week," *New York Herald,* 13 August 1849; *Proceedings of the Board of Aldermen,* 15 October 1849, 37.2:99; "City Intelligence," *New-York Evening Post,* 7 December 1849; New York Board of Health, *Report of the Proceedings of the Sanatory Committee,* 33–36; *Proceedings of the Board of Aldermen,* 12 November 1849, 37.2:237.

61. *Annual Report of the City Inspector,* 1849; "City Intelligence," *New York Herald,* 25 July 1849; "Our Cholera Sermon," *New-York Tribune,* 3 August 1849.

62. "A Rare Curiosity," *New-York Tribune,* 31 January 1852.

63. "Mr. Editor," *New-York Evening Post,* 22 July 1817; "Reform for Filthy New-York," *New-York Tribune,* 6 March 1854.

4. Hog Wash and Swill Milk

1. George Foster, *New York in Slices, by an Experienced Carver: Being the Original Slices Published in the N.Y. Tribune* (New York: W. F. Burgess, 1849), 79–84.

2. Christine Meisner Rosen has a succinct review of the literature on nuisance case law in "'Knowing' Industrial Pollution: Nuisance Law and the Power of Tradition in a Time of Rapid Economic Change, 1840–1864," *Environmental History* 8.4 (2003): 565–597. See also Morton J. Horwitz, *The Transformation of American Law, 1780–1860* (Cambridge, MA: Harvard University Press, 1977), 74–78; Paul M. Kurtz, "Nineteenth Century Anti-Entrepreneurial Nuisance Injunctions: Avoiding the Chancellor," *William and Mary Law Review* 17 (Summer 1976): 621–670; D. M. Provine, "Balancing Pollution and Property Rights: A Comparison of the Development of English and American Nuisance Law," *Anglo-American Law Review* 7 (Jan.–March 1978): 31–56; John P. S. McClaren, "Nuisance Law and the Industrial Revolution: Some Lessons from Social History," *Oxford Journal of Legal Studies* 3.2 (1983): 155–221; E. P. Krauss, "The Legal Form of Liberalism: A Study of Riparian and Nuisance Law in Nineteenth Century Ohio," *Akron Law Journal* 18 (Fall 1984): 223–253; Robert G. Bone, "Normative Theory and Legal Doctrine in American Nuisance Law, 1850–1920," *Southern California Law Review* 59 (Sept. 1986): 1101–1226;

Michael S. McBride, "Critical Legal History and Private Actions against Public Nuisances, 1800–1865," *Columbia Journal of Law and Social Problems* 22 (1989): 307–322; Christine Meisner Rosen, "Differing Perceptions of the Value of Pollution Abatement across Time and Place: Balancing Doctrine in Pollution Nuisance Law, 1840–1906," *Legal History Review* 11.2 (1993): 303–381; William J. Novak, *People's Welfare: Law and Regulation in Nineteenth-Century America* (Chapel Hill: University of North Carolina Press, 1996); Peter Karsten, *Heart versus Head: Judge-Made Law in Nineteenth-Century America* (Chapel Hill: University of North Carolina Press, 1997). For an overview of nuisance case law, see Jesse Dukeminier and James E. Krier, *Property,* 5th ed. (New York: Aspen Law and Business, 2002), ch. 9.

3. "Corporation Proceedings," *New-York Tribune,* 12 June 1850; New York (N.Y.) Board of Aldermen, "Document No. 32," *Documents of the Board of Aldermen of the City of New York* (New York: McSpedon and Baker, 1853), 20.1:590–591.

4. New York (N.Y.) Board of Aldermen, "Document No. 43," *Documents of the Board of Aldermen of the City of New York* (New York: McSpedon and Baker, 1854), 21.1:826–829, 835–843; "Walks among the New-York Poor," *New York Times,* 22 January 1853; "Walks among the New-York Poor," *New York Times,* 4 March 1853. For more on these scavengers or ragpickers, see Chapter 5. In May 1857, a collector was arrested and imprisoned for two days for profiting from offal. City officials were aware that similar violations were occurring regularly. "City Ordinances Violated," *New-York Daily Tribune,* 28 May 1857.

5. "Manures," *The Cultivator* (1834), 1:91–92.

6. New York (N.Y.) Board of Health, *Report of the Proceedings of the Sanatory Committee of the Board of Health in Relation to the Cholera as It Prevailed in New York in 1849* (New York: McSpedon and Baker, 1849), 53; New York (N.Y.), *Proceedings of the Board of Aldermen, From May 8th, to September 17th, 1849* (New York: McSpedon and Baker, 1849), 18 June 1849, 37.1:282; 9 July 1849, 37.1:447–448. The medical community generally accepted that miasmas— strong odors and gases escaping from decomposing plant and animal matter— were the source of most ailments and diseases, including cholera. For more on miasmas, see Chapter 3. See also *Report of the Proceedings of the Sanatory Committee,* 33–36; New York (N.Y.) City Inspector, *Annual Report of the City Inspector, of the Number of Deaths and Interments in the City of New York, during the Year 1849* (New York: McSpedon and Baker, 1850), 501–513. This interpreta-

tion conflicts with Alan I. Marcus's thesis of causation in *A Plague of Strangers: Social Groups and the Origins of City Services in Cincinnati* (Columbus: Ohio State University Press, 1991).

7. *Proceedings of the Board of Aldermen,* 1 August 1849, 37.1:681; *Annual Report of the City Inspector, 1849,* 501–513; New York (N.Y.) Board of Aldermen, "Document No. 32," *Documents of the Board of Aldermen of the City of New York* (New York: McSpedon and Baker, 1854), 20.1:626; "Document No. 32," 20.1:592, 626.

8. *Annual Report of the City Inspector, 1849,* 501–513; New York (N.Y.) Board of Aldermen, "Document No. 43," *Documents of the Board of Aldermen of the City of New York* (New York: McSpedon and Baker, 1854), 21.1:625. On Viele's discussion of the Central Park squatters, see Chapter 5.

9. "Document No. 43," 21.1:792–793; "Document No. 32," 20.1:621–622.

10. "Document No. 43," 21.1:793–794, 798–799; New York (N.Y.) Board of Aldermen, "Document No. 45," *Documents of the Board of Aldermen,* 21.2:867.

11. "Document No. 45," 21.2:878, 888.

12. "Document No. 45," 21.2:876, 882.

13. "Document No. 45," 21.2:866–893.

14. New York (State) Legislature, *An Act Relative to the Public Health in the City of New York, Passed April 10, 1850* (New York: State of New York, Secretary's Office, 1850), 39–43; *Proceedings of the Board of Aldermen* (New York: McSpedon and Baker, 1850), 12 July 1850, 39:425–427; 5 September 1850, 39:648–649; 8 October 1850, 40:42–45; "City Items," *New-York Tribune,* 29 August 1850; "Common Council," *New York Herald,* 6 September 1850.

15. "Court of Common Pleas," *New-York Daily Tribune,* 11 November 1851; "Document No. 43," 21.1:789.

16. "Document No. 43," 21.1:794; *Proceedings of the Board of Aldermen,* 11 November 1850, 40:324–325.

17. Investigators were never able to prove completely that White remained involved, but it was inferred from the continued presence of his friend Morgan. Heman W. Childs, the other silent partner, passed away in June 1851. Despite Childs's corrupt dealings with the firm, he would never have to face public scrutiny. *Proceedings of the Board of Aldermen,* 2 June 1851, 42:525. "Document No. 43," 21.1:771, 791, 794–795. Along with his partners, Reynolds bought out Brady, Baxter, Lent & Co., acquiring their holdings. Some of the holdings were not handed over, and Reynolds ended up taking the firm to court. "Document No. 43," 21.1:765; "Document No. 45," 21.2:896–898.

18. "The City Inspector and the Common Council," *New York Times,* 9 April 1852; "Document No. 43," 21.1:778–792.

19. Azariah Flagg's determination to reform city government and finances is chronicled in his collection of affidavits attesting to the various examples of corruption. New York (N.Y.) Finance Department, *Communication of the Comptroller, Enclosing Affidavits Taken before the Recorder, in the Years 1853 and 1854, Relating to Alleged Abuses in the City Government* (New York: Mc-Spedon and Baker, 1854); "Document No. 43," 21.1:786–792; "Document No. 32," 20.1:601–604.

20. *Proceedings of the Board of Aldermen,* 18 May 1853, 50:498–501; 23 May 1853, 50:531–535; 16 June 1853, 50:657–658; "The Presentment at Last," *New-York Daily Tribune,* 23 October 1855; "City Politics," *New-York Daily Tribune,* 1 November 1855; "The Presentment," *New-York Daily Tribune,* 23 October 1855; Board of Aldermen, "Document No. 38," *Documents of the Board of Aldermen of the City of New York,* 21.1:601–612; "Document No. 32," 20.1:583–600.

21. *Proceedings of the Board of Aldermen,* 17 June 1853, 50:669–670; 6 July 1853, 51:20–22; 8 July 1853, 51:48; 1 August 1853, 51:143; 15 September 1853, 51:421; "Offal Nuisance," *New-York Daily Tribune,* 3 June 1854.

22. Sturtevant was voted out of office after constituents learned about his corrupt dealings with railroad contracts. "Sturtevant Discharged," *New-York Tribune,* 6 February 1854; *Proceedings of the Board of Aldermen,* 19 April 1854, 54:204, 212–213. "The City Finances," *New-York Daily Tribune,* 4 September 1856.

23. The possession of Barren Island continued to trouble the city politicians for years. Barren Island was arguably the best place for the city's offal, and Reynolds demanded a finder's fee of $10,000 in addition to the cost of the lease. Ultimately the courts decided on a price in 1859 and Barren Island became New York's central location for animal processing. *Proceedings of the Board of Aldermen,* 5 May 1854, 54:299–308; 10 August 1854, 55:249–256; 11 May 1855, 58:362–373; "The Presentment at Last," *New-York Daily Tribune,* 23 October 1855; "City Politics," *New-York Daily Tribune,* 1 November 1855; "The Presentment," *New-York Daily Tribune,* 23 October 1855. New York (N.Y.) Board of Aldermen, "Document No. 57," *Documents of the Board of Aldermen of the City of New York,* 21.2: 1745–1750; "Board of Aldermen," *New-York Daily Tribune,* 11 September 1855; "Municipal: Proceedings of the Common Council," *New York Times,* 13 November 1855; "Board of Councilmen," *New-York Daily Tribune,* 13 May 1856; "Public Meetings," *New-York Daily Tribune,*

28 January 1859. Reynolds would later go into business with former City Inspector Thomas K. Downing, forming the firm Reynolds & Downing on 117 Nassau St. Troy City Directory Co., *Wilson's New York City Copartnership Directory, for 1868–1869* (New York: John F. Trow, 1868), 88; *Proceedings of the Board of Aldermen*, 28 September 1854, 55:513–516; 19 October 1854, 56:115–120.

24. "Board of Aldermen," *New-York Daily Tribune*, 26 February 1856. No matter what the city paid, the offal contract was so lucrative that competitors continued to contest it and fight for their own bids that spring. "The Offal Contract," *New York Times*, 11 March 1856.

25. In discussing the corrupt political dealings at the heart of railroad development in the nineteenth century, Richard White artfully weighs the benefits while finding that the losses were ultimately heaviest, a parallel seen here as well. Richard White, "Information, Markets, and Corruption: Transcontinental Railroads in the Gilded Age," *Journal of American History*, 90.1 (2003): 19–43; Richard White, *Railroaded: The Transcontinentals and the Making of Modern America* (New York: W. W. Norton, 2011).

26. W. J. Rorabaugh, *The Alcoholic Republic: An American Tradition* (New York: Oxford University Press, 1979).

27. "Sale of Bad Milk in New York," *New York Herald*, 30 January 1851; "Death in a Jug," *New York Times*, 22 January 1853; John Mullaly, *The Milk Trade in New York and Vicinity* (New York: Fowlers and Wells, 1853), 58–60; "Swill-Fed Cows in New-York and Its Environs—Slaughter of the Innocents—A Hint for the Grand Jury," *New York Times*, 7 September 1857. For a brief history of swill milk from the perspective of the reformers as environmental protesters, see Michael Egan, "Organizing Environmental Protest: Swill Milk and Social Activism in Nineteenth-Century New York City," in Michael Egan and Jeff Crane, eds., *Natural Protest: Essays on the History of American Environmentalism* (New York: Routledge, 2009), 39–63.

28. William Cronon discusses the geographic relationship between various producers such as dairies and the city by relating their locations to Johann Heinrich von Thünen's concept of "rings." Dairies are placed in the closest proximity to cities, as they are part of "intensive agriculture." This remained true in New York, though the distillery men tried to defy this by finding a way to keep the cows in the midst of the city itself. William Cronon, *Nature's Metropolis: Chicago and the Great West* (New York: W. W. Norton, 1991), 46–54. See also Ellen Stroud, *Nature Next Door: Cities and Trees in the American Northeast* (Seattle: University of Washington Press, 2012), 90–91.

29. Mullaly, *The Milk Trade in New York and Vicinity*, 39–48.

30. Mullaly, *The Milk Trade in New York and Vicinity*, 51.

31. "The Adulterated Milk Traffic and Its Injurious Effects," *New York Herald*, 22 March 1854; "Swill-fed Cows in New-York and Its Environs—Slaughter of the Innocents—A Hint for the Grand Jury," *New York Times*, 7 September 1857.

32. Six cents was the average price for swill milk in 1858, according to "The Supply of Milk for the City," *New York Times*, 7 June 1858.

33. "Startling Exposure of the Milk Trade of New York and Brooklyn," *Frank Leslie's Illustrated Newspaper*, 8 May 1858. *Cholera infantum* was possibly an infection caused by bacteria, such as *E. coli*, salmonella, or shigella. It is also possible that it was a viral infection such as a rotavirus. Richard A. Meckel, *Save the Babies: American Public Health Reform and the Prevention of Infant Mortality, 1850–1929* (Baltimore: Johns Hopkins University Press, 1990) 41–43, 49–55; R. T. Trall, "Introduction," in Mullaly, *The Milk Trade in New York and Vicinity*, v. Similar numbers were estimated in 1858: "Swill-Milk and Infant Mortality," *New York Times*, 22 May 1858; Jacqueline H. Wolf, *Don't Kill Your Baby: Public Health and the Decline of Breastfeeding in the Nineteenth and Twentieth Centuries* (Columbus: Ohio State University Press, 2001), 40–41.

34. Robert M. Hartley, *An Historical, Scientific, and Practical Essay on Milk as an Article of Human Sustenance* (New York: J. Leavitt, 1842), 305–306; Samuel Irenaeus Prime, *Life in New York* (New York and Pittsburgh: Robert Carver, 1847), 184–190; Foster, *New York in Slices*, 79–84; "Sale of Bad Milk in New York," *New York Herald*, 30 January 1851; Mullaly, *The Milk Trade in New York and Vicinity*, xii–xvi; "Death in a Jug," *New York Times*, 22 January 1853; "Swill Milk and Bad Writing," *New York Times*, 18 August 1854; "Distillery Milk," *New York Times*, 18 August 1854; "New-York City: The Swill Milk Nuisance," *New York Times*, 23 August 1854. The Board of Aldermen debated restricting the number of cows allowed on any lot below 54th Street in 1854, but they ultimately did not act on the ordinance. *Proceedings of the Board of Aldermen*, 11 September 1854, 55:377–379; 9 April 1855, 58:109–110; Joshua Brown, *Beyond the Lines: Pictorial Reporting, Everyday Life, and the Crisis of Gilded-Age America* (Berkeley: University of California Press, 2002), 8, 17–18, 22.

35. "Frank Leslie to the Public: Startling Exposure of the Milk Trade of New-York and Brooklyn," *New York Times*, 7 May 1858; "Swill Milk," *New York Times*, 12 May 1858, 14 May 1858; "Exposure of the Swill Milk Busi-

ness," *New York Herald*, 3 May 1858; "Swill Milk," *New York Herald*, 5 May 1858; "Swill Milk Is Daily Delivered . . . ," *New York Herald*, 7 May 1858; "Frank Leslie to the Public: Startling Exposure of the Milk Trade of New-York and Brooklyn," *New York Times*, 7 May 1858. The circulation rates are likely slightly inflated, as they were Leslie's estimates. Brown, *Beyond the Lines*, 27–28.

36. Scholars who have studied Frank Leslie's work as a whole note that the success of the swill milk exposé inspired Leslie to change the nature of the *Illustrated Newspaper*. Leslie used illustrations more for news pieces than for humor, focusing on larger events in the months following the exposé, such as the death of President James Monroe, the laying of the Atlantic Cable, and the burning of the Crystal Palace. Budd Leslie Gambee, Jr., *Frank Leslie and His Illustrated Newspaper, 1855–1860* (Ann Arbor: University of Michigan, Dept. of Library Science, 1964), 69–72; Andrea G. Pearson, *"Frank Leslie's Illustrated Newspaper* and *Harper's Weekly:* Innovation and Imitation in Nineteenth-Century American Pictorial Reporting," *Journal of Popular Culture* 23.4 (1990): 82–86. "Startling Exposure of the Milk Trade of New York and Brooklyn," *Frank Leslie's Illustrated Newspaper*, 8 May 1858; "Assault by a Swill-Milk Maid," *New York Times*, 12 June 1858.

37. For more on nineteenth-century depictions of Irish ethnicity and race, see Brown, *Between the Lines*, 87–94; L. Perry Curtis, *Apes and Angels: The Irishman in Victorian Caricature* (Washington, D.C.: Smithsonian Institution Press, 1971), 58–67; Matthew Frye Jacobson, *Whiteness of a Different Color: European Immigrants and the Alchemy of Race* (Cambridge, MA: Harvard University Press, 1998), 45–52; Kevin Kenny, "Race, Violence, and Anti-Irish Sentiment in the Nineteenth Century," in *Making the Irish American*, ed. J. J. Lee and Marion R. Casey (New York: New York University Press, 2006), 364–380.

38. "The Murder of Innocents," *New-York Daily Tribune*, 17 July 1854.

39. "Swill-Milk," *New York Times*, 28 May 1858; "The Swill Milk Question," *New York Herald*, 28 May 1858; "The Swill-Milk Whitewashers Finishing Their Job," *New York Times*, 29 June 1858; New York (N.Y.) Board of Health, *Majority and Minority Reports of the Select Committee of the Board of Health, Appointed to Investigate the Character and Condition of the Sources from Which Cows' Milk Is Derived, for Sale in the City of New York* (New York: Charles W. Baker, 1858), 4–28; "The Board of Aldermen," *New York Times*, 9 June 1858.

40. For more on the professionalization of politicians during this era, see Sam Bass Warner, *The Private City: Philadelphia in Three Periods of Its Growth* (Philadelphia: University of Pennsylvania Press, 1968), 85–86.

41. "City Intelligence," *New York Times,* 1 November 1858.

42. "Meeting of the Board of Health," *New York Times,* 25 May 1858.

43. "Metropolitan Nuisances," *New York Times,* 5 June 1858.

44. "Common Council Proceedings," *New York Times,* 3 July 1854; "Common Council Proceedings," *New York Times,* 11 August 1854; "Municipal," *New York Times,* 27 November 1855.

45. Frederick Law Olmsted, "Passages in the Life of an Unpractical Man," in *The Papers of Frederick Law Olmsted,* vol. 3: *Creating Central Park, 1857–1861,* ed. Charles E. Beveridge and David Schuller (Baltimore: Johns Hopkins University Press, 1983), 84–94. Hogtown was just south of Seneca Village, which was mostly populated by free African Americans. "The Present Look of Our Great Central Park," *New York Times,* 9 July 1856; Roy Rosenzweig and Elizabeth Blackmar, *The Park and the People: A History of Central Park* (Ithaca: Cornell University Press, 1992), 59–91. For more on Central Park, see Chapter 5. "A Monster Nuisance," *New-York Tribune,* 13 July 1858; "Municipal Affairs," *New York Herald,* 20 September 1859.

46. "The Great War on the New York Piggeries," *Frank Leslie's Illustrated Newspaper,* 13 August 1859; "Practical Lesson in Politics," *New-York Daily Tribune,* 21 August 1845. For more on the subjective nature of smell descriptions and parallel issues with reference to nineteenth-century California, see Connie Chiang, "The Nose Knows: The Sense of Smell in American History," *Journal of American History* 95.2 (2008): 405–418; Chiang, "Monterey-by-the-Smell," *Pacific Historical Review* 73.2 (2004): 183–214; Chiang, *Shaping the Shoreline: Fisheries and Tourism on the Monterey Coast* (Seattle: University of Washington Press, 2008).

47. "The Bone Boiling Establishments of New York," *New York Herald,* 20 July 1859; Edwin G. Burrows and Mike Wallace, *Gotham: A History of New York City to 1898* (New York: Oxford University Press, 1999), 852–863.

48. *Proceedings of the Board of Aldermen,* 3 January 1859, 73:58; "The Senate's Sanitary Committee," *New-York Tribune,* 10 November 1858; *Proceedings of the Board of Aldermen,* 30 May 1859, 74:408; 13 June 1859, 74:492; *Proceedings of the Board of Aldermen,* 24 March 1859, 73:988–993; 19 May 1859, 74:314–318; *Proceedings of the Board of Aldermen,* 2 May 1859, 74:113–114; 5 May 1859, 74:142–144; 9 May 1859, 74:196; 12 May 1859, 74:234–235; 19

May 1859, 74:314–330; 23 May 1859, 74:351–352; *Proceedings of the Board of Aldermen of the City of New York*, 19 May 1859, 74:314–318; 23 May 1859, 74:352–360; "Colonel Daniel E. Delavan," *Frank Leslie's Illustrated Newspaper*, 3 September 1859.

49. *Proceedings of the Board of Aldermen*, 23 May 1859, 74:590–591; "Affairs of the City Inspector's Office," *New York Times*, 7 July 1859; "News of the Day," *New York Times*, 7 July 1859; "The Bone Boiling Establishments of New York," *New York Herald*, 20 July 1859. "City Intelligence," *New York Herald*, 26 July 1859.

50. "Further Particulars of the 'Hogtown War,' " *New York Herald*, 29 July 1859; "The Storming of Hogtown," *New York Herald*, 27 July 1859; "City Intelligence," *New York Times*, 7 July 1859; *Proceedings of the Board of Aldermen*, 21 July 1859, 75:148–150; "City Intelligence," *New York Times*, 26 July 1859; New York (N.Y.) Board of Aldermen, *Annual Report of the City Inspector of the City of New York, for the Year Ending December 31, 1860* (New York: Edmund Jones, 1861), 55–57. On the power of Irish voices in municipal politics during the 1850s, see Elliott J. Gorn, " 'Good-Bye Boys, I Die a True American': Homicide, Nativism, and Working-Class Culture in Antebellum New York City," *Journal of American History* 74.2 (1987): 388–410.

51. "The Great War on the New York Piggeries," *Frank Leslie's Illustrated Newspaper*, 13 August 1859; "The Offal and Piggery Nuisances," *New York Times*, 27 July 1859.

52. "The Storming of Hogtown," *New York Herald*, 27 July 1859; "The Great War on the New York Piggeries," *Frank Leslie's Illustrated Newspaper*, 13 August 1859; *Proceedings of the Board of Aldermen*, 19 September 1859, 75:506–520; "Further Particulars of the 'Hogtown War,' " *New York Herald*, 29 July 1859. For more on the lines drawn between bourgeois and lower-class domesticity, see Richard Bushman, *The Refinement of America: Persons, Houses, Cities* (New York: Vintage, 1992), 273–279.

53. *Hunt's Merchants' Magazine and Commercial Review* (New York: Geo. A. & Jno. Wood, 1859), 40:212. For a global view on pig breeds and the markets for fattened hogs, see Sam White, "From Globalized Pig Breeds to Capitalist Pigs: A Study in Animal Cultures and Evolutionary History," *Environmental History* 16 (Jan. 2011): 94–120.

54. "The Offal and Piggery Nuisances," *New York Times*, 27 July 1859; "Further Particulars of the 'Hogtown War,' " *New York Herald*, 29 July 1859; "City Intelligence," *New York Times*, 28 July 1859.

55. "The Hog War: A Policeman in a Tight Place," *New York Herald,* 11 August 1859; "The Great War on the New York Piggeries," *Frank Leslie's Illustrated Newspaper,* 13 August 1859; "The News," *New York Herald,* 27 July 1859; "The Storming of Hogtown," *New York Herald,* 27 July 1859; "Further Particulars of the 'Hogtown War,'" *New York Herald,* 29 July 1859.

56. Edward K. Spann, *The New Metropolis: New York City, 1840–1857* (New York: Columbia University Press, 1981), 364–400.

57. "The Great War on the New York Piggeries," *Frank Leslie's Illustrated Newspaper,* 13 August 1859.

58. "The Offal and Piggery Nuisances," *New York Times,* 27 July 1859; "The Storming of Hogtown," *New York Herald,* 27 July 1859; "The News," *New York Herald,* 27 July 1859; "Another Raid upon the Piggeries," *New York Times,* 9 August 1859; "The Public Health," *New York Herald,* 13 August 1859.

59. "The Public Health," *New-York Tribune,* 10 August 1859; "Removal of the Up Town Piggeries," *New York Herald,* 5 September 1859; "Condition of the Streets: The Right Men for the Right Places," *New York Herald,* 16 August 1859; "Down with the New York Piggeries in Our City: Let Inspector Delavan Keep His Hogs at Home," *Brooklyn Daily Eagle,* 9 August 1859; "The News," *New York Herald,* 15 August 1859; "Colonel Daniel E. Delavan," *Frank Leslie's Illustrated Newspaper,* 3 September 1859.

60. "The War upon the Piggeries: City Inspector's Report," *New York Herald,* 20 September 1859.

61. "Street Cleaning," *New-York Tribune,* 11 August 1859; "The Topics of the Week," *Frank Leslie's Illustrated Newspaper,* 24 September 1859.

5. Clearing the Lungs of the City

1. J. C. Myers, *Sketches on a Tour through the Northern and Eastern States, the Canadas and Nova Scotia* (Harrisonburg, VA: J. H. Wartmann and Brothers, 1849), 50–51; Kenneth T. Jackson and David S. Dunbar, eds., *Empire City: New York through the Centuries* (New York: Columbia University Press, 2005), 209; "City Sounds and Sights," *New-York Spectator,* 23 June 1836; "The Lungs of the City," *New-York Mirror,* 23 July 1842, 239.

2. *The Life of Charles Loring Brace, Chiefly Told in His Own Letters,* ed. Emma Brace (New York: Charles Scribner's Sons, 1894), 58 (hereafter cited as *Life of Brace*). While several historians have discussed the work of Olmsted and of Brace, few have looked at their work together. Given their close com-

munication, intense intellectual debates, the complementary nature of their reform efforts in New York, as well as their leadership among reformers and the bourgeois elite in the nineteenth century, I would argue that their respective efforts to control public space in the 1850s and beyond are very much related and part of a larger trend seen in antebellum New York. Thomas Bender, who discusses the work of both Brace and Olmsted in *Toward an Urban Vision,* is more concerned with their ideas about urban community, the relationship between spontaneity and organization within their respective projects, and the balancing of the natural and the artificial in urban life. Although this intellectual history is certainly apparent in my own treatment of these men and their views on urban life, I focus primarily on the social and environmental context of their attempts to gain power over public space, rather than on their intellectual understanding of cities. Thomas Bender, *Toward an Urban Vision: Ideas and Institutions in Nineteenth Century America* (1975; Baltimore: Johns Hopkins University Press, 1982).

3. *The Papers of Frederick Law Olmsted: The Formative Years* (Baltimore: Johns Hopkins University Press, 1977), 1:6 (hereafter cited as *PFLO*); *Life of Brace,* 58; Charles Capen McLaughlin, "Frederick Law Olmsted: His Life and Work," in *PFLO,* 1:7.

4. Frederick Law Olmsted, *Walks and Talks of an American Farmer in England* (New York: George P. Putnam, 1852), 1: 86–87, 2:103; Charles Loring Brace to Miss Mary Blake, 29 June 1850, Blake Family Papers; Frederick Law Olmsted to Andrew Jackson Downing, 23 November 1850, *PFLO,* 1:363.

5. *Walks and Talks* 1:79–80. In addition to publishing his observations about the Birkenhead Park in *Walks and Talks,* Olmsted also published it in Andrew Jackson Downing's periodical *The Horticulturist,* which was a voice for gentlemen farmers, budding landscape designers, and innovative architects, as well as a platform for Downing's campaign on behalf of public parks in America. Frederick Law Olmsted, "The People's Park at Birkenhead, Near Liverpool," *The Horticulturist,* May 1851, 224–228.

6. *Walks and Talks,* 1:232–234; McLaughlin, "Frederick Law Olmsted: His Life and Work," 10; *Life of Brace,* 91, 120; Frederick Law Olmsted to Charles Loring Brace, 12 November 1850, *PFLO,* 1:358–362. Brace continued his travels after the Olmsteds returned home, publishing his experiences in Charles Loring Brace, *Hungary in 1851, with an Experience of the Austrian Police* (New York: Charles Scribner, 1852); Charles Loring Brace, *Home-Life in Germany* (New York: Charles Scribner, 1853). Brace also published several

articles in journals and newspapers as a means to fund the second leg of his trip.

7. Charles Loring Brace to Mrs. Asa Gray, 6 February 1851, *Life of Brace,* 117; *Walks and Talks,* 2:106; John Hull Olmsted to Charles Loring Brace, [December 1850], *Life of Brace,* 109; Charles Loring Brace to John Hull Olmsted, [undated, 1851], *Life of Brace,* 112–113; *PFLO,* 2:5, 9; Frederick Law Olmsted to Charles Loring Brace, 1 November 1853, *PFLO,* 2:232–236. As a result of these travels, Olmsted not only published articles in the *New-York Daily Times,* but also published a series of books on the South, including Frederick Law Olmsted, *Journey in the Seaboard States, with Remarks on Their Economy* (New York: Dix and Edwards, 1856); and Frederick Law Olmsted, *The Cotton Kingdom: A Traveller's Observation on Cotton and Slavery in the American Slave States,* 2 vols. (New York: Mason Brothers, 1861).

8. Edward K. Spann, *The New Metropolis: New York City, 1840–1857* (New York: Columbia University Press, 1981), 384.

9. *Life of Brace,* 153; Frederick Law Olmsted to Charles Loring Brace, 26 July 1847, quoted in *PFLO,* 1:69.

10. "The Country—Where Is It?" *New-York Spectator,* 30 April, 1835; New York (N.Y.) Board of Commissioners of Central Park, *Second Annual Report of the Board of Commissioners of the Central Park: January 1859* (New York: Wm. C. Bryant, 1859), 59–68; *Life of Brace,* 82–83. Brace wrote a similar, undated letter to Horace Bushnell's wife, saying that he hoped to bring "public attention to that immense class—the children of New York . . . who never have a finger reached out to them." Charles Loring Brace to Mrs. Bushnell, [undated], Blake Papers, Box 1, Folder 28, Manuscripts and Archives, Yale University.

11. Robert Ernst, *Immigrant Life in New York City, 1825–1863* (New York: King's Crown Press, 1949); Spann, *New Metropolis,* ch. 2; Hasia R. Diner, " 'The Most Irish City in the Union': The Era of the Great Migration, 1844–1877," in *The New York Irish,* ed. Ronald H. Bayor and Timothy J. Meagher (Baltimore: Johns Hopkins University Press, 1996), 87–106; Asa Greene, *A Glance at New York* (New York: A. Greene, 1837), 12–13; Charles Dickens, "American Notes for General Circulation," in *The New World,* 8/9.2, ed. Park Benjamin (New York: J. Winchester, 1842), 40; E. Porter Belden, *New York, Past, Present, and Future; Comprising a History of the City of New York, a Description of Its Present Condition, and an Estimate of Its Future Increase* (New York: G. P. Putnam, 1849), 44–45.

12. Christine Stansell, *City of Women: Sex and Class in New York, 1789–1860* (New York: Knopf, 1986); *Documents of the Assembly of the State of New-York, Eightieth Session, 1857* (Albany: C. Van Benthuysen, 1857), 3: doc. 205, 14, 22. See also Graham Hodges, "'Desirable Companions and Lovers': Irish and African Americans in the Sixth Ward, 1830–1870," in *The New York Irish,* ed. Ronald H. Bayor and Timothy J. Meagher (Baltimore: Johns Hopkins University Press, 1996), 107–124. For more on antebellum American fears of miscegenation, see Joshua Rothman, *Notorious in the Neighborhood: Sex and Families across the Color Line in Virginia, 1787–1861* (Chapel Hill: University of North Carolina Press, 2003); Ariela J. Gross, *What Blood Won't Tell: A History of Race on Trial, 1787–1861* (Cambridge, MA: Harvard University Press, 2008).

13. Leslie M. Harris, *In the Shadows of Slavery: African Americans in New York City, 1626–1863* (Chicago: University of Chicago Press, 2003), 79–81, 217–219; Carla Peterson, *Black Gotham: A Family History of African Americans in Nineteenth-Century New York City* (New Haven: Yale University Press, 2011), 147–187; Graham Russell Hodges, *New York City Cartmen, 1667–1850* (New York: New York University Press, 1986), 158–160.

14. *Documents of the Assembly of the State of New-York, Eightieth Session, 1857* (Albany: C. Van Benthuysen, 1857), 3: doc. 205; "Beware of Five Points," *New-York Spectator,* 22 May 1834; Nathaniel Parker Willis, *The Complete Works of N. P. Willis* (New York: J. S. Redfield, 1846), 582–583. Regarding urban renewal in Five Points, see Chapter 2. For more on Five Points, see Tyler Anbinder, *Five Points: The 19th-Century New York City Neighborhood That Invented Dance, Stole Elections, and Became the World's Most Notorious Slum* (New York: Free Press, 2001). Jason Jindrich traces the history of New York's shantytowns in the later part of the nineteenth century in "The Shantytowns of Central Park West: Fin-de-Siècle Squatting in American Cities," *Journal of Urban History* 36.5 (2010): 672–684. Revealing the legal and economic climate that allowed squatting to exist in New York and Brooklyn, Jindrich argues that it was an integral, though forgotten part of urban development. "Our Squatter Population," *New York Times,* 15 July 1867; *A Clear and Concise Statement of New-York, and the Surrounding Country: Containing a Faithful Account of Many of Those Base Impositions, which Are So Constantly and Uniformly Practiced upon British Emigrants, by Crafty, Designing, and Unprincipled Adventurers* (New York: Printed for the Author; and sold by John Wilson, No. 22 William-Street, Opposite the Post-Office, 1819), 26–28; I. N. Phelps Stokes, *The Iconography of Manhattan Island, 1498–1909* (New York: R. H. Dodd,

1915–1928), 5:1608–1609; Edwin G. Burrows and Mike Wallace, *Gotham: A History of New York City to 1898* (New York: Oxford University Press, 1999), 750; John Punnett Peters, ed., *Annals of St. Michael's: Being the History of St. Michael's Protestant Episcopal Church, New York, for One Hundred Years, 1807–1907* (New York: G. P. Putnam's Sons, 1907); Katherine Burton, *The Dream Lives Forever: The Story of St. Patrick's Cathedral* (New York: Longmans, Green, 1960).

15. One need only look at guidebooks and city histories for evidence of how authors purposely erased shantytowns from descriptions of the city: "The Crystal Palace," *New-York Daily Times*, 25 March 1853; H. Phelps, *The Lions of New York: Being a Guide to Objects of Interest in and around the Great Metropolis* (New York: Phelps, Fanning, 1853); Benson John Lossing, *History of New York City* (New York: Perine Engraving and Printing, 1887), 2.2:603. Though the term "suburbia" is contested, defined alternatively as communities independent of their neighboring metropolis or intrinsically part of their growth, as bedroom communities or edge cities, I am using it here to describe communities on the outskirts of New York that were neither fully urban nor fully rural and where residents often, though not always, relied on the city for their employment.

Given that shantytowns are unplanned and grow outside the control of governments, scholars often exclude them from studies of urban growth or suburbs. For instance, in *Building Suburbia*, Dolores Hayden depicts the growth of antebellum suburbs as primarily a bourgeois effort. While she describes the mixture of land uses, ranging from industries to country villas in the urban "borderlands," she dismisses the idea that the shanties themselves could be considered suburban communities. Scholars who have challenged this exclusion include Leonie Sandercock, James Holston, and Richard Harris. See Dolores Hayden, *Building Suburbia: Green Fields and Urban Growth, 1820–2000* (New York: Pantheon Books, 2003), 21–44; Richard Harris, *Unplanned Suburbs: Toronto's American Tragedy, 1900–1950* (Baltimore: Johns Hopkins University Press, 1996); James Holston, "Spaces of Insurgent Citizenship," in *Making the Invisible Visible: Multicutural Planning History*, ed. Leonie Sandercock (Berkeley: University of California Press, 1998); Leonie Sandercock, *Cosmopolis II: Mongrel Cities of the Twenty-First Century* (New York: Continuum, 2003).

For definitions of what counts as a suburb, see also Kenneth T. Jackson, *Crabgrass Frontier: The Suburbanization of the United States* (New York: Oxford

University Press, 1985), 12–19; Robert Fishman, *Bourgeois Utopias: The Rise and Fall of Suburbia* (New York: Basic Books, 1987); Sam Bass Warner, *Streetcar Suburbs: The Process of Growth in Boston, 1870–1900* (Cambridge, MA: Harvard University Press, 1978). For the adjectives used to describe shanty suburbs, see New York (N.Y.) Board of Commissioners of Central Park, *Second Annual Report of the Board of Commissioners of the Central Park: January 1859* (New York: Wm. C. Bryant, Printers, 1859), 59–68; W. H. Guild, Jr., *The Central Park: Photographed with Descriptions and a Historical Sketch by Frederick B. Perkins* (New York: Carleton, 1864), 13; "Aspect of the New Ward," *New York Herald,* 27 February 1846; "The New-York Tenants," *New-York Tribune,* 24 February 1848.

16. "Our Squatter Population," *New York Times,* 15 July 1867; Roy Rosenzweig and Elizabeth Blackmar, *The Park and the People: A History of Central Park* (Ithaca: Cornell University Press, 1992), 77; "City Squatters," *New-York Daily Times,* 12 July 1854; "Walks among the New York Poor," *New-York Daily Times,* 19 April 1854; "Dutch Hill," *New-York Daily Times,* 21 March 1855; "Our Squatter Population," *New York Times,* 15 July 1867. Squatters and their chaotic developments continue to face similar criticisms. Scholars focusing on the shantytowns of the global south continue to find evidence of these stereotypes. See, for instance, Janice Perlman, *Favela: Four Decades of Living on the Edge in Rio de Janiero* (New York: Oxford University Press, 2010); Robert Neuwirth, *Shadow Cities: A Billion Squatters, A New Urban World* (New York: Routledge, 2005).

17. "Walks among the New York Poor," *New-York Daily Times,* 19 April 1854. For evidence of the varied locations of mid-nineteenth-century shantytowns throughout New York, see Citizens' Association's Record of Sanitary Inquiry, 1864–1865, Ward 19, Manuscripts Collection, New-York Historical Society.

18. "Dutch Hill," *New-York Daily Times,* 21 March 1855; "Our Squatter Population," *New York Times,* 15 July 1867.

19. "Walks among the New York Poor," *New-York Daily Times,* 19 April 1854; "Dutch Hill," *New-York Daily Times,* 21 March 1855; "Our Squatter Population," *New York Times,* 15 July 1867; "The Murder of the Innocents," *New-York Tribune,* 9 February 1859. The municipal legislators never specifically targeted poultry during this period, but hogs and goats were banned from roaming free in the city. George W. Morton, *Laws and Ordinances Relative to*

the Preservation of the Public Health in the City of New York (New York: Edmund Jones, 1860), 108–110; Charles Loring Brace, "Early Diary of Charles Loring Brace, 1853–1855," Victor Remer Historical Archives of the Children's Aid Society, Manuscript Collections, New-York Historical Society, 5 April 1854.

20. Frederick Marryat, *A Diary in America, with Remarks on Its Institutions* (New York: D. Appleton, 1839), 16–20; "Dutch Hill," *New-York Daily Times,* 21 March 1855. For more on hogs and dogs, see Chapter 1; for more on manure, see Chapter 3. For more on the economy of ragpicking in the late nineteenth and early twentieth century, see Susan Strasser, *Waste and Want: A Social History of Trash* (New York: Henry Holt, 1999), 69–109.

21. "Our Ragpickers," *New York Times,* 21 November 1869; *New-York Evening Post,* 3 March 1843, quoted in Stokes, *Iconography of Manhattan Island,* 5:1779; "Walks among the New-York Poor," *New-York Daily Times,* 19 April 1854; *New-York Evening Post,* 3 March 1843; Samuel Irenæus Prime, *Life in New York* (New York: Robert Carver, 1847), 221–224; G. G. Foster, *New York by Gas-Light, with Here and There a Streak of Sunshine* (New York: Dewitt and Davenport, 1850), 120–123; "Walks among the New-York Poor," *New-York Daily Times,* 22 January 1853; Charles Loring Brace, "Early Diary of Charles Loring Brace, 1853–1855," Victor Remer Historical Archives of the Children's Aid Society, Manuscript Collections, New-York Historical Society, 9 July 1853, 11 October 1854.

22. "Walks among the New-York Poor," *New-York Daily Times,* 22 January 1853; "Walks among the New-York Poor," *New-York Daily Times,* 4 March 1853; *Documents of the Assembly of the State of New-York, Eightieth Session, 1857* (Albany: C. Van Benthuysen, 1857), 3: doc. 205, 20.

23. "Walks among the New-York Poor," *New-York Daily Times,* 22 January 1853; New York (N.Y.) Common Council, *By-laws and Ordinances of the Mayor, Aldermen, and Commonalty of the City of New-York* (New York: William Townsend, 1839), 336–343; For an anti-Semitic account of the Jewish owners of pawnshops and the goods they traded in, see Foster, *New York by Gas-Light,* 57–59. Ned Buntline, in *The Mysteries and Miseries of New York,* claimed that the offal collected on the street was repurposed at eateries in poor neighborhoods. If this was indeed the case, it seems to be an exception. Found food was of course sometimes used by collectors, but it seems to have been sold to piggery owners, fat melters, and bone boilers through the bone collectors who daily came through the neighborhoods with carts. Ned Buntline,

The Mysteries and Miseries of New York: A Story of Real Life (New York: Berford, 1848), 75–77.

24. Stansell, *City of Women*, 205; *Semi-Annual Report of the Chief of Police, from May 1 to October 31, 1849* (New York, 1850), 58–61, 62–66.

25. "Walks among the New-York Poor," *New-York Daily Times*, 22 January 1853; "Our Ragpickers," *New York Times*, 21 November 1869; "Pop Corn," *New-York Daily Tribune*, 14 December 1857.

26. Paul Boyer, *Urban Masses and Moral Order in America, 1820–1920* (Cambridge, MA: Harvard University Press, 1992), 69; Stokes, *The Iconography of Manhattan Island*, 3:525–526; Benson John Lossing, *History of New York City* (New York, 1887), 1.3:372–376; Stokes, *The Iconography of Manhattan Island*, 5:1745; "The Police, Once More," *New-York Spectator*, 21 February 1837; "Court of General Sessions," *New-York Spectator*, 17 March 1837; "The Honorable Board of Aldermen," *Morning Courier and New-York Enquirer, for the Country*, 26 March 1839; "City Police," *Morning Courier and New-York Enquirer, for the Country*, 7 January 1840, "The Croton War," *Morning Courier and New-York Enquirer, for the Country*, 10 April 1840; "Serious Riot," *Morning Courier and New-York Enquirer, for the Country*, 8 May 1840; Joel Tyler Headley, *The Great Riots of New York, 1712–1873* (1873; New York: Thunder's Mouth Press, 2004); George Foster, *New York in Slices: By an Experienced Carver: Being the Original Slices Published in the N.Y. Tribune* (New York: W. F. Burgess, 1849), 3–5, 22–25. Dickens, "American Notes for General Circulation," 14–17; "Beware of Five Points," *New-York Spectator*, 22 May 1834; Foster, *New York by Gas-Light*, 56–57, 59–61; "Walks among the New-York Poor," *New-York Daily Times*, 11 October 1852; "Walks among the New-York Poor," *New-York Daily Times*, 18 October 1852; Willis, *Complete Works*, 582–583; Dickens, "American Notes for General Circulation." For more on the genre of writing that grew up around describing the urban poor, see Stansell, *City of Women*, 195–197.

27. Dickens, "American Notes for General Circulation"; Foster, *New York in Slices*, 84–86; Foster, *New York by Gas-Light*, 11, 124–127; Karl Jacoby, "Slaves by Nature? Domestic Animals and Human Slaves," *Slavery and Abolition: A Journal of Slave and Post-Slave Studies* 15.1 (1994): 89–99.

28. "Walks among the New-York Poor," *New-York Daily Times*, 18 October 1852; "Walks among the New-York Poor: "Rotten Row," *New-York Daily Times*, 19 April 1853.

29. Children's Aid Society, *Second Annual Report of the Children's Aid Society, February, 1855* (New York: M. B. Wynkoop, 1855), 3–7; Hasia R. Diner,

" 'The Most Irish City in the Union': The Era of the Great Migration, 1844–1877," 101–102.

30. Bender, *Toward an Urban Vision,* 132–136; Boyer, *Urban Masses and Moral Order in America,* 94–96; David J. Rothman, *The Discovery of the Asylum: Social Order and Disorder in the New Republic* (Boston: Little, Brown, 1971); Robert S. Pickett, *House of Refuge: Origins of Juvenile Reform in New York State, 1815–1857* (Syracuse: Syracuse University Press, 1969); *Life of Brace,* 154; Children's Aid Society, *Second Annual Report,* 3–7, 33–35.

31. Charles Loring Brace, *The Dangerous Classes of New York, and Twenty Years' Work among Them* (New York: Wynkoop and Hallenbeck, 1872), 61–62, 136–139, 175; Children's Aid Society, *Second Annual Report,* 9–13; "Walks among the New-York Poor," *New-York Daily Times,* 22 January 1853.

32. Stansell, *City of Women,* 209–215; Brace, *Dangerous Classes,* 158; *Life of Brace,* 163. There is a vast literature surrounding the Children's Aid Society, especially the "Orphan Train" or placing-out aspect of their work: Miriam Z. Langsam, *Children West: A History of the Placing-Out System of the New York Children's Aid Society, 1853–1890* (Madison: State Historical Society of Wisconsin, 1964); Stephen O'Connor, *Orphan Trains: The Story of Charles Loring Brace and the Children He Saved and Failed* (New York: Houghton Mifflin, 2001); Henry W. Thurston, *The Dependent Child: A Story of Changing Aims and Methods in the Care of Dependent Children* (New York: Columbia University Press, 1930).

33. In many ways, Brace's ideas about the way America should solve its urban social problems were in keeping with George Henry Evans's and Horace Greeley's promotion of a homestead law that would grant any American 160 acres if he or he was willing to improve the land. They, too, believed that social strife could be alleviated if workers and their families had the option of leaving the city and supporting themselves elsewhere. Robert V. Hine and John Mack Faragher, *The American West: A New Interpretive History* (New Haven: Yale University Press, 2000), ch. 11. Brace, *Dangerous Classes,* 225. See also *Life of Brace,* 58; Children's Aid Society, *Second Annual Report,* 3–7.

34. Boyer, *Urban Masses and Moral Order in America,* 98–99; *Proceedings of the Board of Aldermen,* 1 July 1831, 1:151–154; "Support of the Poor," *New-York Spectator,* 6 December 1831; Proceedings of the Board of Assistants, 25 June 1832, 2:53; Lydia Maria Child, *Letters from New-York* (New York: Charles S. Francis, 1943), 55–56; Dickens, "American Notes for General Circulation," 14–17; Foster, *New York in Slices,* 84–86; "The Country—Where Is It?" *New-York*

Spectator, 30 April 1835; "New-York Mechanics and the West," *New-York Spectator,* 11 April 1837.

35. Many poor immigrants, especially the Irish, grew skeptical of Brace's goals, believing that the project was aimed at turning their Catholic children into Protestants by sending them to Protestant farmers. Brace repeatedly denied this, but the fear affected the ability of the Children's Aid Society to work with many of the Irish communities. For more on the control of public space in the mid-nineteenth century, see Nick Yablon, *Untimely Ruins: An Archaeology of American Urban Modernity, 1819–1919* (Chicago: University of Chicago Press, 2009), 137–138; Stansell, *City of Women.*

36. Charles Loring Brace, "Parks and Chapels for the Poor," *New-York Daily Tribune,* 3 May 1855.

37. "The Lungs of the City," *New-York Mirror,* 23 July 1842; William Cullen Bryant, "A New Public Park," *New-York Evening Post,* 3 July 1844. *Proceedings of the Board of Aldermen of the City of New York* (New York: McSpedon and Baker, 1854), 6 March 1854, 53:421–435; Andrew Jackson Downing, "The New-York Park," *The Horticulturist,* 1 August 1851. Historians and contemporaries have long given credit to multiple sources for the origins of the idea for Central Park. For more on this debate, see Rosenzweig and Blackmar, *The Park and the People,* ch. 1.

38. "A New Park," *New-York Daily Times,* 21 May 1852; "The Health of New York: Necessity of a Great Central Park," *New York Herald,* 3 May 1853.

39. Downing, "The New-York Park," *New-York Evening Post,* 10 July 1851; "Parks for the People," *New-York Tribune,* 22 June 1853; "The Two Parks," *New-York Tribune,* 28 June 1853; New York (N.Y.) Board of Commissioners of Central Park, *First Annual Report on the Improvement of the Central Park, New York: January 1, 1857* (New York: Chas. W. Baker, 1857), 77–78.

40. For more on the parks of the 1830s, see Chapter 2. Charles Loring Brace, "Parks and Chapels for the Poor," *New-York Daily Tribune,* 3 May 1855; Frederick Law Olmsted, "The People's Park at Birkenhead, Near Liverpool," *The Horticulturist,* May 1851. *Proceedings of the Board of Aldermen,* 7 January 1850, 38:18–19; 6 March 1854, 53:421–435; Board of Commissioners of Central Park, *First Annual Report,* 79–80, 116–129. "The Upper Ten" was a phrase coined by Nathaniel Parker Willis in 1852 and used widely during the mid-nineteenth century; it referred to the wealthiest 10,000 New Yorkers.

41. "The New Parks," *New-York Tribune,* 30 January 1854; Rosenzweig and Blackmar, *The Park and the People,* 45–54.

42. Rosenzweig and Blackmar, *The Park and the People,* 20–45; "Document No. 83," *Documents of the Board of Aldermen,* 18.2, reprinted in Board of Commissioners of Central Park, *First Annual Report,* 137–158; "The Present Look of Our Great Central Park," *New-York Daily Times,* 9 July 1856.

43. "Document No. 83," *Documents of the Board of Aldermen;* Board of Commissioners of Central Park, *First Annual Report,* 130–134.

44. For more on the ways governments have mapped or altered land in order to gain control through legibility, see James Scott, *Seeing Like a State: How Certain Schemes to Improve the Human Condition Have Failed* (New Haven: Yale University Press, 1998). Board of Commissioners of Central Park, *First Annual Report,* 46–76. The fact that the buildings were missing in earlier versions of the map is noted in an 1856 letter from the chief clerk to the Commissioners of Central Park. The letter suggested that it was difficult to keep track of all the buildings and residents in the park because they were missing from the surveyor's maps. "New-York City," *New-York Daily Times,* 12 December 1856.

45. Egbert L. Viele, "Topography of New-York and Its Park System," in *The Memorial History of the City of New York,* ed. James Grant Wilson (New York: New-York History Company, 1893). 4:556–557; New York State Legislature, "An Act Relative to the Purchase and Laying Out of Certain Lands for a Public Park in the Nineteenth Ward of the City of New York, and the Powers and Duties of the Mayor, Aldermen, and Commonalty in Relation Thereto, Passed July 21, 1853," in Board of Commissioners of Central Park, *First Annual Report,* 91–97; "In the Matter of the Application of the Mayor, &c., of New York, Relative to Opening, &c., a Public Place, between Fifty-Ninth and One Hundred and Sixth Streets, and Fifth and Eighth Avenues," in Board of Commissioners of Central Park, *First Annual Report,* 71–76, 99–102; "In the Matter of the Application of the Mayor, &c., of the City of New York, Relative to the Opening and Laying Out of a Public Place, between Fifty-Ninth and One Hundred and Sixth Streets and the Fifth and Eighth Avenues, in the City of New York," in Board of Commissioners of Central Park, *First Annual Report,* 103–111. For more on the legal standings of the park's residents and for a more detailed description of the people living in Seneca Village, see Rosenzweig and Blackmar, *The Park and the People,* 59–91; Harris, *In the Shadows of Slavery,* 74–75; Leslie M. Alexander, "Community and Institution Building in Antebellum New York: The Story of Seneca Village, 1825–1857," in Angel David Nieves and Leslie M. Alexander, eds., *"We Shall Independent Be": African American Place*

Making and the Struggle to Claim Space in the United States (Boulder: University Press of Colorado, 2008), 23–46.

46. "The Central Park," *New-York Herald,* 5 June 1856.

47. New York (N.Y.) Board of Commissioners of Central Park, *Second Annual Report,* 59–68; W. H. Guild, Jr., *The Central Park: Photographed with Descriptions and a Historical Sketch by Frederick B. Perkins* (New York: Carleton, 1864), 13; Frederick Law Olmsted and Calvert Vaux, "Greensward Plan," in *PFLO,* 3:153; Editorial, *New-York Daily Times,* 9 July 1856; Rosenzweig and Blackmar, *The Park and the People,* 76–77.

48. "The Present Look of Our Great Central Park," *New-York Daily Times,* 9 July 1856; *Annals of St. Michael's,* 90–96; 393–397; "Board of Assistants," *Morning Courier and New-York Enquirer, for the Country,* 8 February 1839. The buildings located on the property allocated for the new reservoir can be seen in a set of maps published in 1853. *Maps and Profiles of Ground for New Reservoir Situated between 86th & 96th Streets and 5th & 7th Avenues,* New York Public Library, Lionel Pincus and Princess Firyal Map Division. The Seneca Village Project has been working to expand on the work done by Rosenzweig and Blackmar in *The Park and the People.* They've unearthed many details about the families and buildings in Seneca Village, while also performing some archaeological digs. Among other things, they have discovered that the community, though mainly African American, included several Irish families as well as other Euro-American families. See www.mcah.columbia.edu/seneca _village/.

49. Board of Commissioners of Central Park, *First Annual Report,* 36–45, 71–76, 88–90, 99–102; "An Ordinance for the Regulation and Government of Central Park," printed in Board of Commissioners of Central Park, *First Annual Report,* 135–136; "The Central Park," *New York Herald,* 5 June 1856; "The Present Look of Our Great Central Park," *New-York Daily Times,* 9 July 1856; "New-York City," *New-York Daily Times,* 12 December 1856; "Central Park," *New-York Daily Times,* 30 July 1856; "Central Park Police," *New-York Daily Times,* 25 July 1856. Other residents were arrested for selling the park's rocks for pavement materials. Rosenzweig and Blackmar, *The Park and the People,* 91. For a similar transformation of accepted practices into illegal behavior in the context of late-nineteenth-century conservation efforts, see Karl Jacoby, *Crimes against Nature: Squatters, Poachers, Thieves, and the Hidden History of American Conservation* (Berkeley: University of California Press, 2001). Besides illegal plunder of park resources, the "nocturnal depredations" apparently included the

reception of stolen goods and the operation of dance halls. "A Central Park Dance House," *New-York Tribune,* 5 August 1856.

Heath Schenker's *Melodramatic Landscapes* investigates cultural understandings of the park by discussing it in relation to various books and plays of the era that similarly focused on society in mid-nineteenth-century New York. This helps to unpack how bourgeois New Yorkers understood the park and the ways that class anxieties were expressed in cultural forms, but I think it misses the chance to talk about the actual class battles that took place in the park. Schenker opens her book, for instance, with a vignette about a police sergeant who found a man warming himself at a bonfire on park grounds in 1877. Schenker muses that urban parks of the era "required some interpretation for a public unschooled in the finer distinctions of romantic sensibility" (3). While this interpretation certainly explores the bourgeois understanding of the park, it does little to provide historical context for why poor New Yorkers might consider it their right to use the land in this unapproved way, or how the man's presence was less a cultural gaffe than a political statement or expression of economic need. Heath Massey Schenker, *Melodramatic Landscapes: Urban Parks in the Nineteenth Century* (Charlottesville: University of Virginia Press, 2011).

50. "Document No. 3, May 26 1857," *Documents of the Board of Commissioners of Central Park* (New York: Wm. C. Bryant, 1858); *New York Times,* 9 July 1857; *Annals of St. Michael's,* 95; "Document No. 9, September 23, 1857," *Documents of the Board of Commissioners of Central Park;* "Central Park," *New-York Daily Times,* 30 July 1856.

51. The Commissioners netted almost $5,000 in 1859 from the sale of the park's buildings. *New York Times,* 5 September 1857; "Progress of the Central Park Improvements," *New-York Daily Times,* 7 September 1857; Board of Commissioners of Central Park, *Second Annual Report,* 1–7; *New York Times,* 4 November 1857; Board of Commissioners of Central Park, *Second Annual Report,* 9–68; "Document No. 5," *Documents of the Board of Aldermen of the City of New York* (New York: Charles W. Baker, 1859), 25:2.

52. Frederick Law Olmsted to Asa Gray, 20 August 1857, *PFLO,* 3:77; Frederick Law Olmsted, "Passages in the Life of an Unpractical Man," in *PFLO,* 3:84–94; Andrew Jackson Downing, *A Treatise on the Theory and Practice of Landscape Gardening, Adapted to North America,* 6th ed. (New York: A. O. Moore, 1859), 45–68. The extent to which Downing influenced Olmsted and Vaux can be seen in their attempt to pay homage to Downing by erecting a memorial in Central Park: "Circular Proposing the Erection in Central Park

of a Memorial to Andrew Jackson Downing," in *PFLO,* 3:251–252. In the proposal for the memorial, they quote heavily from Downing, selecting a passage that emphasizes the way a park can serve to uplift and educate the masses, taking up "popular education where the common school and ballot-box leave it." A. J. Downing, *Rural Essays* (New York: George P. Putnam, 1853), 101–109; Board of Commissioners of Central Park, *First Annual Report,* 36–45; Alexander Jackson Downing, "Mr. Downing's Letters from England," *The Horticulturist,* 1 June 1851, 281–287.

53. Peter Schmitt erroneously notes that attempts to farm the land had failed by the time Olmsted and Vaux set about transforming it. Peter J. Schmitt, *Back to Nature: The Arcadian Myth in Urban America* (New York: Oxford University Press, 1969), 69.

54. Olmsted, "Passages in the Life of an Unpractical Man," 84–94; Rosenzweig and Blackmar, *The Park and the People,* 95–120; Spann, *New Metropolis,* 341–400. Vaux continued working alongside Olmsted as a designer, though without any official title. Board of Commissioners of Central Park, *Second Annual Report,* 1–7. The literature on Frederick Law Olmsted and Central Park is vast. His work on the park has received a great deal of attention in the past forty years, partly as a reaction to the decline of Central Park in the 1960s and 1970s and the resulting quest to restore the park to his vision. In addition to those who have celebrated his work, others have critically reevaluated his role in the park. Most central to this study have been Rosenzweig and Blackmar, *The Park and the People;* and David M. Scobey, *Empire City: The Making and Meaning of the New York City Landscape* (Philadelphia: Temple University Press, 2002). See also David Schuyler, *The New Urban Landscape: The Redefinition of Urban Form in Nineteenth-Century America* (Baltimore: Johns Hopkins University Press, 1986), Albert Fein, *Frederick Law Olmsted and the American Environmental Tradition* (New York: George Braziller, 1972); Bender, *Toward an Urban Vision,* ch. 7. For biographies, see Laura Wood Roper, *FLO: A Biography of Frederick Law Olmsted* (Baltimore: Johns Hopkins University Press, 1973); Melvin Kalfus, *Frederick Law Olmsted: The Passion of a Public Artist* (New York: New York University Press, 1990); Witold Rybczynski, *A Clearing in the Distance: Frederick Law Olmsted and America in the Nineteenth Century* (New York: Scribner, 2000); Justin Martin, *Genius of Place: The Life of Frederick Law Olmsted* (New York: Da Capo Press, 2011).

55. New York (N.Y.) Board of Commissioners of Central Park, *Tenth Annual Report of the Board of Commissioners of the Central Park, for the Year Ending*

December 31, 1866 (New York: Wm. C. Bryant Printers, 1867), 39–40; New York (N.Y.) Board of Commissioners of Central Park, *Third Annual Report of the Board of Commissioners of the Central Park: January 1860* (New York: Wm. C. Bryant Printers, 1860), 7–29; New York (N.Y.) Board of Commissioners of the Central Park, *Seventh Annual Report of the Board of Commissioners of the Central Park, for the Year Ending with December 31, 1863* (New York: Wm. C. Bryant Printers, 1864), 28; New York (N.Y.) Board of Commissioners of the Central Park, *Fourteenth Report of the Board of Commissioners of the Central Park or the Period from January 1 to April 20, 1870* (New York: New York Printing Company, 1871), 16–17.

56. "The Central Park and Other City Improvements," *New York Herald,* 6 September 1857; "The Central Park," *Harper's Weekly,* 28 November 1857.

57. Frederick Law Olmsted to James T. Fields, 21 October 1860, *PFLO,* 3:269–274; "Cities and Parks, with Special Reference to the New York Central Park," *Atlantic Monthly* 7 (April 1861), 428.

58. "Central Park Report: Report of the Minority of the Select Committee on the Bill Relative to a Public Park in New York," in Board of Commissioners of Central Park, *First Annual Report,* 178–179; *PFLO,* 3:63, 219–221; Board of Commissioners of Central Park, *Fourth Annual Report of the Board of Commissioners of the Central Park: January 1861* (New York: Wm. C. Bryant Printers, 1861), 99–101.

59. Board of Commissioners of Central Park, *Fourth Annual Report,* 99–101, 106–109; Frederick Law Olmsted to Andrew Haswell Green, 3 November 1860, in *Forty Years of Landscape Architecture: Central Park,* ed. Frederick Law Olmsted, Jr., and Theodora Kimball (Cambridge, MA: MIT Press, 1928), 412–413; Board of Commissioners of Central Park, *Third Annual Report,* 7–29; *PFLO,* 3:279–280.

60. Board of Commissioners of Central Park. *Fourth Annual Report,* 99–101; Board of Commissioners of Central Park, *Sixth Annual Report,* 42–43; Board of Commissioners of Central Park, *Seventh Annual Report,* 29–32; Matthew Lumb, Journal of Three Voyages from England to America and Back (1863), James Marshall and Marie-Louise Osborn Collection, Beinecke Rare Book and Manuscript Library, Yale University. Several scholars write about the decline of public space in twentieth-century America, often looking back nostalgically to Olmsted's vision for Central Park as a more democratic use of space, while overlooking the level of social control involved in its administration. Mike Davis, *City of Quartz: Excavating the Future of Los Angeles* (New

York: Verso, 1992); Michael Sorkin, *Variations on a Theme Park: The New American City and the End of Public Space* (New York: Hill and Wang, 1992); Edward Soja, *Postmodern Geographies: The Reassertion of Space in Critical Social Theory* (New York: Verso, 1989). Mona Domosh has done work to counter this nostalgia in "Those 'Gorgeous Incongruities': Polite Politics and Public Space on the Streets of Nineteenth-Century New York," *Annals of the Association of American Geographers* 88.2 (1998): 209–226; as has Don Mitchell in "The End of Public Space? People's Park, Definitions of Public, and Democracy," *Annals of the Association of American Geographers* 85.1 (1995): 108–133.

61. New York (N.Y.) Board of Commissioners of the Central Park, *Sixth Annual Report of the Board of Commissioners of the Central Park: January, 1863* (New York: Wm. C. Bryant Printers, 1863), 49–50; New York (N.Y.) Board of Commissioners of the Central Park, *Eighth Annual Report of the Board of Commissioners of the Central Park, for the Year Ending with December 31, 1864* (New York: Wm. C. Bryant, 1865), 52–54.

62. Frederick Law Olmsted to Charles Loring Brace, 1 December 1853, *PFLO*, 2:232–236.

Epilogue

1. "The Draft," *New-York Tribune*, 14 July 1863. Paul A. Gilje, *The Road to Mobocracy: Popular Disorder in New York City* (Chapel Hill: University of North Carolina Press, 1987); Joel Tyler Headley, *The Great Riots of New York, 1712–1873* (New York: E. B. Treat, 1873).

2. From 1860 to 1863, retail prices rose 43 percent but wages rose only 12 percent, a disparity that led to a drastic change in workers' standard of living. Adrian Cook, *The Armies of the Streets: The New York City Draft Riots of 1863* (Lexington: University Press of Kentucky, 1974), 50.

3. Iver Bernstein, *The New York City Draft Riots: Their Significance for American Society and Politics in the Age of the Civil War* (New York: Oxford University Press, 1990), 9–10, 27–28. Adrian Cook argues that the racial tensions of the war had little to do with labor threats but were, rather, based in racial hatred. Bernstein's argument about the perceived threat is compelling, especially given the context of the longshoremen's strike that spring. Bigotry and economic threat are not mutually exclusive. Cook, *The Armies of the Streets*.

4. A. Hunter Dupree and Leslie H. Fishel, Jr., "An Eyewitness Account of the New York Draft Riots, July 1863," *Mississippi Valley Historical Review* 47.3

(1960): 472–479; Cook, *The Armies of the Streets;* Bernstein, *The New York City Draft Riots,* 17–42; Edward K. Spann, *Gotham at War: New York City, 1860–1865* (Wilmington, DE: SR Books, 2002), 93–106.

    5. Bernstein, *The New York City Draft Riots,* 24–25; Graham Hodges, "'Desirable Companions and Lovers': Irish and African Americans in the Sixth Ward, 1830–1870," in *The New York Irish,* ed. Ronald H. Bayor and Timothy J. Meagher (Baltimore: Johns Hopkins University Press, 1996), 107–124; Cook, *The Armies of the Streets,* 195. James Hughes, a swill milkman, and Peter Quinn, a piggery owner, were both killed by gunfire in the riots. John Nicholson, who had been found hiding in a pig pen as a vagrant child over two decades earlier, was shot by an African American he was chasing down Clarkson Street and charged with the murder of William Jones on the same street. Thomas Donahue and Francis Duffy, both squatters, were arrested for their part in the riots, as was John Ling, a piggery owner. Thomas McGuire, who had been arrested in 1857 for purchasing a diseased hog with the intent of butchering it, was also arrested for his role in the riots. I cross-listed these names, obtained from my research database of squatters and piggery owners, with Cook's lists of rioters. Cook, *The Armies of the Streets,* 215, 216, 230, 238, 244, 246, 248, 252. "Swill-Milk," *New York Times,* 28 May 1858; "The War on the Pigs, Piggeries and Bone Boiling Establishments," *New York Herald,* 9 August 1859; "City Intelligence: Police Office," *New-York Tribune,* 15 April 1841; "A Raid on Squatterdom," *New York Times,* 16 August 1867; "Pork—Bacon—Ham—Sausages," *New-York Daily Tribune,* 6 June 1857.

    6. Children's Aid Society, *Second Annual Report of the Children's Aid Society, February, 1855* (New York: M. B. Wynkoop, 1855), 3–7; Charles Loring Brace, *The Dangerous Classes of New York and Twenty Years' Work among Them* (New York: Wynkoop and Hallenbrook, 1872), 29–30; New York Association for Improving the Condition of the Poor, *Twentieth Annual Report* (New York: John F. Trow, 1863), 21–36.

    7. "New York Citizens' Association," *New York Herald,* 30 November 1864. In *The Monied Metropolis,* Sven Beckert argues that New York's upper class remained divided until the 1890s, when their interests began to coalesce. While they certainly continued to be divided religiously and politically, this bipartisan group of wealthy New Yorkers shows that the elite had been able to come together over issues of environmental control thirty years before. Sven Beckert, *The Monied Metropolis: New York City and the Consolidation of*

the American Bourgeoisie, 1850–1896 (New York: Cambridge University Press, 2001).

8. Citizens' Association of New York, *Report of the Council of Hygiene and Public Health of the Citizens' Association of New York upon the Sanitary Condition of the City* (New York: D. Appleton, 1865), xv, xvi, lxviii, lxxiii–lxxiv, 64–65; Citizens' Association of New York, Council of Hygiene and Public Health, Record of Sanitary Inquiry, 1864–1865, Manuscript Collection, New-York Historical Society.

9. Citizens' Association, *Report of the Council,* liii.

10. Citizens' Association, *Report of the Council,* 339–340.

11. Citizens' Association, *Report of the Council,* lxxxii, cxiv, cxxv, cxxvii.

12. John Duffy, "The Fight for Reform," in *The History of Public Health in New York City, 1625–1866* (New York: Russell Sage Foundation, 1968), 540–571; Richard Plunz, *A History of Housing in New York City* (New York: Columbia University Press, 1990), 21–24; Robert W. DeForest and Lawrence Veiller, eds., *The Tenement House Problem: Including the Report of the New York State Tenement House Commission of 1900* (New York: Macmillan, 1903), 1:71–118.

13. See Jacob A. Riis, *How the Other Half Lives: Studies among the Tenements of New York* (New York: Charles Scribner's Sons, 1890), 50–52; Jason Jindrich, "The Shantytowns of Central Park West: Fin-de-Siècle Squatting in American Cities," *Journal of Urban History* 36.5 (2010): 672–684; Roy Rosenzweig and Elizabeth Blackmar, *The Park and the People: A History of Central Park* (Ithaca: Cornell University Press, 1992).

Acknowledgments

When you write a history that involves turning human waste into fertilizer and feeding offal to livestock, you're bound to bring a few dinner conversations to a halt. I'm thankful (and apologetic) to everyone I've ever eaten with who has innocently asked me how my work was going.

At Yale, when I began this project, Johnny Faragher took me under his wing, providing invaluable guidance that helped me to think about the narratives I was developing. With his help, what started off as a story about urban pigs turned into something bigger. Joanne Freeman's constant good humor and sharp writing advice was truly invaluable. David Blight's enthusiasm for reimagining New York as something less polished and cosmopolitan than it is today was contagious as I continued writing. Though not officially on my committee, Paul Freedman proved a wonderful mentor and advocate as we both worked on the opposite ends of New York cuisine. I also had the opportunity to work with John Demos, and a kinder and more thoughtful writer is hard to find. In addition, Paul Sabin provided both great advice and a close reading of an early version of the first chapter.

I continued talking about my stories of filth and bad food over lunches with the Westerners at Yale—a group that kindly embraced me each Wednesday despite the fact that my research was far from actually Western. Jay Gitlin and George Miles were always particularly supportive of my project and helpful with advice. George sought out sources for me at the Beinecke Rare Book and Manuscript Library, and together we unearthed a surprising amount of material about New York. The Lamar Center helped to fund my research, providing truly invaluable aid. Jim Scott and the Agrarian Studies Program were also incredibly supportive, offering financial assistance and a wonderfully interdisciplinary community in which to discuss my work.

Out of the goodness of their hearts, several scholars who were otherwise not bound to help me have done exactly that, over coffee, email, or Skype. Matthew Klingle, first and foremost, became an invaluable resource to me as I finished this project and turned it into a book. His close reading of the text and subsequent advice were something that scholars can only dream of, and I hope to pay that forward some day. Dan Czitrom drove down to New Haven from Massachusetts multiple times, once even in a blizzard, to give me some insightful advice about complicated nineteenth-century New York politics. Virginia Scharff, William Deverell, Martha Sandweiss, Michael Rawson, and Seth Rockman all provided valuable advice at crucial points. Andrew Robichaud, Joseph Ciadella, Melanie Kiechle, and Sean Kheraj are among the scholars I've been lucky to meet at conferences of the American Society of Environmental Historians, the Urban History Association, and the Organization of American Historians, and they've been great resources and friends ever since.

One of my fondest memories from grad school involves the delicious potluck dinners that my writing group put together. Luckily, my discussions of disease and rotting carcasses tended to come long after we were finished eating. Francesca Russello Ammon, Helen Curry, Kathryn Gin, Julia Guarneri, Sara Hudson, and Robin Morris gave me some of the most detailed and useful critiques that I have ever received, and helped me to work through such mysteries as strange nineteenth-century turns-of-phrase and how one might hide a hog under a hoop skirt. Fran, in particular, continued to exchange drafts with me long after our writing group began scattering across the country. This book has certainly benefited from her close readings. Other friends from Yale and beyond have provided support, advice, and laughs over the years, especially Adam Arenson, Kathleen Belew, Christine DeLucia, Yassine Diboun, Peter Douglas, Ziv Eisenberg, Shiri Goren, Alicia Cahill Ha, Sinead Hunt, Barry Muchnick, Jennifer Scheib, Matthew Underwood, Helen Veit, Erica Wagner, Roxanne Willis, and Alice Wolfram.

I spent a wonderful and productive year as a Bernard and Irene Schwartz Postdoctoral Fellow at the New-York Historical Society and the New School. The faculty at the New School and the librarians and staff at the New-York Historical Society were a great resource. Special thanks are due to Valerie Paley, Ted O'Reilly, Marybeth Kavanagh, Joseph Ditta, and Nina Nazionale. One of the best parts of that position was the true fellowship I found with the other fellows there: Dael Norwood, Robin Vandome, Kevin Butterfield, and Andrew Lipman. Dael proved a particularly helpful sounding board as I revised drafts and worked through possible titles.

My new colleagues at Portland State University's Department of History have been particularly welcoming and encouraging of my work. I've been grateful to be a part of this community as I've worked through the completion of the book. In particular, I've benefited from the advice and suggestions of Tim Garrison, David Johnson, Laura Robson, Jennifer Tappan, Ken Ruoff, John Ott, Brian Turner, Patricia Schechter, Katrine Barber, Thomas Luckett, Bill Lang, Carl Abbott, Chet Orloff, Nathan McClintock, the faculty and students of the College of Urban and Public Policy, the Institute for Sustainable Solutions, and the faculty and students of the Architecture School. Discussions with students in my urban environmental history courses were wonderful for thinking through larger themes and issues. Perhaps it was fate, but soon after settling into my new office, I learned that an urban pig regularly went on walks through the university's park blocks. With that strolling hog and the numerous sheep bleating and chickens clucking on my block in the summertime, Portland has proven a fantastic place to think about urban animals and agriculture.

The enthusiasm that Andrew Kinney, my editor at Harvard University Press, has had for this book has made him an ideal advocate and supporter. It's been a pleasure to work with both him and the Press. I'm indebted to the Press's outside reviewers, Michael Rawson and Tyler Anbinder, whose sharp critiques and advice helped to guide my revisions. Portions of Chapter 1 were originally published in Catherine McNeur, "The 'Swinish Multitude': Controversies over Hogs in Antebellum New York City," *Journal of Urban History,* vol. 37, no. 5 (September 2011): 639–660. I am grateful for permission to reprint it here. That article, as well as my larger project, benefited greatly from the comments of Brett Mizelle and an anonymous reviewer, as well as from the guidance of the journal's editor, David R. Goldfield.

I've been lucky to have an education filled with inspiring teachers, without whom I perhaps would not have continued on the path that led to a Ph.D. and a book. Ines Basso Glick was there early on, and her enthusiasm and encouragement cannot be matched. Benton Stark, my high school history teacher who introduced me to urban history and gave me a passion for close reading, continues to be an inspiration today. Robert Gerver, my high school math research teacher, instilled in me a love of organized, expansive projects. Last but hardly least, at New York University Mosette Broderick awakened my interest in New York City history and opened my eyes to the layers of history embedded in any urban landscape. She personally took the time to introduce me to the archives at the New-York Historical Society and has been a close friend and mentor ever since.

An education is always rooted at home, and I cannot thank my parents, John and Clare McNeur, enough for filling my life with a passion for stories. Their unwavering support and love has powered me through this journey. My brothers, Josh and Luke, who've groaned as I've gone on about street filth over Thanksgiving dinners, deserve my thanks, as do John and Ashley, my nephew and niece. My grandmother Phyllis McNeur has read drafts of this book from an early stage. Many thanks to the extended McNeur family as well. Special thanks are also due to my in-laws, Sherry Pellegrini, Jim Pellegrini, Sara Pellegrini, and Keith Fox, as well as the extended Pellegrini, Watts, Tozian, and Poulos families.

Dan Pellegrini has been an ideal partner as I've turned this project into a book. He's lived with it as long as I have, has endured countless dinners with inappropriate discussions of sewage, and has been the greatest supporter I could possibly imagine. Our daughter Nora was born in the midst of this project and has grown up getting much-too-long answers about what pigs eat and how we define domesticated animals. Her little sister, Julia, doesn't know what she's in for. It is for all that and much more that I dedicate this work to the three of them. Thank you.

Index